THE RADICAL FICTION OF ANN PETRY

THE RADICAL FICTION OF ANN PETRY

KEITH CLARK

LOUISIANA STATE UNIVERSITY PRESS
BATON ROUGE

Published by Louisiana State University Press

Manufactured in the United States of America
First printing

DESIGNER: Michelle A. Neustrom
TYPEFACE: Livory
PRINTER: McNaughton & Gunn, Inc.
BINDER: Dekker Bookbinding

LIBRARY OF CONGRESS CATALOGING-IN-PUBLICATION DATA

Clark, Keith, 1963–
The radical fiction of Ann Petry / Keith Clark.
pages cm
Includes bibliographical references and index.
ISBN 978-0-8071-5066-5 (cloth : alk. paper) — ISBN 978-0-8071-5067-2 (pdf) — ISBN 978-0-8071-5068-9 (epub) — ISBN 978-0-8071-5069-6 (mobi) 1. Petry, Ann, 1908–1997—Criticism and interpretation. I. Title.
PS3531.E933Z63 2013
813'.54—dc23

2012039922

The paper in this book meets the guidelines for permanence and durability of the Committee on Production Guidelines for Book Longevity of the Council on Library Resources. ♾

For my parents, Morris and Millicent Lowery Clark.
And for their siblings: Constantine Wilson, Sylvia Leach, Winston Lowery, William Lowery, Terry Edwards, John Lowery, and Theodore Clark . . . Marvelous aunts and uncles whose lifelong love, guidance, and support have provided inestimable blessings.

Contents

Acknowledgments

I am immensely indebted to many since I first undertook this true labor of love, researching and writing on an author who has written passionately, painstakingly, and undeterred about topics that make her a true literary maverick. So I begin by thanking Ann Petry for her artistry and commitment to unvarnished truth.

I owe my unreserved gratitude to colleagues at my home institution, George Mason University. Robert Matz, chair of the Department of English, has been an unwavering friend and exemplary colleague who has always believed in this project, even during those moments when my energy and enthusiasm started to ebb; I will forever be especially grateful for his heartfelt desire to "see this book published," as he declared during one of my many trips to his office seeking moral support. Amelia Rutledge, another colleague, generously read the "Gothic" sections of the manuscript and offered incisive criticism and suggestions, taking a portion of her own summer research time to do so. Friend and colleague John Burt Foster made himself available to discuss my work, offering insights and genuine enthusiasm about the project, so much so that he took it upon himself to read *The Narrows*, Petry's most ambitious and *longest* work, after which he read my chapter on the novel. Deborah Kaplan and Devon Hodges, the department's former chair and associate chair, respectively, have been consummate role models and guiding lights, generous in their support of me not only professionally but personally as well. A special nod to the students from George Mason's Osher Lifelong Learning Institute (OLLI); they graciously lobbied for me to teach a course on Petry and responded effusively to her fiction and my ideas about it. Finally, I am exceedingly grateful for the Faculty Study Leave GMU granted during the 2006–7 academic year; this invaluable year off provided me the time to do copious amounts of research and to begin formulating the book's critical blueprint.

In addition to my George Mason colleagues, I am indebted to scores of friends/colleagues throughout the wider scholarly community. Hilary Holladay (James Madison University), a pathbreaking Petry scholar herself and a valued friend since those exhausting but invigorating days as doctoral students at the University of North Carolina at Chapel Hill, read the manuscript, offering what she deemed the "strong medicine," the candor that every writer needs; she has been and remains my most punctilious and valued reader. J. Lee Greene (retired from University of North Carolina, Chapel Hill), my former professor who has continued to be a mentor and intellectual beacon long after graduation, offered his tough but always on-point analysis of my work. I thank Sheila Smith McKoy (North Carolina State University), another cherished friend from graduate school and a razor-sharp critic of African American and Diasporan literature whose insightful comments on my work and staunch love/support have meant more to me than I can truly express. In a similar vein, Joy Myree-Mainor (Morgan State University) has been a dear, dear friend who on a daily basis has provided unflagging intellectual support, jokes, the proverbial shoulder on which to cry, and most of all, a love for me that extends well beyond the academic. Another buddy, writer/critic Kenyatta Dorey Graves, sincerely believed in the value of this work. He may have forgotten the day I texted him wondering if my work on a writer not named Morrison or Wilson would ever see light of day beyond my own laptop: he simply but convincingly assured me, "It will be published"; to be sure, I've never forgotten this simple but genuine declaration of encouragement at a time when I truly needed it. I am grateful for the work of Hazel Arnett Ervin, a devoted Petry scholar whose work on her has proved invaluable to scores of critics. I remember brother-scholar Aimé Ellis (Michigan State University), a towering intellect and passionate voice who departed this earth heartbreakingly too soon. My beloved compatriot Jonas DeWitt Webster (George Mason University) has modeled for me courage and perseverance.

I am indebted to scores of friends/colleagues: Karla Slocum (University of North Carolina, Chapel Hill) generously opened her home to me during several summers when she left town to conduct her own research; Karla's unofficial "scholar's colony" enabled me to spend vital time in the Triangle, the environment most conducive to my thinking and writing. These summer sojourns gave me intellectual and leisure time with friends/colleagues whom I treasure: sister-friend/scholar Alisa Ann Johnson (Meredith College) and her husband, dancer L. D. Burris (I'll never forget "Dames" or the spectacular "Pilobolus"); and the brilliant and always kind Maurice Wallace (Duke University). I give an appreciative acknowledgment to a cadre of devoted friends in the profession: Trudier Harris (University of Alabama, Tuscaloosa), Helena Woodard (University of Texas, Austin), James W. Coleman (University of North Carolina, Chapel Hill), E. Patrick Johnson (Northwestern University), Antiwan Walker (Georgia Gwinnett College), Angelo Robinson (Goucher College), Scott Trafton (University of South Carolina, Columbia), and Warren Carson (University of South Carolina, Upstate).

Friends outside the academy have buoyed me tremendously: I thank Brian Scott, Carolyn and Robert Cannon, Donald Burch, John Southall, and Ron and Sandy Wilmore for their inquiries about the progress of my work and their abiding interest in it.

My heartfelt appreciation to the staff at the Louisiana State University Press—especially the retired John Easterly, who early on saw the value and potential importance of this project, and Margaret Lovecraft, his successor who so ably shepherded my work through the lengthy and occasionally anxiety-inducing publication process with a calm but steady hand.

Last but not least, much thanks to the baristas at my favorite coffeehouse-workspace: you know who you are.

THE RADICAL FICTION OF ANN PETRY

Introduction

THE "LITERARY BONES" OF ANN PETRY

Excavating and Re-situating a Reluctant Icon

My introduction to Ann Petry's most widely acclaimed novels, *The Street* and *The Narrows*, occurred in an early 1990s graduate seminar at the University of North Carolina at Chapel Hill. Until that time, my knowledge of Petry's works had been limited to the short story "Like a Winding Sheet," which was included in the estimable Richard Barksdale/Keneth Kinnamon anthology *Black Writers of America*—a volume that paved the way for the many African American literature anthologies we are so fortunate to have. Prior to deciding to concentrate on Petry's writings as the basis of my next scholarly project, I had actually conducted extensive research on black southern writers; I had even spent hundreds of dollars on primary and secondary works. Since I had taught undergraduate and graduate courses on this topic, declaring it the subject of my next scholarly endeavor made perfect professional sense.

However, a trip to Boston dramatically changed my research agenda. A close friend writing a dissertation on Petry and Dorothy West invited me to accompany her to Boston University's Gotlieb Archival Research Center, where she'd arranged to examine Petry's papers. I was astounded by the volume of material Petry had left to BU: in addition to handwritten drafts of several works, the twenty or so boxes included a trove of writings and other memorabilia: original versions of nonfiction she'd published in the *Crisis* and *Opportunity* magazines, letters she'd written to politicians (including President Richard M. Nixon), letters from elementary students whose classes Petry had visited, correspondences with members of the literati (Carl Van Vechten et al.). This cornucopia of personal and professional artifacts revealed a literarily prolific, politically engaged, socially conscious, and even *radical* Petry, a far cry from the prominent perception of her as aloof if not outright disdainful when it came to the spotlight and social engagement. Indeed, she was a far cry from the prototypical damned scribbling black New England woman writer cloistered in the Old Saybrook, Connecticut, home she shared with her husband, George.

Poring through scores of black-and-white-specked "composition" notebooks containing drafts of her work, I was especially amazed to find a draft of the work I truly consider an unheralded American classic, her 1953 novel *The Narrows*—what would be published as a four-hundred-plus-page novel she'd drafted entirely in longhand. This was a truly epiphanic moment, for it brought into sharp relief the tenacity and sheer will it must have taken to fill those notebooks. Indeed, this moment convinced me that here was an indefatigable writer whose work warranted wider critical attention, not to mention a larger readership.

Another determining factor in my decision to redirect my scholarly energy exclusively to Petry relates to the politics of canon formation and periodization. For several decades, Petry was known almost singly for her million-copy-selling first novel and for her short story "Like a Winding Sheet" (1945); the latter continues to be published regularly in American/African American literature anthologies. I've always been bothered by how this story, much like James Baldwin's "Sonny's Blues," functions almost synecdochically while Petry's prodigious output has remained undervalued and understudied. Does the story's inordinate focus stem from its "sensational" conclusion, in which a long-suffering African American male factory worker pummels his innocent and defenseless wife—she playfully calls him a "hungry nigger"—after he arrives home from the graveyard shift of his mind-numbing, physically debilitating factory job (he couldn't attack his white boss for her not-so-playful use of this racial epithet; hence, his wife Mae becomes the object of his suppressed rage). Is the story so frequently anthologized because it adheres to the dictates of naturalistic literary discourse and can therefore be extracted from her canon as somehow *representative* of both her entire body of work and the period in which it was produced? Or is it continually anthologized because it fits snugly into the rubric of literary identity politics as a tale dramatizing black male and black female victimization—in short, does it function as a token narrative that has come to eclipse Petry's more complexly drawn other short fiction, which cannot be limited to the enshrined category of protest?

In my "re-situating" of a writer I've labeled a "reluctant icon," I think it important to locate Petry within her literary milieu, what critic W. Lawrence Hogue calls the "dominant literary establishment" of the 1930s and 1940s—the hegemonic apparatus that governed literary production, publication, and consumption. Then and through the 1980s, Petry was routinely considered part of the "Richard Wright School of Social Protest," a referent which may have captured the Zeitgeist in terms of constitutive literary histories but one which simultaneously revealed the masculinizing of literary production and the exclusion of women writers like Zora Neale Hurston and Margaret Walker, not to mention the tragicomic uniqueness of a voice such as Chester Himes. Petry's de rigueur positioning as Wright's "native daughter" speaks directly to what feminist critic Joyce Warren argues in her introduction to *Challenging Boundaries: Gender and Periodization:*

> Although feminist critics have worked successfully to recover neglected women writers and to place them in the canon along with established women writers, generally these critics have not been able to dislodge the periods into which American literature [I'd include African American literature here as well] is divided. Typically, women writers are simply wedged into established literary periods that hardly suit them. For example, Emily Dickinson is sometimes located in the so-called American Renaissance, a category of all-male writers that was created by F. O. Matthiessen in the 1940s for his own and the nation's purposes and that, although frequently challenged, still dominates studies of nineteenth-century American literature. Only by being considered a disciple of the much lesser poet Ralph Waldo Emerson can Dickinson be added to this literary period, and even then she is out of place. (ix)

Given the comparable categorizing of mid-twentieth-century African American literature as "protest/naturalist," Petry, like her native New England–born literary forebear Dickinson, was "wedged" into a conclave of male contemporaries—Wright, Himes, William Attaway, and Willard Motley. Petry was summarily lumped into this coterie as another of Wright's literary acolytes who critics insisted mimicked the grand master in portraying blacks' abject dehumanization, which eventually thwarts their quest for personhood. While on some level a reductive categorization for each of these unique writers, it takes on particularly worrisome gender implications when the lone woman gains admittance because of her seeming "ability" to write like one of the (black) boys, in the grim, racially combative protest register that Irving Howe would claim "black boys" were obligated to do—to write in the name and style of the literary patriarch Wright.[1]

In writing about *Native Son*'s privileged status as representative of mid-century African American literature, Hogue concludes that it achieved such a position because Wright was "writing about certain themes—social maladjustment, the individual and his environment, criminals, murder, violence, and death—that dominant critical practices, at least at this period in American literary history, defined as more worthy and 'universal' than the quest for identity, personal freedom, and happiness" (Hogue 30). On the one hand, I would take issue with Hogue's dichotomization—*Native Son* is nothing if not the cataloging of Bigger's "quest for identity, personal freedom, and happiness" in a venomous America. On the other hand, Hogue's larger point is valid: naturalism and its various synonyms—environmentalism, determinism, protest—still represented the discursive brush that would tar and taint the reception of Petry's immensely nuanced and, unbeknownst to many readers and critics, transgressive and progressive body of writing.

To be sure, instead of limiting Petry's oeuvre to the simultaneously apposite and pigeonholing realm of naturalism, I would contend that the trajectories of her fiction are much more expansive than such confining referents suggest. I concentrate primarily on what I am calling her radical aesthetic agenda—that often-overlooked dimension of her artistic project in which she, for instance, vociferously contests essentialist definitions of gender for *male* protagonists (chaps. 2 and 3, which focus on masculine identity in *The Narrows* and in several short stories, respectively) and employs the conventions of terror literature to show how the lives of WASPs occupying a seemingly halcyon New England hamlet can be as nightmarish and pathological as those blacks confined to a plantation-like, predacious Harlem (chaps. 4 and 6, on *The Street* and *Country Place*, respectively). The author's interest in conjure and the supernatural interfaces with gothic tropes in two short stories set in the drearily depressing North, regardless of whether their inhabitants reside in grim urban milieus or equally gloomy provincial locales (chap. 5). The final chapter commingles the study's twin concerns with masculine ontology and horror in treating "In Darkness and Confusion," while the conclusion contains brief discussion of "The New Mirror," "Mother Africa," and two largely neglected stories, "The Migraine Workers" and "The Moses Project"; in the latter two works the prophetic Petry fictivizes issues that have proven combustible in our increasingly volatile twenty-first century: the wretched plight of migrant workers in an increasingly black and brown America, and the state's use of technology to monitor those deemed criminal and threatening.

Though clearly conversant with the conventions of black masculinist protest/naturalism of the 1940s, Petry modally departs from this discourse, reifying a distinction literary critic Karla Holloway makes between black male and female writers' discursive strategies: She writes, "The province of the word for black women commands a perspective that does not isolate it from its community source" and "Black women writers seem to concentrate on shared ways of saying, black males concentrate on individual ways of behaving" (*Moorings and Metaphors* 7). Holloway pinpoints what I consider the matrix of Petry's entire oeuvre: her "sharing" of the word accounts for the postmodern dimensions of her work—her multiple points of view, her narrative discontinuities and breaks, her improvised variations on a singular scene, her reliance on parallelism in lieu of causality. One might rightly rejoin that this makes Petry more Faulknerian than Wrightian, but her emphasis on "shared" stories and voices distinguishes her from both of these Anglo- or African American "masters." The author herself explicates her technical design in at least two instances. First, in an illuminating autobiographical essay, she highlights the paramount value of familial storytelling during her upbringing in a less-than-pristine New England milieu:

> These stories transmitted knowledge, knowledge on how to survive in a hostile environment. They were a part of my education. As a writer, I am really the endproduct [sic] of what Reynolds Price (*A Palpable God*) calls a "powerful oral-narrative tradition. . . . A need to hear and tell stories is essential to the species—second in necessity after nourishment and before love and shelter. Millions survive without love or home, almost none in silence—the sound of story is the dominant sound of our lives." (Petry, "Ann Petry" 259)

Petry's heartfelt emphasis on storytelling and story transmission provides the technical stanchion for all of her work. As Hilary Holladay observes, "Petry's abiding interest in the relationships between tellers and their tales, made explicit in 'Has Anybody Seen Miss Dora Dean?' and *Country Place*, informs all her works. Her experimentation with a variety of narrative techniques, especially multiple points of view, illustrates her devotion to the art of writing" (133). These two works in particular are tours de force in the mechanics of storytelling—how the teller's perspective, biases, and motivations are as important as the tale she/he renders.

In addition to specifying how family narratives anchor her fiction, Petry cites a distinctly black expressive form as part of her stylistic architecture. In response to Petry scholar Hazel Ervin's query in a 1987 interview, "In *The Narrows*, Mamie Powther is like a blues lady. Then, there are jazz scenes in *The Street* and jazz scenes in the short stories 'Marie of the Cabin Club' and 'Solo on the Drums.' How were you introduced to jazz?" Petry replies, "I've been a jazz buff, or a fan, ever since I was a teenager—many a long year ago" (Ervin, "Just a Few Questions" 102). Though Petry's answer is typical of her less-than-loquacious responses to interviewers' forays into her life and work, these comments suggest the basis of her works' jazz sensibilities; her canon abounds with actual or would-be musical artists: Lutie Johnson aspires to work as an interpreter of jazz standards with a big band; Mamie Powther is clearly fashioned after the blues singer Mamie Smith (the character's maiden name is, in fact, Smith); and Kid Jones in "Solo on the Drums" performs frenetically while sublimating the pain of being jilted by his girlfriend.[2] Petry's interlarding of both storytelling and jazz is a precursor to Ellison's pioneering treatise on literature and music, *Shadow and Act*, where he declares that "true jazz is an art of individual assertion within and against the group. . . . Each solo flight, or improvisation, represents (like the successive canvases of a painter) a definition of his identity: as individual, as member of the collectivity and as link in a chain of tradition" (234).

Considering the reductive though continually evolving view of her as simply a literary "native daughter" moored in Wrightian protest—a truncating identity which neglects the breadth and trajectory of her oeuvre—I hope *The Radical Fiction of Ann Petry* will play a role in the "excavation" of a reluctant and understudied literary icon. I'm guardedly optimistic given that more scholars have trained their critical eyes on this truly original and sonorous literary voice: from the pioneering foundational scholarship of Hazel Arnett Ervin (*Ann Petry: A Bio-Bibliography*, 1993) and Hilary Holladay (*Ann Petry*, 1996), to recent essay collections such as Alex Lubin's *Revising the Blueprint: Ann Petry and the Literary Left* (2007), to Elisabeth Petry's memoir *At Home Inside: A Daughter's Tribute to Ann Petry* (2008), Petry is now beginning to garner the critical if not popular interest that moves beyond the monocentric emphasis on "Like a Winding Sheet" and *The Street*, which for several decades were read as performing the "socially correct" work of dramatizing the bleakness of black life in mid-twentieth-century America. The work of no mere male impersonator or writer of the environment, Petry's jazz-inflected forms further showcase her radical departures from standard discursive praxes in the 1940s and 1950s, which too often pigeonholed black literary expression.

1

FROM GANGSTA TO GOTHIC

Ann Petry's Unbounded Aesthetic Universe

> It is, indeed, to be expected that our first eminent Southern author [Poe] discover that the proper subject for American gothic is the black man, from whose shadow we have not yet emerged.
>
> —Leslie A. Fiedler, *Love and Death in the American Novel*

> Interviewer: Are there any black writers that you remember reading either in high school or in your own early years as a writer?
>
> Petry: There were two in particular: *Narrative of the Life of Frederick Douglass* and James Weldon Johnson's *Autobiography of an Ex-Colored Man.*
>
> —*MELUS* Interview with Mark K. Wilson

The "darker brother" of whom Langston Hughes sang in the poem "I, Too"—the unrecognized native son relegated to the "kitchen" of America's racial house—has always been the foreboding presence in our culture, the inscrutable br/other whose presence is indelible but irrepressible. Thus, gothic's literal and metaphorical emphasis on "darkness" lends credence to Leslie Fiedler's delimiting, though legitimate claim—delimiting because it confines blackness to the white literary imagination. So Pauline Hopkins's bold declaration in 1900 that "*we* [African Americans] *must ourselves develop the men and women who will faithfully portray the inmost thoughts and feelings of the Negro with all the fire and romance which lie dormant in our history*" (14; author's emphasis) is proleptic vis-à-vis Fiedler's assertion, for she calls on the black writer to embrace the challenge of fictionalizing blackness in its multiple hues and dimensions. Hopkins's exhortation, in fact, undercuts Fiedler's claim—gothic, a subgenre that teems with "fire and romance," must also be a part of the African American fictive imagination. Given Petry's recognition of Douglass and Johnson, authors who wrestled with both the "horror" of slavery and the epidermal maligning of "darkness" as they especially related to black male subjects, one can extrapolate the gothic-masculinity nexus which provides the basis for what I deem Petry's unbounded aesthetic universe and thereby her *radical* fictive voice.

"What's Wrong with Negro Men?": Gangsta and Familial Masculinity in the Black Female Imaginary

On its surface, one would take the late Nellie McKay's assessment of Petry's prodigious fictionalization of black female subjectivity as unimpeachable: without question, "Petry has played a significant role in the development of the strong female characters in the works of contemporary black women writers like Morrison, Paule Marshall, Gloria Naylor, and Alice Walker" (McKay, "Introduction" xvii–xviii). But unlike a spate of critics who focus on Petry's ostensibly gynocentric concerns, I turn my attention to her multifaceted portraitures of black masculinity.[1] On the one hand, Petry's satirical 1947 piece published in *Negro Digest*, "What's Wrong with Negro Men?," can be read as a quasi-black feminist broadside upbraiding black men for their "attitude toward women [that] comes straight out of the Dark Ages" (4). Just as Zora Neale Hurston would articulate new protocols for black masculine literary subjectivity, Petry too denounced black men's "belief in the God-given superiority of the male" (6). But more than a sardonic call for black men to terminate their chauvinistic ways, this modest proposal underscores Petry's long-standing concern with black literary masculinity, another topic indicative of her willingness to move beyond interracial conflict to more fully display her thematic and discursive repertoire.

Moreover, Petry's spirited critique of black men does not mitigate her unequivocal admiration for black male writers. When an interviewer queries her about Richard Wright, she replies: "No, I had no contact with Richard Wright, though I read his novels and short stories as they were published. And I also read the work of Langston Hughes, James Baldwin, and Ralph Ellison—with admiration for all of them, including Wright. *Invisible Man* is a truly great novel" (Wilson 80). Without hesitation, Petry claims these men as literary kin in a charitable display of appreciation far more gracious than these same writers' occasionally puerile "anxieties" and attendant disclamations of literary consanguinity. Within Petry's unvarnished feminist declaration lies a deep-seated interest in black masculine identify formation and subjectivity, one that adumbrates Toni Morrison's comparable interest in black masculinity not simply as an undeviating version—or mimicry—of white masculinity, but as a complicated and often vexing subject open to an array of interpretations. Petry agilely complicates literary masculinity, imaging a range of characters who have received scant critical attention when, too often, the gender of the author directs our critical eye almost myopically to characters of that same gender. Multiscopic male representation becomes another distinguishing feature of a writer whose work resists confinement to reductive literary bins—protest writer, feminist writer, New England writer.

By invoking the term *gangsta* throughout this study, I realize that I'm treading on potentially hazardous discursive and vernacular terrain. In the lingua franca of rap/hip-hop, the term has come to mark an aggressively stylized hypermasculinity, one marked by sexual profligacy and privilege, verbal braggadocio, and, often, violence—black male on black male, black male on black female. Groups such as N.W.A. (Niggaz with Attitude) in the late 1980s are recognized as the form's most accomplished (?) practitioners. If the likes of Will Smith and Vanilla Ice represented rap at its squishy, *crossover* center, N.W.A., Biggie Smalls, and pre-*Law and Order* Ice-T (who penned the incendiary rap tune "Cop Killer" in the early 1990s) typified its hard, *authentic* black edge—*the* blackness of blackness, to invoke Ellison. Cultural critic Robin D. G. Kelley summarizes the pervasive gangsta rap ideology: "Indeed, its masculinist emphasis and pimp-inspired vitriol toward women are central to gangsta rap. While its misogynistic narratives are not supposed to be descriptions of everyday reality, they are offensive and chilling nonetheless" (185). In addition to lyrics that too often teem with misogynistic content, Kelley further points out, black expressive/oral culture is laden with narratives that celebrate phallocentrism and antiwoman violence: "While young African American males are both products of and sometimes active participants in the creation of a new masculinist, antifeminist cultural current, we cannot be too quick to interpret sexist and misogynist lyrics as a peculiarly modern product. African American vernacular has a very long and ignoble tradition of sexism evidenced in daily language and other more formal variants such as 'the dozens,' 'toasts,' and the age-old 'baadman narratives'" (214).[2]

To be sure, African American vernacular culture has recuperated and often celebrated the most phallocentric, antiwoman elements of gangsta culture. From this perspective, Kelley's concluding point about "baadman narratives" is apropos; inarguably, black folk culture abounds with larger-than-life, ruthless figures who faced off against both white and black foes without trepidation, from High John the Conqueror to Black Bart to John Henry to Railroad Bill.[3] In many instances, the "baad man" or "baad nigga"—the forerunner of the contemporary "gangsta"—comes to embody radicalized racial resistance, a lone voice challenging entrenched patriarchal white supremacy albeit often simultaneously instantiating the most execrable forms of patriarchal excess. Within the black female literary imagination, Zora Neale Hurston's pioneering folklore recouped the most laudable elements of "baad man/gangsta" culture in works such as *Mules and Men* where she researched and (re)presented figures such as High John the Conqueror and John Henry (worth noting is Petry's own familiarity with a folkloristic history too often solely associated with black southern writers—one of her early essays is entitled "New England's John Henry"). As well, Hurston's extensive excursions into masculine representation have direct bearing on Petry's expanded, nuanced portraitures that transcend too often monolithic depictions of black male literary subjectivity in the 1930s and 1940s.

Now considered iconic and trailblazing, *Their Eyes Were Watching God* (1937) anticipates the multivalent masculinities that will flower in Petry's oeuvre. As she is routinely celebrated for achieving, Hurston unreservedly inscribed black female intersubjectivities—African American women's economic, emotional, spiritual, and, perhaps most significantly, sexual lives. But she accomplished something else, though perhaps more subtly: widening the lens through which to view black male subjectivity. Incontestably, Hurston exposes the wretched failure of marriage as panacea: Janie Crawford Killicks Starks Woods chafes under the patriarchal tyranny of men who berate her (Logan Killicks: "Heah you got uh prop tuh lean on all yo' bawn days, and big protection, and everybody got tuh tip dey hat tuh you and call you Mis' Killicks, and you come worryin' me 'bout love" [22]) and silence her (Jody Starks: "You gettin' too moufy, Janie. . . . Go fetch me de checker-board *and* de checkers" [71]). Only with the considerably younger Verigible "Tea Cake" Woods does she find a veritable—true?—neo-black man, or at least one not inclined to view women alternatively as property; pedestalized, infantilized "baby dolls" (Killicks's phrase); and mutes. But alas, Janie's third husband is not quite the savior she imagined, for he too clings to the most loathsome form of patriarchal domination: "Before the week was over he had whipped Janie. Not because her behavior justified his jealousy, but it relieved that awful fear inside him" (140). Critic Ann duCille is dead-on in her appraisal of the novel's gender politics and the limitations of Hurston's "feminism": "Indeed, *Their Eyes* critiques, challenges, and subverts male authority . . . but female subjectivity does not win out over patriarchal ideology" (121). I would add that what Hurston ultimately achieves, then, is not the construction of a wholly "new black man" liberated from the shackles of androcentric domination, but a *tableau* of what such a man could entail.

Petry, in effect, expands Hurston's neo-masculine black subject in kaleidoscopic depictions that will add sexual orientation, "moderated masculinity," and male domesticity to the plurality of *masculinities* that inform black male subjectivity, these in addition to culturally anachronistic forms that sanction male sexual prerogative, authority, and violence.[4] Historically, then, we can discern at least two accurate though discrepant constructions of manhood—the more recent neologism *gangsta* suggesting hypervirility, violence, and misogyny; while the conjunctive, "old school" term for *gangsta*, "baad nigga," encompasses a combative masculinity more often rooted in racial heroism and resistance. I maintain that Petry vehemently interrogates and often derogates the former notion while countenancing and occasionally embracing the latter. I now turn to her instructive biographical essay, which contains several anecdotes featuring scores of male kin. While some could easily be categorized as gangsta in their unflinching responses to different degrees of racial animus, others reenvision maleness in terms that are defiantly anathema to the more socially and historically enshrined but parochial and hackneyed constructions.

First, she recalls her maternal grandfather, Willis Samuel James, a runaway slave: “He escaped from a plantation in Virginia shortly before the Civil War. He came north via the Underground Railroad and settled in Hartford” (Petry, “Ann Petry” 255). Though her keen recollection here is typically “Petrian” in its terseness, her point is clear: like the lionized Douglass about whom she read in school, her grandfather marshaled the strength to break the physical, psychological, and economic fetters of this too peculiar institution. She then offers an anecdote on her father Peter Clark Lane, Jr., who opened a drugstore in an all-white Connecticut town in 1902. When a “small white man” entered the store and warned him that the residents “don't want no black druggist in this town. If you ain't gone by to-morrow night they're going to run you out of town, run you right out of here,” Petry recounts:

> My father said, “What?” And the little man repeated the message. My father grabbed the little man by the throat and shook him and shouted at him, talking faster and faster, saying, “You brought a message? You take a message back. You tell *them* that I close my store every night at nine o'clock and I walk down this street alone to the house where I live at the corner of Maple Avenue. And as soon as my wife gets here I'm going to be living in this building. Meantime any night *they* think *they* can run me out of town tell 'em to try. Mebbe they can run me out of here. But you tell *them* that I come from Madagascar and we slit throats. We're stranglers. If I have to leave here I'll be back. And I'm going to bring my great-grandfather, and my grandfather, and my father, and my ten brothers with me. And this damn town will never look the same again. (256)

One can hear echoes of Black Bart and John Henry in Peter Lane, Jr.'s impassioned, resolute brand of black masculinity, as he stakes out his family's and ancestors' turf and dares anyone to invade it, lest he return with a posse of black men spanning multiple generations. Reminiscent of the lexical masking and signifying that mark fellow New England ancestor Wheatley's most famous poem, “On Being Brought from Africa to America,” which coyly seems to cast her native Senegal as “pagan,” Lane cunningly exploits racial fears by appropriating the Western myth of Africa as uncivilized and barbarous; his audacious declaration is comparable to some rappers' reclamation and "bending" of the slur "nigger" into "niggaz" (e.g., Niggaz with Attitude)—the latter representing a transformation of the former from enslaved object into radicalized subject. Though we can never be certain of the degree to which daughter Petry might have been embellishing these *his*tories or the accuracy of her memory, these short biographical profiles nevertheless provide the framework for the dauntless men (and women) she imagines, men who belie dyadic categories of victim and victimizer, saint and sinner.

Several characters throughout her fictive corpus mirror the multiple figurations of gangsta masculinity embodied in her male relatives. Most representative is Bill Hod from what I consider her greatest artistic achievement, *The Narrows* (I analyze him extensively in chap. 2). A combination race man–hoodlum (*Hood*?), Hod at once instills in the preadolescent Link Williams a race pride sorely lacking in his adopted mother Abigail Crunch; however, Hod will undermine this invaluable racial re-education when he subsequently pummels the budding teenager for venturing into a brothel that Hod himself operates. To further illustrate Petry's incarnation of the outlaw, I'll elaborate briefly here on a character who at first glance seems ancillary, Boots Smith from *The Street*.

Boots, the bandleader at the nightclub Lutie frequents, is a synthesis of the contemporary "gangsta" and the more laudatory "baad nigger" version—the socially astute race man who can articulate blacks' derogated space in the American racial consciousness while asserting some form of pushback. Narrated from Lutie's perspective during their first meeting, this glimpse signals his unsavory and potentially ravenous personality: "And his eyes on her face were so knowing, so hard, that she thought instantly of the robins she had seen on the Chandlers' lawn in Lyme, and the cat, lean, stretched out full length, drawing itself along on its belly, intent on its prey" (150); shortly thereafter, she notices a "thin scar on his left cheek" (152). That Lutie juxtaposes Boots with the morally bankrupt though wealthy white suburban (Connecticut) family for which she works presages what is later revealed about his chauvinistic, occasionally violent relationships with women; just as moneyed whites prey on economically impoverished blacks like Lutie, Boots wields physical and financial power over her, exercising what he would consider his masculine prerogative. Not content to sketch a monovisual portrait of black masculinity, Petry will later draw a more complex picture of him when he reveals why he would never allow himself to be drafted during World War II. In a conversation with Junto, the white nightclub owner for whom he works, Boots demands that the former "fix" the draft notice he has just received; Boots then riffs on America, war, and the black man's alienation: "Because, no matter how scared they are of Germans, they're still more scared of me. I'm black, see? And they hate Germans, but they hate me worse. If that wasn't so they wouldn't have a separate army for black men" (258–59). Here Petry uses Boots to denounce a racist military establishment generally and, more specifically, the venomous attitudes of white Americans who regard fellow blacks as worse than the putative "enemy." While Boots's social castration begets a compensatory hypermasculinity—his eventual slapping of Lutie undermines his racially incisive invective—Petry consistently provides a multilateral view of him and other black males.

While it is not my intention to argue that Petry singularly re-imagined black literary masculinity, it is still imperative to delineate what I've called "multiple masculinities" in her work, her role in moving black male representation beyond static notions of social pathology and victimage.[5] In terms of 1950s black literary discourse, critics rightly acknowledge James Baldwin's role in clearing fictive ground for a deeper examination of black men's intersubjectivities—other dimensions of their interiority that transcended their exteriorized position as socioracial subjects. The publication of *Go Tell It on the Mountain* in 1953 was certainly pathbreaking not alone for its nuanced exploration of an adolescent black male's coming-of age in a racially hostile America; Baldwin's maiden novel also particularized how the confluence of social, sexual, familial, and psychic forces shapes a black adolescent male's maturation. However, what is often excised from an overwhelmingly male-centric literary record is the appearance of Petry's *The Narrows* in the same year, a book arguably comparable to *Mountain* in its intricate embroidering of black male childhood/adolescence that moves beyond interracial conflict as the sole determinant in their evolution—or devolution. The spectrum of masculine portraits in this novel alone evinces Petry's radical intervention upon often-homogeneous representations of black men as what bell hooks has labeled "fucked up" because of their presumed inability to "fulfill the phallocentric masculine ideal as it has been articulated in white supremacist capitalist patriarchy" (*Black Looks* 89). Alternatively, Petry images them in a variety of roles and formations—as engaged fathers, as surrogate parents, as comrades, as abusive spouses, as nurturing husbands, as sexually tormented, as gender bending. Her depictions reflect multiple coordinates on the black masculine axis, her depictions rooted in the upbringing she accentuates and celebrates.

Petry's recollections of the pivotal role black men played throughout her life become a sort of anterior narrative, for the vividness of her stories elucidates her multihued configurations of black masculinity. Her reverence for her male influences is most effusively expressed in these word-pictures of her father:

> My father was Peter Clark Lane, Jr. (1872–1949), licensed pharmacist (1895), storyteller, tenor in the choir of the Congregational Church, fancy figure skater, expert swimmer, collector of old drug bottles, occasional gardener; he wore the highly polished shoes of a city dude. In the summer he wore bow ties and stiff straw hats, known as boaters. (Petry, "Ann Petry" 259)

And in an interview, she added further:

> He helped raise the money to build this town hall. He and three other men used to sing stuff from Gilbert and Sullivan all over the country. In other words, he was part of the community, and yet not part of it. He had a big family, warm and close-knit. . . . There was always this separate private world that had nothing to do with the town. (Wilson 77)

These miniature bio-sketches of her father elucidate Petry's textured depictions of black masculinity, for they parallel her overall body of fiction:

like them, Peter Lane defies categorization and resides comfortably in a multitude of identities and roles. A living and breathing male quilt, he was at once entrepreneur, powerbroker, and fashion plate; an artist and an athlete. To be sure, his biography recalls that of another twentieth-century black renaissance man, Paul Robeson.

What I find most striking about Petry's recollections is how they express Peter Lane, Jr.'s unwillingness to be encased by essentialist gender constructions. On the one hand, he is the quintessential dandy, an *arbiter elegantiae* in his fashion sense; on the other, his pastimes of "fancy figure skater" and "occasional gardener" place him in roles that are often considered "feminine" and, to a lesser extent, nonblack as well. In essence, he became a "walking palimpsest" for Petry's fecund literary imagination; firsthand, she witnessed that black male subjectivity was truly multifarious and need not be hemmed in by hackneyed signifiers of socially sanctioned male behavior—competition, pugilism, individualism, isolation.[6] He thus corporealizes Petry's complex rendering of the asymmetries of black masculinity, those dimensions of it which deviate from socially orthodox norms. Some characters who resemble her father—for instance, the effete butler John Forbes in "Has Anybody Seen Miss Dora Dean?" whose racial and sexual anxiety may have contributed to his suicide—are less than ideal. However, they are balanced by men such as the nurturer Weak Knees in *The Narrows*, a cook who becomes the de facto parent of the aforementioned child Link Williams, who is neglected by his adoptive mother upon her husband's death. Such men reify alternative forms of black masculinity that depart from "authentic" representations purveyed by Wright, Ellison, and other major midcentury authors who viewed black masculinity as afamilial, acommunal, oppositional, aggressive—indeed, inexorably American. As Addison Gayle incisively points out, Petry "paved the way for future black writers . . . to examine the relationship between black man and black man, instead of those that primarily concern man and society" (197). Her men transcend the dwarfing notion that white masculinity is the sole touchstone for black male subjectivity; alternatively, she insists that the totality of black men's lives—in relation to family, community, and each other—is worthy of fictive exploration.

"Moving like Sleepwalkers": Gothic Eruptions and the Dread of Blackness—and Whiteness

Given the accurateness of Judith Wilt's assertion that the gothic "is a faithful record of human engagement with visible, political, cultural issues—race, class, gender, science, empire, authorities of all kinds" (41), I will now lay the groundwork for what I see as the corresponding crucial component in Petry's broadened black discursive universe. Coexistent with her refiguration of African American male subjectivity is her abiding concern with the "blackness of blackness," not in an Ellisonian affirming sense, but in terms of black people's lives in America as being encased in abjection. Lest one conclude that this state is entirely racial, however, white Americans' lives can be as besotted with horror: one of her most gothic works, in fact, interrogates a commensurable "terror" that accompanies whiteness—her second novel, the "raceless" *Country Place.*

Though I have not done a word count, the word "horror" reverberates throughout her first novel, *The Street;* correlatively, throughout her entire fictive corpus, words like *terror* and *fear* are not employed for effect, but deliberately used to draw parallels between black lives and a discourse not historically associated with them, the gothic. Note, for instance, Lutie Johnson's brisk nocturnal trek through downtown Harlem, past stores that peddle fetid meat and produce to a community where economic racism is legion: "It was a good thing that she had walked past these mean little stores with Boots Smith because the sight of them stiffened her determination to leave streets like this behind her—dark streets filled with shadowy figures that carried with them the horror of the places they lived in, places like her own apartment" (153). Such dismal environs are the economic appendages of Harlem's squalid tenements. A miasma of dread courses through this passage, a testament to Petry's lingering concern with the geographic place–psychic space nexus, which she no doubt witnessed firsthand as a reporter for the Harlem-based *Amsterdam News* from 1938 to 1941. Later, Lutie's gaze is drawn to a "curious procession" of black adolescents—"sixteen, seventeen, eighteen, nineteen—and they were moving like sleepwalkers" (204–5). They are escorting a teenage girl whose face has just been "cut to ribbons!" to the hospital: "The bright red blood turned what had been her face into a gaudy mask with patches of brown here and there where her skin showed through. Lutie got that same jolting sense of shock and then of rage, because these people, all of them—the girl, the crowd in back of her—showed no horror, no surprise, no dismay" (205). The language of nightmarish violence, where zombie-like black youth have become inured to their own mutilation, exhibits the gothic eruptions that pervade Petry's fiction.

Thus, when she responds to an interviewer's query about which writers she remembers reading in high school thusly—"Yes, Poe, some of the short stories. Let's see. Oh yes, and Hawthorne" (Wilson 74)—I see more than an author paying perfunctory homage to great white dead literary fathers. On the contrary, these gothic fore-writers consciously or unconsciously influence Petry's art, evidenced by the above-quoted passages from *The Street*. While I refrain from arguing that Petry is as much a consciously gothic writer as a Charles Brockden Brown or a Charlotte Perkins Gilman, I would make a parallel argument to Allan Lloyd-Smith's claim about nineteenth-century American writer James Fenimore Cooper: novels such as *The Spy* (1821) or *The Prairie* (1827) "are not so much working to *adapt* the Gothic mode; instead the Gothic emerges from the conditions they seek to describe" (4). Analogously, the visceral, often macabre violence Petry describes in an amalgam of forms—economic, psychic, physical, spatial—and its attendant debilitating, even catatonic effects hearken to a tradition not often associated with the black writer but one whose primary themes/conventions permeate Petry's writing. Moreover, these gothic eruptions are an outgrowth of her expressed interest in preternatural and alternative epistemological and ontological praxes. Just as one could read Chesnutt's "conjure tales" as the gothic forerunners of works like *Beloved*, Petry herself has acknowledged the role of this unequivocally African/Diasporan, non-Western epistemological base when she recalls the family legends and stories that molded her fictive imagination, kinsfolk like her great-great-aunt Hal, "a conjure woman who sold roots and herbs in Hartford" (Petry, "Ann Petry" 259); and in the same context, she unashamedly declares "I am a conjure woman" (268).[7] Therefore, her *Tituba of Salem Village* (1964), a book written for adolescents that recounts the life of the black "witch" whose powers led to her persecution in seventeenth-century New England, bears out the author's cosmological concerns and opens the space for unearthing the gothic terrain that underlies so much of her work.

Just as Petry's recollection of Hawthorne and Poe is not a mere token gesture, neither is another memory from her adolescent reading list—that of *Narrative of the Life of Frederick Douglass*—insignificant or fleeting. Her interest in slavery would eventually result in her publication of a second book for young people, *Harriet Tubman, Conductor on the Underground Railroad*, in 1955 (the first being *The Drugstore Cat* in 1949). But it is Douglass's archetypal autobiography that presages the masculine and gothic components most evident in works such as *The Street*. Commenting on the slave narrative's native discursive kinship to the gothic, critic Justin Edwards adduces that "Harriet A. Jacobs's *Incidents in the Life of a Slave Girl* recounts bludgeoning, flogging, burning, selling, and confinement of slaves to suggest how actual events can produce gothic narratives. She thus uses gothic discourse to paint the slave master and the oppressive institution as a source of terror that must be eliminated" (xxii). As well, Edwards's delineation of the gothic in Jacobs applies equally to Douglass, whose narrative is perhaps the black *ur*-gothic text that chronicles in wrenching, fervid prose all of the ghastliness Edwards particularizes.

In one of the most evocative passages in all of American literature, one that vivifies the harrowing, gruesome violence that provided slavery its infrastructure, Douglass recounts an epiphanic moment from his childhood: the barbaric whipping of his Aunt Hester by their master, Anthony Auld, after she disobeyed his directive that she not pursue an intimate relationship with another slave. Concealed in a closet during what he would call "this horrible exhibition" (51), Douglass recollects:

> And after rolling up his sleeves, he commenced to lay on the heavy cowskin, and soon the warm, red blood (amid heart-rending shrieks from her, and horrid oaths from him) came dripping on the floor. I was so terrified and horror-stricken at the sight, that I hid myself in a closet, and dared not venture out till long after the bloody transaction was over. I expected it would be my turn next. It was all new to me. I had never seen any thing like it before. I had always lived with my grandmother on the outskirts of the plantation, where she was put to

> raise the children of the younger women. I had therefore been, until now, out of the way of the bloody scenes that often occurred on the plantation. (52)

Indisputably, this cataclysmic moment is "one of the most well-known scenes of torture in the literature of slavery, perhaps only second to Uncle Tom's murder at the hands of Simon Legree" (Hartman 3); it is also the benchmark for his subsequent spiritual and psychic resuscitation, when a sixteen-year-old Douglass upends the overseer "Mr. Covey," who unsuccessfully tries to batter his charge into submission. To be sure, the closet episode resonates on so many levels: the eroticized, sadomasochistic violence; the literal and metaphorical attention to the visual, emphasizing Douglass's powerless role as spectator; the *seen/scene* rhetorically reinforcing the visual as well as the staged or performative qualities of the passage. For purposes of linking Petry's invocation of the gothic to a work that figured so prominently in her youth, however, I emphasize the theme of sequestration/confinement and the potentially psychically disintegrative effect of this episode on young Douglass's identity formation.

Though her work is not synonymous by any means, Petry portrays boyhood terror in a vein reminiscent of young Douglass's dolorous remembrances. Consider another passage from *The Street*, where eight-year-old Bub Johnson, being raised solely by Lutie, must spend his evenings alone while his mother chases an ill-conceived career as a nightclub singer.

> When she wasn't there, he was filled with a sense of loss. It wasn't just the darkness, for the same thing happened in the daylight when he came home from school. The instant he opened the door, he was filled with a sense of desolation, for the house was empty and quiet and strange. At noon he would eat his lunch fast and go out to the street. After school he changed his clothes quickly and, even as he changed them, no matter how quick he was, the house was frightening and cold. But when she was in it, it was warm and friendly and familiar. (214)

Far from being simply an Oedipal-tinged passage recording a mama's boy's baseless fears, this excerpt is almost Poevian, capturing the sepulchral quality of the apartment and the foreboding isolation that loneliness and fear animate; for Bub, the foreboding street is preferable to this cloistral dungeon of a home. While young Frederick's physical confinement concretized the impact of the psychological violence unknowingly inflicted upon him by his master/father, Petry delineates Bub's emotional deprivation and dis-ease through a comparable spatial metaphor: the mausoleum-like apartment, more tomb than nurturing womb. In Petry's quasi-gothic mise-en-scène, we see germinating in Bub a *gothic masculinity*, a hideously deformed psychic state most vividly engendered in psychically and physically monstrous characters like black William "Supe" Jones and white Junto (discussed in chap. 4).

Petry's punctilious dramatization of a black boy's interiority—the invisible self that coexists with his exterior, *raced* self—is the by-product of her journalistic experiences, when she regularly encountered "the horror" of Harlem life that had both racial and nonracial dimensions:

> You don't have to work on a Harlem newspaper to get a picture of the violence and poverty there. Just go into some of the houses. You'll see rooms so small, and halls so narrow, it won't seem possible they were designed for humans to live in. Just live in one of those houses for a week. Any night you're liable to wake up and hear somebody screaming his head off—because he's sick, or because he's been being beaten. You'll hear rats scratching around the walls. (qtd. in Theodore Gross 43)

The images of constriction, immobility, and agony that Petry describes invariably evoke the Middle Passage, where slave ships became nautical interment sites because of the many deaths brought on by overcrowding, deprivation, and disease.

Considered alongside the passage from *The Street*, Petry's haunting description of Harlem captures a dominant thematic and stylistic dimension of much of her fiction: the dread of isolation and the black community's failure to address the psychological health of its male children; and her utilization of gothic tropes to dramatize the psychic malaise externalized in the tomb-like spaces the characters inhabit. Not content to reductively make blackness *the* source of her characters' multiple maladies, Petry goes beyond race in exploring how isolation, abandonment, and sequestration debilitate the psyches of black and white people alike, with grave consequences.

Thus, I employ the term *Afro-Gothic* to capture Petry's appropriation and reconfiguring of the tropes associated with horror in *The Street*. Not only does she evoke the primordial genre of terror in the African American literary imagination, the slave narrative, but she anticipates works like *Beloved*, a neo-black gothic tour de force that foregrounds issues of infanticide, enslavement, physical and psychic brutality, the spectral, geospatial confinement, and, ultimately, geopsychic liberation. Indeed, given her distinctly Anglo- and African American literary bloodlines, Petry owes as much to her white New England literary forefathers as she does to her presumed literary patriarch Wright. The contours of blacks' nightmarish racial history and white New England and gothic writers' fascination with the subaltern, nether regions of the American psyche inflect her work, adding yet another layer of discursive complexity to a writer who traverses multiple literary modalities.

In addition to limning the urban hell of Harlem in *The Street*, Petry continues her utilization of gothic tropes and conventions in *Country Place*, her second novel, where she depicts a morally depraved *white* bucolic community (examined in chap. 6). In addition to *The Street*, stories such as "The Bones of Louella Brown" are awash in gothic and otherworldly features, as she condemns the segregationist practices of white New England cemetery owners who are haunted by the rollicking laughter of a black maid whom they callously buried in the rear of the cemetery. On the one hand, such a story humorously exposes the illogic of racial caste, but on the other hand, more somberly, the repression/oppression of blackness becomes the inescapable nightmare that invades the white characters' psyches; think here of Chesnutt's gothic tale of racial inversion, "Mars Jeems's Nightmare," where the eponymous slave master realizes his worst fear when he is turned black, the horror of which occasions an enlightenment and consequent purging of racial animus. Petry's Afro-Gothic fiction showcases her ability to interpolate "white" forms with unequivocally black content. Petry signifies on the gothic form, elastically contorting it for both racial and nonracial ends. While she inarguably uses it to explore standard gothic themes—the scabrous Harlem landscape in *The Street* as emblematic of black emotional torpor as well as psychosexual deformities and repressed desires—she also Anglicizes it in *Country Place* to explore how similar maladies infect upper- and middle-class white New Englanders, thereby displaying the portability of the form in her oeuvre.

Thus, I have titled this foundational chapter "From Gangsta to Gothic: Ann Petry's Unbounded Aesthetic Universe" to signal this study's central concerns: multivalent configurations of maleness with respect to gender and sexuality, along with the various forms of terror that underline setting and beset characters regardless of their race, gender, or sexuality. Subsequent chapters will explore the multitudinous ways in which Petry complicates notions of black masculinity and her invocation of gothic discourse to inform these reinscriptions and to vivify what she casts as the inapprehensible horror of black life in several works—and *white* life in at least one under-read one. While I've referenced the inter- and extratextual relationships between Petry and scores of authors—her predecessors and contemporaries alike—I ultimately conclude that hers is a sui generis voice. The breadth of her fictive imagination, which defies and explodes literary taxonomies, reveals itself in her multilayered approach to gender and literary form. By emphasizing and illuminating her innovative fictionalizing of seemingly divergent concerns—masculine ontology, gothic epistemology—I interpret her fictive repertoire as counter-discursive and radical, neither subsumed by the dictates of racially correct "protest" discourse nor detached from the racially tormented and tormenting lives of scores of black and white people alike, be they the haunted Harlem denizens in *The Street* or the equally disembodied white residents of Lennox, Connecticut, in *Country Place.*

2

BLACK BOYS, HOODS, AND WANNABES

Images of Imperiled Black Manhood in The Narrows

> *Negro* brought forth [in response to queries posed to white Europeans] biology, penis, strong, athletic, potent, boxer, Joe Louis, Jesse Owens, Senegalese troops, savage, animal, devil, sin.
>
> —Frantz Fanon, *Black Skin, White Masks*

> Interviewer: Is there any "correct" point of view in *The Narrows*? I think of this in relation to the themes of guilt and time. Abbie thinks that the past determines everything and that she, personally, is responsible for the evil that has occurred. Miss Doris thinks that everyone is responsible. Bill Hod and Weak Knees think of racism as being the cause of the evil. Is any one of these wholly correct?
>
> Petry: I suppose not, though racism comes closer to being *the* cause.
>
> —John O'Brien, *Interviews with Black Writers*

Given Ann Petry's reply to an interviewer's 1988 query as to whether or not she considers herself a feminist—"I don't like labels like that. . . . But I am an ally of feminists, there's absolutely no question about that" ("An Interview" 100)—one might be inclined to attribute it to any number of things. While I'm not necessarily questioning the author's sincerity—I think most writers bristle when critics attempt to pigeonhole them as a biologist might classify different forms of Japanese beetles—I take license here to complicate her assertion a bit. Perhaps it speaks to many African American women's long-standing incredulity regarding what they perceive as a "privileged white woman's movement" that marginalizes women of color and appears disproportionately anti–black male; writers as diverse as Ishmael Reed and Toni Morrison have echoed Petry's skepticism, albeit in vastly different keys. And while a certain racial skepticism might underlie Petry's eschewing of "feminist" as a discomfiting "label," I would conclude that it says less about race than it does about the scope of her literary imagination. Let me be clear: I'm not suggesting that "feminist" is synonymous with a narrowness of artistic vision. But Petry's response indicates that, at least in her artistic grammar, it becomes lexically and aesthetically binding if not prescriptive, a freighted term that circumscribes a writer and imposes a preset ideological perspective. As I noted in the opening chapter on Petry's literary reception and position, her most lauded novel, *The Street*, was and is often still read as a landmark achievement of "black protest" and "black feminist literature," both a female counterpart of *Native Son* and a gynocentered intervention upon and "corrective" of Wright's startlingly anti-black-woman classic.

Hence, I'm posing an alternative to the bifurcated way of thinking about "feminist" as a zero-sum discursive proposition. Notwithstanding her discomfort with the term, I read Petry's fictive corpus as both feminist *and* male-centered—as opposed to the *masculinism* of Wright and other male authors from the 1940s. If feminist implies empathy for the material lives of real black women and the obdurate constrictions that result from the triple oppressions of race, class, gender, then Petry's oeuvre engages these concerns as they relate to black men as well. Informed by Arthur Flannigan Saint-Aubin's idea that "any theory of masculinity in this culture must ask the following: How is masculinity shaped by racism, capitalism, patriarchal hegemony, and heterosexist assumptions?" (1057), I contend that Petry's pathbreaking representations not only dramatize black men's formations as social subjects (e.g., interpellated by race and class), but that she steadfastly probes the psychosexual dimensions of black masculine identity. In her complicating of black literary masculinity, she foregrounds the multisubjectivity of what have often been hierarchialized or compartmentalized identities, where the socioracial subsumes the sexual and emotional. Counterpoising what many black male and female authors were doing in the 1940s and early 1950s, she challenges the orthodox heteronormative framework from which black authors presumably operated, with its attendant elision of the "fissures" of black male subjectivity, its components which might be considered "non-normative" or deviations from the heterosexist ideal.

Looked at retrospectively, Petry's kaleidoscopic approach to black literary masculinity is not surprising vis-à-vis both her personal life and her nonfiction, which have received scant if any commentary.[1] Recall her reverence for the cavalcade of male family members who affected her—from her childhood in all-white Connecticut to her blossoming as an artist who tapped into a treasure trove of experiences with and stories about several male relatives: her choir-singing and gardening father, her runaway-slave grandfather, her fearless uncles who defended her and her sister against white children's assaults during their girlhood walks to school. Her short prose pieces exhibit her interest in black men past and present: if her satirical sketch "What's Wrong with Negro Men" in a 1947 issue of *Negro Digest* upbraided black men for their "belief in the God-given superiority of the male" (6), her paean to Venture Smith in the same periodical, "New England's John Henry," reflects her admiration for both the former slave whose indefatigable efforts made him a successful entrepreneur and for the legendary folk hero who remained undaunted in the face of white capitalist attempts to render him obsolete. Finally, an anecdote from another interview bears mentioning, for it encapsulates her progressive gender politics and her sensitivity to how men, like women, can be hemmed in by chauvinistic mind-sets. She recalled that during an artistic residence at the University of Hawaii, "One of the first questions that people would ask me was, 'What does your husband do?' And I would look them right in the eye and say, 'If I were a man, would you ask me what my *wife* did?'" (Mrtek 88). Her unvarnished candor underscores her sensitivity to and abiding artistic concern with the manifold nature of black male subjectivity, many parts of which are often elided in the overemphasizing of racial pain.

Monovalent versus Multivalent Black Masculinities: A Prolegomenon

African American masculinity as cultural subject and scholarly topos has mushroomed into a veritable cottage industry since the 1990s. Whether it be films such as actor/director Bill Dukes's disappointingly homophobic 2007 *Cover*; or Oprah gloomily decrying the "DL" (Down-Low) phenomenon, where self-professed "straight" brothers wantonly prevaricate and spread AIDS to "innocent" sisters; or madding throngs of sports journalists decrying the profligacy of the drug, money, and sex-addled "modern" (read *black)* athlete; the profusion of studies about and symposia on black men in any number of arenas (hip-hop, prison, the presidency); or black men as the subjects of special series in America's flagship newspapers—the African American male has been probed nearly to death.[2] With little variation, however, the epigraphic quotation from Frantz Fanon's 1967 landmark work *Black Skin, White Masks* has as its contemporary analog the following micro-text of the black male subject:

> The experience of the black-as-body becomes, not merely a Self-Other conflict, nor simply Hegel's torturous Master-Slave dialectic, but a variation on both these conditions, intensified by the particularity of the body's appearance as black, as "stained," *lacking interiority*. . . . The body as opaque and consciousness as invisible is developed in [Eldridge] Cleaver's brief essay ["The Primeval Mitosis" from *Soul on Ice*]. And if that consciousness is not experienced by the Other as invisible, it is the repository for the offscum of racial relations—to black subjectivity is attributed the contents that white consciousness itself fears to contain or confront: bestial sexuality, uncleanliness, criminality, all purported "dark things." (C. Johnson 228; emphasis added)

Not surprising is the commensurability of both Fanon's and novelist Charles Johnson's meditations, notwithstanding the almost thirty years separating them. One need only look at black maleness as theorized by founding father Thomas Jefferson, where he pseudo-scientifically reaches any number of odious conclusions; indeed, his musings on black men, who are "more ardent after their female: but love seems with them to be more an eager desire, than a tender delicate mixture of sentiment and sensation" (139), laid the groundwork for eighteenth- and nineteenth-century "studies" documenting the black body's congenitally savage physiognomy.

To be sure, African American writers have addressed the constancy of black masculine misrepresentations in the cultural and popular white American imaginary. Indelibly etched in our collective historical-literary imagination is Richard Wright's Bigger Thomas, the *ueber*-nigger who murders a white heiress and his black girlfriend. Ascribing to Bigger the inaccurate label "Negro sex-slayer," the press copy reads thusly: "Though the Negro killer's body does not seem compactly built, he gives the impression of possessing abnormal physical strength. He is about five feet, nine inches tall and his skin is exceedingly black. His lower jaw protrudes obnoxiously, reminding one of a jungle beast" (260). Not to be outdone in the life-mimicking-art category, a swarm of Los Angeles policemen over fifty years later would describe police brutality victim Rodney King as a "bear . . . emitting bearlike groans" (Gooding-Williams 166); offending officer Stacy Koon provided the specious rationale for his and fellow officers' barbarous assault, concluding that they had to keep pounding King because he was "like something out of a monster movie" (qtd. in Flannigan Saint-Aubin 1071). Cumulatively, the dominant racial-cultural episteme images the black male body as implacably feral and predatory, his subject or object position of little consequence.

I provide this thumbnail overview of popular and literary black masculinities to tease out the antinomic assumptions underlying these timeless, overarching configurations: a deeply held fear of both the black dick and the black fist legitimates their containment by any means necessary (imprisonment, battering, killing); and, concomitantly, this fear robs the black male of any form of agency, his sociophysical objectification foreclosing any ability to position himself as acting subject. Though we can uniformly repudiate the multiple mutilations of the black male body—whether simply "literary" or detestably "real"—too often neglected in both representation and analysis is what Johnson called the "interiority" of black maledom, their variegated emotional and psychic lives beyond the realm of the corporeal. Contesting often dwarfing and monochromatic notions of black masculinity is thus central to Petry's fictive refigurations.

Petry's plurality of black men anticipates critic Marlon Ross's intervention upon what he considers a deficiency in black masculinity studies: he signals his work's departure from analyses which "view black manhood as either a reactive identity overdetermined by the hegemony of white masculinity or as a parallel, if marginalized, cultural formation mimetically patterned on white masculinity" (*Manning the Race* 6–7). To be sure, Petry's narrative strategies in depicting black male subjects are much more hetero- than homogeneous—meaning that she foregrounds black men in an array of roles and situations not confined to "facing off" against the omnipresent nefarious (white) *Man*. In fact I see the convention-defying Petry laying the groundwork for authors as diverse as Morrison, Rita Dove, Gloria Naylor, and Suzan-Lori Parks: her multivisual portraitures paved the way for black women literary descendants who would devote much of their creative energies to exploring black male interiority. In proleptic relation to works such as *Song of Solomon* (1977), *Thomas and Beulah* (1986), *The Men of Brewster Place* (1998), and *Topdog/Underdog* (2002), Petry's fiction emerged in sharp relief to male contemporaries Wright and Ellison, who didn't quite imagine black women with as keen a critical eye as that which informs Petry's multivalent black masculinities.

"It Was a Queer Story": Maimed and Mammified Masculinities in The Narrows

When interviewer John O'Brien sought in 1973 to pin Petry down on the precise "cause of the evil" that infects the hamlet of Monmouth, Connecticut, in *The Narrows*, she declared that "racism comes closer to being *the* cause" (162). Specifically, it is the plague which catalyzes the young black protagonist Link Williams's death at the hands of moneyed and vengeful whites. In a 1988 interview, where she elaborated on the difficulty she had in crafting his death, she expounds further on Link's centrality: "Well, because it seemed to me that here was this man who in so many ways had to battle to survive; and he *had* survived—and had survived, I would think, fairly whole as a person. And that the end of his life should have been like that—I had trouble with that" (Wilson 79). When further queried regarding this "trouble," she addresses the specific event that impels his kidnapping and assassination: his multiply transgressive affair with the exceedingly wealthy—and white—munitions heiress Camilo Sheffield: "So when it came to this young man who, I think, was great . . . But on the other hand, the instant that he had said to these people [Camilo's mother and husband, who hatch and execute the kidnapping/murder], 'We were in love,' it was a death sentence; and there was no way, logically, that he would not be killed" (Wilson 79). Comparable to her discursive positioning of *The Street* within the boundaries of naturalistic/protest fiction, Petry is also aware of the currency and popularity of the miscegenation plot in American and African American culture. From Harriet Jacobs's *Incident in the Life of a Slave Girl;* to D. W. Griffith's racially incendiary *The Birth of a Nation;* to Chesnutt's fictions of the "color line"; to comparable novels such as *Autobiography of an Ex-Colored Man, Passing,* and *Light in August;* to Jack Johnson's serial breaches of the sexual-racial color line; to our crazed, unquenchable obsession with O. J. ad infinitum, ad nauseum—miscegenation has been America's sweetest taboo, the love that when spoken stokes fear, fascination, loathing, tragedy.

Given the exigencies of a dominant literary establishment that profits from our miscegenistic obsession, Petry on the one hand appropriates the black man-white woman discursive formation, which she suggests provides the novel its narrative spark. But I also think that Petry, wittingly or otherwise, is further engaging in a bit of discursive sleight-of-hand: by privileging what Iago sneeringly deemed "making the beast with two backs," she positions her novel within an already viable and marketable category, thereby fueling both critical and popular interest in her work. This dimension of *The Narrows* makes it a precursor of Baldwin's more celebrated *Another Country* (1962), a Byzantine novel that, among various other themes, centers dizzyingly numerous interracial couplings both homo- and heterosexual. Expanding the juxtaposition, I would argue that Link, like his artist counterpart Rufus Scott, is bedeviled by his own insoluble Anglophobia-Anglophilia, which becomes the fictive engine that propels the novel. Following Petry's positioning of Link at the text's locus, I will begin my discussion of *The Narrows* by tracing and deconstructing the cardinal moments in his life, concentrating somewhat on his racial identity but emphasizing his and other black males' formation as gendered, psychological subjects—what Charles Johnson deemed the *interiority* of black male subjects that includes but also goes beyond their racialized status.

Though the action of the novel commences when Link is twenty-six, Petry constructs it episodically as an arabesque of nonlinear flashbacks and flash-forwards. Perhaps the most crucial moment in Link's life occurs when, as an adult, he conflates a troika of particularly visceral events that involve his adoptive mother, white lover, and black surrogate father: "Abbie: Out of my house. Camilo: Black bastard. Bill Hod: I'll cripple you for life" (*Narrows* 260). This deceptively translucent comment becomes a sort of *mise-en-abîme*, a mini text that encapsulates the defining moments that engender his psychological and ultimately physical death. Significantly, the ostensible threads that connect this sequence—Abbie's violent reaction to and expulsion of Link and Camilo upon finding them in Link's bedroom; Camilo's equally vitriolic response to Link regarding Abbie's rage, which Camilo blames on him; and his surrogate father's vicious assault on him when he catches the sixteen-year-old Link at the brothel Hod himself operates—are race, sex, and violence in multiple manifestations. But on a deeper psychological level, in each moment Link is deprived of agency and voice, thereby relegating him to an inexorable status as subjected subject, as each of these moments, as well as one or two others, leave ephemerally physical but permanently emotional scars. He is a walking vortex of different types of pain.

Petry brackets the novel with references to one of its most pivotal moments, referenced in its opening and its conclusion. First, from the omniscient narrative perspective we glean Abbie's ruminations: "If Link had been her own child instead of an adopted child, would she, could she, have forgotten him for three months, three whole months?" (4). This sentiment is reiterated on the text's penultimate page by her closest confidante, undertaker Frances Jackson, who dissuades Abbie's threat to stop then-sixteen-year-old Link from playing a "violent" sport: "You may have forgotten that he was an orphan adopted by people who were strangers. But he hasn't forgotten it. And you may have forgotten that you rejected him, completely, totally, when the Major died. But he hasn't forgotten it. He never will. Football is good for him" (427). These women, Link's "two mommies" in the wake of his adoptive father's death, bespeak the depth of Link's emotional/spiritual deficits: Abbie retrospectively chides herself for being so paralyzed by her husband's (the "Major") death that Link became emotionally as well as physically expendable, while Frances implores her not to harm him any further by forbidding his participation in an activity that fosters male bonding. Petry uses as the novel's thematic moorings Link's position as racial and gendered metonym: his orphaning, his devalued position as a "black bastard," and the multiple violations visited upon him because of this derogated status. But underlying Abbie's and Frances's remorse is a plethora of concerns—home/homelessness, parenting, abandonment, gender identity, homosociality—that undergirds and propels the novel. Petry delves into the interstitial dimensions of black male subjectivity, those spaces and gaps that don't simply focus on social alienation as much as the interlocking connections between the constitutive parts that make up his whole self.

As Link's adoptive parents, Abbie and the Major hold antipodal racial philosophies. Though Petry herself described Abbie as "intelligent and kindly, really, at heart" (Wilson 79), Abbie liberally sprinkles her speech with antiblack insults, revealing her internalized Negrophobia. Some remarks that stand out among a litany of demeaning ones include her neologism "Aunt Mehalie," which she explains to an impressionable young Link isn't a specific person but "just a very old and rather funny way of describing all slovenly black women. When a colored woman looks old and fat and rumpled and not too clean we say she looks like Aunt Mehalie" (113). She frequently refers to Bill Hod, the proprietor of the Last Chance Bar, which is adjacent to the Crunch home, and his cook, Weak Knees, as "that man" and "the other one" (116), respectively but disrespectfully. Though she abhors what they represent, eight-year-old Link precociously detects the foolishness of her inconsistencies:

> Bill Hod's hair was straight, absolutely straight, and Abbie thought it was wonderful when a colored person had straight hair. His skin was light, and Abbie thought that was good, too, in a colored person, even though she herself wasn't exactly light, and neither was the Major. Then he remembered that what Abbie thought, or said, no longer counted with him. (116–17)

These sentiments are self-explanatory: black artists as diverse as George Schuyler, Lorraine Hansberry, and Spike Lee have exposed many blacks' calumnious belief that light skin and "good" hair are unassailable attributes, external markers of a blackness that closely approximates whiteness.[3] When Link asks about Weak Knees, Abbie dismissively responds, "I don't know anything about him. He's not the kind of person I'd be apt to know" (105). Abbie holds the same intolerant, supercilious racial and class biases associated with the quintessential white New Englander, views which Abbie mimics and holds sacrosanct. I will shortly argue that while young Link is disdainful of Abbie's deprecatory comments about the "unwashed" class of black folk, her views take a foothold in his consciousness, especially in his gender formation and the choices he makes in regard to sexual intimacy.

To counterbalance Abbie's miscalibrated racial metric, the Major offers both her and their adopted son a much more affirming view of black people; this evinces again Petry's recollections and integration of her male relatives' fondness for narrative and family history.[4] In the 1988 *MELUS* interview, Petry recalls that her own father "was a great storyteller, and he loved to tell stories about his family" (Wilson 72); she also remembers her uncles' stories as "just plain wonderful. . . . I grew up with these stories, and I've told them over and over again in various ways." These men's collective stories involve black people in myriad circumstances, but two stand out: blacks as conjurers and folk healers, and black people standing down hostile whites. These relatives are clearly models for the Major, a "born storyteller" (34) who regales first Abbie and later Link with legendary tales of male and female heroism. The Major heartily boasts that his "people were swamp niggers" and that his great-grandfather, Theodore Crunch, "bit an Irishman's ear off in a fight in the dooryard of an inn" (36). Without question, "unlike Abbie, he [the Major] sees no reason to minimize his racial heritage or to censure his ancestors for their free-spirited ways" (Holladay 81–82). So when Abbie denigrates Hod and Weak Knees to a young, impressionable Link, the Major offers a necessary if somewhat holier-than-thou admonition: "Abbie, if you believe that the Lord watches over and cares about a sparrow, then you must also believe that He watches over and cares about Bill Hod" (107). Predictably, Abbie chafes at the Major's remembrances of this unrepentantly black outlaw family history, admitting to herself that "you didn't like the stories. He made those people live again. They were an emotional primitive people, whose existence even in the past seemed somehow to be an affront to the things you believed in, and stood for" (36). In fact, the Major's name, Dory, denotes Petry's intention for him to embody a formidable, noble black history and folk tradition: Given that the novel was published only a few years after World War II, he is quite possibly named for Dorie Miller, the first heroic figure of any race to emerge from the war.[5]

Thus, the text positions the Major as the lone Crunch family member espousing an oppositional *Weltanschauung* trumpeting African Americans' resistance in the face of insurmountable racial oppression and one that should be transmitted to future generations. Unsurprisingly, his death unsettles and traumatizes both Link and Abbie. Link's visceral response to viewing the Major's corpse in their living room is one of ineffable dread: "All of him thinner, smaller. Link bent over the coffin and there was a queer, sweetish, sickening smell that made him gasp" (111). Since he has no language to express this unspeakable pain, emotional malaise and disease become insufficient but default responses. This surely affects young Link's gender formation, underscoring Anthony Rotundo's observations regarding boys' clotted emotional lives: "As boys learned to master pain, fear, and the need for emotional comfort, they were encouraged to suppress other expressions of vulnerability, such as grief and tender affection" (44). And Abbie, enveloped in her own crippling grief, doesn't simply fail to console Link; she completely disregards his very existence, causing her subsequent abiding guilt. The Major's death—inadvertently caused by Abbie, who ignored Bill Hod's insistence that she should call a doctor; she made the grave mistake of assuming that the Major was drunk when in fact he was suffering a fatal stroke—coupled with Abbie's understandable but neglectful abdication of her parental duty, inaugurates Link's emotional if not actual death.

The cataclysmic moment occurs after Link has viewed the Major's body and experienced a dread so profound that he skipped the funeral:

> They [Abbie and Frances] hadn't even missed him. They didn't know he hadn't been at the Major's funeral. They had shut him out of their lives, cut him off from them. He didn't care about Miss Jackson and what she did or didn't do. But Abbie had been his whole existence, she had watched over him, listened to everything he said, told him

> what to wear, what to eat, when he should go to bed, had loved him. Now she had forgotten all about him. It was like being nowhere. Lost. Nowhere at all. (113)

Thus, Link's emotionally occlusive response to death, coupled with Abbie's callous if not willful exclusion of him from the mourning ritual, could potentially have a negative impact on his gender development. Given the child's earlier infatuation with Abbie, whom he "was going to marry when he grew up" (102), Link's prostrate position here harkens back to Frederick Douglass's viewing of his Aunt Hester's brutalization at the hands of his master/father; while obviously not synonymous, Link, too, is unable to fulfill the presumed role as "protector," since his mother's grief is so impenetrable. Link's gendered response to visceral emotional pain—silence, physical inertia, and failure to fulfill his "masculine" responsibility—leaves indelible psychic scars that throb throughout the remainder of his childhood/adolescence, surfacing at two additionally pivotal moments.

If the Major's tales of the historically inestimable power and will of African Americans are meant to nullify Abbie's deprecatory beliefs, Link's "formal" instruction provides lessons unequivocally meant to foster a corrosive self-image. Petry's depiction of school as an institution that devalues black children and fails to educate them recurs throughout her fiction and reflects her own girlhood experiences: she recollects that she and her high school English teacher "weren't particularly fond of each other" (Wilson 73).[6] From a racial and pedagogical perspective, Petry denounces the fallacious presentation of enslavement: "I read the sections [in American history textbooks] that had to do with slavery, and I was appalled. I thought, 'Now, look at all these youngsters growing up in this country, whose only knowledge, really and truly, of black people is what they read in these books.' The blacks were always portrayed as happy in slavery. They could all sing and dance. They were immoral, for the most part" ("An Interview" 99). Correlatively, Petry is relentless (perhaps a bit overzealous) in portraying the educational establishment's cancerous attitudes toward African American children through her portrayal of Link's teacher, "Miss Dwight" (i.e., "white").

Given Link's demeaned status as a black child in a predominantly white New England school, the deluge of racist acts he experiences is de rigueur. Miss Dwight stages a minstrel show to raise money for the P.T.A., assigning Link the role of "Sambo," though she opines, "We won't have to use any burnt cork on Link though" (135); when she reads Link's lines during rehearsal, the other children "laughed until they almost cried. He was the butt of all the jokes, he was to say all the yessuhs and the nosuhs, he was to explain what he was doing in the chicken house" (134); and when she finally insists that his father "teach you the buck and wing," he pitifully replies "My father's dead" (135). The unrelenting cruelty that Miss Dwight disseminates is reenacted by the children themselves, who would "band together in a tight invulnerable group, welded together by their whiteness," and sneer "Lookatthecoon" and take to "calling him Sambo, during school hours, after school hours, on Saturdays" (133, 136). I relate these episodes not merely to rehash the unintended downside of integration—ironically, the book appeared a year before the seismic Brown vs. Topeka Board of Education decision and two decades before Boston's busing conflagrations—but to further emphasize Abbie's role in Link's emotional destabilization, specifically how her actions make her complicit with a racist educational apparatus that some still feel is particularly injurious to young black males. Moreover, if one accepts the premise that "schools are essentially feminine institutions" (Sexton 25), one could conclude that Link's school is a space where white women wield untrammeled power over black children. Therefore, we can observe the nexus between the Major's death, Abbie's neglect, and the systemic impeding of Link's intellectual and racial-gender development.

Abbie's incurious reaction to the jaundiced educational system marks yet another breach in her and Link's steadily rupturing relationship. Link responds to the torrent of racial humiliations in a way reminiscent of the physical and psychic dis-ease he experienced upon the Major's death: "He decided that he would get sick . . . so sick that he wouldn't be able to be Sambo" (135). Link displays here a keen resourcefulness, possibly drawing upon the Major's lessons about his ancestors' native survivalist instincts; his feigned illness becomes a deft resistive maneuver to counteract the racially malignant Sambo role that he's assigned. Regrettably, however,

Link's canny tricksterism degenerates into a palpable melancholy that leads to truancy and despondency at school: "He stopped trying to learn anything. There wasn't any use. He thought she [Miss Dwight] might forget about him if he acted as though he were deaf, dumb, blind" (142). As well, Abbie's abandoning him has now taken a foothold in his consciousness—invisibility now being preferable to the visceral psychoracial pain that his white teacher inflicts with impunity.

Link's explicable but self-abnegating response has its roots in clinicians' etiological work on how anger manifests itself in African American males: These researchers conclude that many young black males "have erected elaborate defense mechanisms and developed dysfunctional behavior in order to prevent their rage from overwhelming them or causing them constant distress" (Gibbs 115). Presented with the opportunity to advocate on Link's behalf, Abbie supinely accepts the principal's "remedy": "Link would soon have to go in the class for the mentally retarded, the dummies as the kids said, because he was now behaving as though he were halfwitted" (142). Again, Petry is prophetic in diagnosing the school system's pathologizing of black boys, a standard practice that persists even today. When a frustrated Abbie wonders if "there's something wrong with his mind" (143), we can detect the harmful alliance between our culture's bedrock institutions, the family and the school system, which are intended to serve as children's physical, emotional, and intellectual custodians. Thus, Link's intellectual and emotional fates are sealed, his discredited status as a black male subject mapped out by those entrusted with his welfare.

Undeniably, Abbie's role in Link's imbricated identities—racial, gendered, social, sexual—cannot be overstated, for she is the young boy's anchor. Geographer Yi-Fu Tuan's study *Space and Place* is instructive here, as he particularizes the psychospatial dimensions of mother-child relations:[7] "If we define place broadly as a focus of value, or nurture and support, then the mother is the child's primary place. . . . Their [mothers'] image is one of stability and permanence. The mother is mobile, but to the child she nonetheless stands for stability and permanence . . . she is his familiar environment and haven. A child is adrift—placeless—without the supportive parent" (29). I don't quote Tuan here to heap incommensurate blame on Abbie for Link's psychological disequilibrium and subsequent demise; Frances's black housekeeper, Miss Doris, functions as the black neighborhood's chorus in her solecistic but crystalline summation of Link's demise and ultimate murder: "It were everybody's fault" (415). And in the ensuing section, I will argue that his proximity to the most execrable elements of patriarchal masculinity compound the psychoracial damage Abbie has inflicted.

But, to borrow from Tuan, it is Link's very "adriftness," his inability to find a safe harbor throughout his desultory journey—his voyage to an Ivy League school, Canada, the Navy, and back to the Narrows—that epitomizes his psychospiritual homelessness. In keeping with the nautical imagery here, it is not coincidental that when Frances expels him from the grieving ritual, he seeks refuge at the dock (the Narrows neighborhood is on a river that runs through Monmouth), where he sits "like an old man" who "felt like crying" (111). Reminiscent of scores of real and literary black men—from a young Langston Hughes, who threw his books into the sea and set sail as a merchant marine, to Cory in August Wilson's *Fences*, who joins the army to escape his martinet of a father—Link enacts a fervent desire to sever the ties of home and school, seen as predominantly feminine spaces; officially sanctioned male-dominated spheres provide the most accessible escape route. But in another discursive intervention and re-imagining of masculine space, Petry relocates the grieving and rudderless eight-year-old Link to a port that is initially nurturingly homosocial and domestic but ultimately harmful to his burgeoning manhood.

Unwittingly exiled, Link finds shelter at the "Last Chance," the neighborhood bar/restaurant adjacent to the Crunch home. Most noteworthy is Petry's re-envisioning of both space and family. The wayfaring Link "went and stood beside Bill Hod, not saying anything, just standing beside him, in the hope that being near a grownup would help some of the misery, some of the lonesomeness to leak out of him" (114). At this juncture, Hod becomes Link's de facto father, ushering him into the bar's kitchen, which is "warm" with "lots of light" (115). Lovingly served by Weak Knees, Link devours the nourishing soul food that replenishes him physically but, more importantly, emotionally: "He gulped down a plate of fried chicken and rice and gravy and kale and four biscuits and swallowed a glass of milk" (115). Petry's emphasis on the kitchen's "warmth" renders it a psychic and spiritual womb for Link; this neo-natal space differs appreciably from Abbie's "dark, cold house" (118). To be sure, "here is the vitality, warmth, and joy of black culture; it is a kitchen in which smells represent the Sunday morning cooking smells of The Narrows as a whole, the heart of the black community" (Weir 86).

Not only does this homo-gendered environment sate his physical hunger, but Hod and Weak Knees—his unofficial adoptive parents—grant him the space to mourn: Link's cathartic "shivering and sobbing," borne out of the Major's physical death and Abbie's emotional desertion, mark both a spiritual-emotional exorcism and a regeneration. After sleeping in Hod's bed,

> when he woke up the next morning, warm and relaxed, the room was full of sunlight. No curtains at the windows, no pictures on the walls, walls painted white, and so there was sunlight or reflected light everywhere. As he looked around, Bill Hod came into the room, naked, nothing on his feet. He stared at him, surprised, a little shocked, because he had never seen a grownup without any clothes on. (119)

Hod's saloon becomes an oasis, an andro-centered Eden that not only fulfills Link's emotional deficits; the literal and metaphorical enlightenment of Link's new *home* more than countermands the racial and emotional endarkenment that engulfed the bleak Crunch *house*—Abbie's house no longer the hallowed, safe haven her name inheres. Link's peering at the starkly naked Hod harkens back to a halcyon, prelapsarian moment free of racial and gender prohibitions and taboos; Petry alchemizes the saloon into a seaside version of Twain's tropological raft.

Hod and Weak Knees' re-christening of Link as "Sonny" precedes a more monumental achievement: They "re-educated him on the subject of race," disrupting and correcting the school system and Abbie's conflating of blackness and pathology by "prov[ing] to him . . . that black could be other things, too" (144–45). The author herself pinpointed Link's life-altering three months at the Last Chance as a continuation of the Major's "race man" function in the Crunch home: "Weak Knees and Bill Hod are trying to give Link a sense of pride in order to survive. What they are using is a survival tactic" (Ervin, "Just a Few Questions," 103). To be sure, Petry presciently illustrates the indispensable role black men play in black boys' psychoracial development, as this same-gendered environ can be as nurturing as any socially sanctioned and deified heteronormative unit. As Nellie McKay notes in her introduction to the 1988 reprinted text, "This multiple parenting (which further integrates Link into his community) also implies an interesting critique of nontraditional versus traditional child-rearing practices in most Western societies" (xii). While gender roles are not necessarily jettisoned—Hod exhibits the more socially determined "masculine" traits, and Weak Knees has the more socially defined "feminine" ones (in addition to cooking, he's also described as having a "funny highpitched voice" [104])—Petry does anticipate writers like Toni Morrison and Albert Murray who, in the novels *The Bluest Eye* and *Train Whistle Guitar*, respectively, also depict the indispensable role of same-gender environments on young black males' evolution as racial and gendered subjects.

Still, the Last Chance, with its enigmatic name simultaneously suggesting potential reinvigoration and inevitable doom, is a complicated, even conflicted space. Thus, in spite of its seminal role in young Link's emotional rebirth—he goes as far as hiding when Abbie's grief-induced haze dissipates and she and Frances try to retrieve him—Hod's saloon does not remain a homo-gendered oasis as Link matures. Contrarily, the Last Chance will manifest the worst practices of nuclear families that are moored in antedated gender roles, specifically, its reinforcement of patriarchal privilege. Regrettably, it will aggrandize masculine prerogative, power, and phallocentrism, reifying the "patriarch paradigm" that bell hooks at once calls out and deconstructs: "Reliance on a single male authority figure is dangerous because it creates a climate of autocracy where the politics of coercion (and that includes violence) are used to maintain that authority" (*Killing Rage* 68). Petry's naming of Hod, I imagine, is not by happenstance; given that it rhymes with "God" and can also be bent into "hood" captures the incongruous behavior he exhibits as simultaneous surrogate father and merciless tyrant.

As evidence of the Last Chance's and Hod's vexing and vacillating positions, consider that the bar is described as "safe as a convent. . . . Cozy. Homelike" (82); the adult Link refers to Hod as "Father Hod"(98); Link's aforementioned gazing at the naked Hod clearly evokes the story of Noah and his son Ham—Noah's offspring being the prototypical dispossessed nigger, banished for viewing his drunken, unclad father; and in a description that conjures up Christ's role as "light of the world," young Link rhapsodizes that "this man, Bill Hod, had taken him out of the dark and put him in the sun" (119). More damningly, this veritable godhead is also the "father" of vice in the Narrows, running his bar without a permit and operating brothels as well. Later, Link will describe his eyes as "hooded, like the eyes of a snake" (268); and Link also asks Weak Knees, "Why does King Hod walk around The Narrows with a gun strapped under his armpit?" (272). Thus, Hod's seemingly "holy" acts are defiled, for these latter descriptions set the stage for what becomes a cataclysmic moment in Link-Hod's relationship: the latter's violent beating of his adolescent charge. Inverting the Bible's temporal sequence, where the Old Testament's codification of vengeance and punishment are tempered by the New Testament's doctrine of love and mercy, Hod initially displayed warmth and compassion to eight-year-old Link, only to nullify these acts by the barbarity he visits upon him exactly eight years later. Ironically enough, it is the infuriatingly naïve Abbie who discerns Hod's execution of Old Testament, "Moses' Law"-type justice when she presumes that Hod will avenge Link's murder by killing his white lover Camilo Treadway Sheffield, whom Hod holds responsible: Abbie perceptively observes, "He has always taken an eye for an eye, and a tooth for a tooth" (424).

Hod's ascension in the neighborhood, where he reigns as a less-than-beneficent kingpin and arms himself in the manner of a small-time hood, has crushing consequences for sixteen-year-old Link's gender formation. Indeed, Hod's display of inflamed, extreme manhood conforms to what Joseph Pleck calls the "hyper-masculinity hypothesis," which entails "delinquency and violence, conservative social attitudes (for example, authoritarianism and homophobia), and bodybuilding" (96). While Link "always returns to the time he was eight," when an inconsolable Abbie was oblivious to his very being, there is another event he can't escape: the ferocious beating his surrogate father will administer when Link visits one of his brothels. Tipped off by the madam, "vast, fat, yellow of skin" China (278), Hod circumvents Link's sexual initiation by "violently, suddenly" pushing open the door and ordering him to "get out of here." While Hod's reprimand is understandable, his pugilistic assault is not:

> Bill walked toward him, took hold of his arm, twisted it, kept twisting it, so that he had either to bend toward him or resist him by not bending, and resistance meant the bone in his wrist would snap, he could have sworn he felt it give, and so he bent toward him, and the pain that shot up his arm took his breath away. . . . And twisted his arm again, and the pain ran up his shoulder into his neck, reached into his spine, and he thought he's trying to break my back, break my spine. (278–79)

This moment is indelibly seared into the adult Link's consciousness, as he recalls being examined by a doctor who conjectures that he had been beaten with a "rawhide"; the doctor concludes that "a man capable of doing this sort of thing to a sixteen-year-old-boy ought to be put in prison. If I were Mrs. Crunch, I would have him arrested. He's a mad dog. He ought to be locked up" (258). Finally, the physical pain that Hod metes out is accompanied by an equally vituperative warning to his adolescent charge: "You stay out of that beer parlor [the Moonbeam, another Hod-operated bar] up the street. You go in there one more time and I'll come up there and smack you all over the place as though you were a twobit whore" (277). Hod's imposition of patriarchal domination analogizes a proto-Freudian situation, where "the law of the Father prevents the disruption that would be caused by the child's desire. In this vein, one can understand the Father's impulse to perpetually infantilize the concupiscent child, to prevent his evolution into man" (Flannigan Saint-Aubin 1061). From this perspective, it becomes evident that Hod consolidates his own tenuous black male subjectivity by not only snuffing out sixteen-year-old Link's budding sexuality but by degradingly castrating—*feminizing*—him in the process while also revealing Hod's own predictable misogyny; without question, there shall be no other "hard" males before Hod in this tacit sexual competition.[8] Hod's quelling of Link's natural sexual awakening and subsequent brutalization are indeed psychosexually debilitating.

Taken together, Hod's physio-lingual thuggery and Link's processing of it—think of Morrison's notion of *re-memory*—constitute the locus of Link's psychosexual d/evolution; consequently, this fateful event engenders his sense of devitalized, deformed masculinity. In effect, Hod is transmogrified into the most detestable emblem of autocratic white patriarchal hegemony, which is intimated in Link's description of the naked Hod: "The skin on his body was almost white, the forearms, and his face, tan by contrast" (119). Thus, it's not farfetched to imagine Hod as the incarnation of an incongruously mulatto, sadistic slavemaster. Ironically enough, the adult Link becomes a historian who aspires to write "a rather specialized, but very brief, study of slavery and the Civil War" to correct his race's collective disenfranchisement, which previously and personally played out in his adolescent enslavement under the phenotypically "white" Hod's reign (325).

In addition to its African American historical resonances, Hod's fanatical, violent treatment of Link reflects some intriguing parallels between it and Aboriginal initiation ceremonies, which Harold Schechter examines in his essay "Symbols of Initiation in *Adventures of Huckleberry Finn*." Synthesizing studies of myth/anthropology by Joseph Campbell, Mircea Eliade, J. L. Henderson, and Arnold Van Gennep, he observes:

> "The novices [initiates] are seized by their guardians and carried off to the forest." The elders who perform this ritual kidnapping, moreover, are terrifying figures, for they are usually colored white—smeared with white clay or ashes or covered with bird down [sic] (Campbell 1969)." . . . Speaking of these "white clay men," Henderson (1967a) explains that "although impersonating death in its ghostly aspect, they are also harbingers of that life which springs anew from the original source of all things. . . . This white is an ambiguous color and would seem to embody just that spirit of paradox which is the essence of the death and rebirth experience. . . ." What we find at the beginning of the puberty rites, then, is the boy being torn from the maternal sphere—from the

> control of the women—and spirited off to the forest by a "resurrected," deathly white bogeyman. (69–70)

Despite geo-cultural gulfs between African American and Aboriginal boys' rites of passage, the fact that the Aborigines, like black Americans, have been historically marginalized and subjected to epidermalized oppression connects these pubescent-male initiation rituals. While Link serendipitously found in Hod/Weak Knees an alternative family, his surrogate father degenerates into a "terrifying figure" who dispenses savage physical and psychological punishments. In effect, Hod incarnates the "spirit of paradox," embodying the sacred and the profane, the divine and the demonic [Petry's comparing his eyes to "the eyes of a snake" (268); at one point he's even described as "looking as evil as Satan" (299)], liberator and enslaver, paterfamilias and ogre.

As the evocative commingling of the gangsta and the gothic, Hod foists upon Link the deplorable codes of a hypermasculine ontology, rooted in belligerence and control; in effect, he severely annuls both the nurturance and black-affirming re-education that marked Link's arrival into Hod and Weak Knees' alternative, same-sex family. I return to bell hooks' analysis to underscore the ultimate peril of Link's second adopted home: "Patriarchal families are not safe, constructive places for the development of identities and kinship ties free of the crippling weight of domination. Patriarchy is about domination" (*Killing Rage* 73). Inculcating "Father Hod's" lesson that domination is the cornerstone of masculine identity, young Link reenacts it by concocting a plot to avenge Hod's psychic emasculation and physical pummeling: "The trouble with me is a man who isn't my father tried to kill me. Because that was the summer I was sixteen, the summer I stole F. [Frances] K. Jackson's gun because I was going to kill King Hod because he caught me in China's place again, and, justifiably, from his point of view, and, justifiably, according to his theory of educating a young male, damn near beat me to death" (323). Though half-cocked in its conception, Link's testosterone-induced response shows that he is his faux-father's son, having adopted Hod's vigilante, eye-for-an-eye ethos. One need only consider the deplorable statistics on black male-on-black male brutality to discern the cyclical nature of homo-racial, homo-gendered violence and its psychically crippling impact.[9]

Petry's own judicious assessment of Hod—she proclaims that he, like other characters in her work, is not "all evil" but instead "mixtures of good and evil" (O'Brien 162)—reflects her balanced conceptualization of literary masculinity, irrespective of race. For instance, while *The Narrows* is relatively free of central white male characters, one peripheral character, Bob White, merits mention. As Link's high school history instructor, it is White who invests him with the challenge of researching and writing a history on slavery and the Civil War. Reflecting on White's mentoring, Link recalls one of his teacher's maxims in particular: "Once a man knows who he is, knows something of his own history, he can rid himself of selfdoubt, of belittling comparisons" (324). Here, Petry demonstrates that white masculinity, like its black counterpart, can't be reduced to caricatures and monochromatic portraitures; inarguably, White's is an extension of the late Major's project: imparting the wisdom that the past is neither ignoble nor glorious, but that it can contain precious information about one's culture that can elevate one's sense of self. Thus, White balances more unsavory white male figures—characters such as Camilo's husband and Link's murderer, Captain Bunny Sheffield. A far cry from Miss Dwight and Hod, White models for Link an alternative to both his former teacher's malignant racism and his surrogate father's equally perverted hypermasculine belligerence.

As this arabesque novel makes evident, characters such as Hod too are balanced by the more solicitous Weak Knees, who exemplifies an alternative to Hod's brutality and vindictiveness. Their quasi-marriage, in fact, softens Hod's "hard" persona and reinforces how homo-gendered "families" such as this one and Abbie-Frances's are the cornerstone of the novel. Indeed, this epitomizes what I consider the author's forward-thinking, radical status. And though Hod's combatively masculinist modus operandi seems to win out, the arc of Petry's masculine representations includes variations, men for whom domination and power are not their raison d'être, or men who grapple with such codes of male conduct. For these men, gender and gender roles are unstable; this is where Petry, to borrow from Ellison's iconic Invisible Man, traverses the "lower frequencies" of black masculinity, which too often are short-circuited by many midcentury writers' acceptance of the culturally enshrined, univocal conception of manhood that leaves little room for variance. Within the sphere of the novel's central male characters, the ostensible "moderated" alternative to the more socially sanctioned Hodian model of masculinity is the Treadways' butler, Malcolm Powther.

Powther's assertion that "it was a queer story" (333) upon reading the newspaper's account of the false rape charge Camilo lodges against Link reverberates with sexual-gender undertones. If local lore situates Hod as the unofficial CEO of the licit and illicit in the Narrows—"In the barber shop, they said he was the owner of The Last Chance, that he was a gambler, an operator of houses of ill fame, a numbers king, probably nearer the truth, that nobody really knew what illegal enterprises he directed or controlled but that he was unquestionably a racketeer" (202)—Powther, at least in demeanor and bearing, represents his polar opposite. Known throughout the community as the butler at Treadway Hall, various descriptions of both his actions and attire provide a composite sketch. Physically, he's often pictured as: a "polite, precisely dressed, little man" (11); "Little Mr. Powther" (11); a "polishedlooking person" (14); and "a funny little man" (189). Moreover, his clothing consists of "sharply creased trousers, starched white shirt, carefully knotted black necktie, highly polished black shoes suggest[ing] conservatism, neatness" (331). As Margaret Jordan observes in her study on historical and literary representations of black servants, "The figure of the African American servant delineates the rules of social engagement, precisely defining the limitations and circumstances under which 'American' identity is constructed and maintained, or to which one is entitled to lay claim to being an American" (24). I would add only that the implications of Powther's presence in several spheres go beyond race, striking at notions of masculinity, phallocentricity, and power.

A more modernized black retainer, he attends to the explicit and unexpressed domestic demands of the Treadways. When the chauffeur, Al, falls ill, Powther so seamlessly replaces him that Camilo's mother, whom Powther affectionately calls "The Madam," replies, "You managed this so quickly, Powther. Thank you" (162); simultaneously, he "nursed

Al through a four-day illness and looked after his own work as well, running out to the garage to sponge him off, to give him the liquids and the medicine the doctor had ordered." While one might be tempted to make a correlation between Powther and other prototypical literary mammies such as Faulkner's Dilsey Gibson, one marked difference is Powther's willingness to perform such domestic duties for his wife Mamie and their three children (the Powthers rent an apartment in Abbie's house). For instance, after dinner, he "found an apron, tied it tight around his waist, and set to work, clearing the table, washing the dishes, scouring the pots, then scouring the sink, boiling the dish towels" (174), all before tucking the kids in and spinning an elaborate fairy tale for their amusement. And in perhaps the most plangent expression of this role, Powther, upon hanging up his coat in the bedroom closet and sulking over his inability to deter Mamie and Hod's openly adulterous relationship, "in a petty unreasoning kind of anger, born of what he could not say, . . . pushed the newestlooking dress from its hanger and watched it fall, in a heap, on the closet floor. Tomorrow morning, if he had time, he would rearrange the closet before he went to work. Mamie liked having him fix up her clothes. He pressed her dresses, sewed on buttons, repaired the split seams under the arms" (167). This passage particularly lends itself to an array of interpretive possibilities—Powther as wife, Powther as cuckolded husband, even the space possibly hinting at the prissy Powther as "closet" homosexual. His characterization reveals the possibility of all of these identities; incontestably, his primness and domesticity are his most enduring traits, for they provide a window into what I deem his tertiary anxieties of sexuality, gender, and race.

In Powther Petry imagines a character who breaches society's rigid gender taxonomies in both his personal and professional lives. His departure from the socially ordained patriarchal and phallocentric constructions of masculinity to which Hod adheres clearly liminalizes him; Petry spatially amplifies this notion when Powther, listening to Al's racist-sexist harangue regarding how Camilo was "askin' to be raped by a nigger" in "Niggertown," is "standing half in, half out of the kitchen" (337). Powther's dissident masculinity, as he straddles the threshold of the most prototypically feminine space, dovetails with E. Anthony Rotundo's accurate diagnosis of society's dis-ease with "masculine domesticity," a scourge that "presumed that men could—and should—carry out female tasks for which their male nature did not fit them" (263). Concomitantly, society is quick to affix any number of scurrilous labels to men who "perform" femininity, be it in dress or presumed "women's roles"—sissy, pansy, nellie, faggot, bitch, "woman" itself being the worst "epithet" one "real" man could hurl at a man-manqué. Even the overly decorous Abbie mocks Powther's feminine persona in the rhyme "Little Mister Powther/ Sat on a sowther" (12), conjuring images of the put-upon Little Miss Muffet. Appropriately enough, Powther will later embroider for youngest son J.C. the fanciful fairytale of a "princess with golden hair who was kept chained deepdown in a dark cold dungeon" (174–75); this diaphanous fable barely veils his own various confinements—in a marriage to a brazenly adulterous wife, in the butler's pantry at the Treadways, in the attic apartment he rents from Abbie—as an excessively prim man in a culture that sanctions various forms of masculine excess (physical violence, sexual license), as an Anglophilic black man relegated to "Niggertown." But a more apt descriptor for the fastidious Powther might be that of *dandy*, a figure who defies socially prescribed notions of gender in wardrobe and demeanor.

Jessica Feldman's innovative study on dandies in modernist literature provides a fitting framework for Powther's alternative male subjectivity:

> The dandy is . . . artificial in dress and deportment, always elegant, often theatrical. He creates "la mode," style itself. . . . Aloof, impassive, vain, the dandy has a defensive air of superiority that shades into the aggression of impertinence and cruelty. Military in bearing and discipline, the dandy is also as fragile and whimsical as a butterfly. Outwardly cool, he burns inwardly. A man, he pursues an ideal of charm and personal beauty which the dominant culture, against which he poses himself, labels feminine. (3)

Never one to shape characters according to a preset social template, Petry's configuration of Powther both coincides with and deviates from various elements in Feldman's schematization. While one can detect his effete persona, he simultaneously measures himself against a hegemonic white culture that he reveres and, just as important, he also mentally dissociates himself from the subordinated and disempowered black one in which he resides; clearly he parrots Abbie in consistently disparaging it. His comments about the Narrows rehearse the dominant hermeneutical practice of pathologizing black people and black spaces. Not only does he hastily and inaccurately believe, without any tangible evidence, that "Mrs. Crunch's unscrupulous young nephew" "immediately attacked" Camilo, but he categorizes the neighborhood in simplistic sociological argot that demeans blacks: "Dock Street at the corner of Dumble meant poverty, colored people, tenements, whether you called it Dark Town, Little Harlem, The Narrows, or The Bottom" (334). Powther's marginalization within the black community is made even starker by the hypermasculine Hod, who presides over both legitimate and illegitimate enterprises in the space where Powther physically resides but emotionally despises.

Petry's twinning of Powther's raced-gendered anxieties is illustrated most profoundly in his employment by and affiliation with the Treadways. Ironically enough, Feldman's observation regarding the dandy's "militaristic" proclivities speaks to his position within this omnipotent white family, which owns and operates the town's munitions factory. But while the Treadways wield material, consequential power by fueling and profiting from the American war industry, Powther's faux-power consists of overseeing domestic duties at Treadway Hall. In fact, this quasi authority shores up Powther's diminished conception of his masculinity vis-à-vis Hod's communal reign, Hod and Mamie's uninhibited adulterous relationship, and Mamie's frequent reproaches (e.g., "Oh, for God's sake, Powther, why don't you shut up?" 173):

> Once again he reminded himself, as he always did whenever he felt a little low in his mind, that though he was constantly defeated at home, he was a conqueror, a victor, at Treadway Hall. His predecessor at the Hall had been an Englishman, and though he knew he was the equal if not the superior of the Englishman, he also knew that he would have to fight and win a war against the other servants before he was accepted. (163)

Powther's inconsequential authority at Treadway Hall becomes compensatory, assuaging his failure to fulfill society's enshrined role of sovereign in his own home ("a man's home is his castle"). And his replacing of an "Englishman" and presumed sense of superiority more than offset his compromised racial and class status. However, Powther's domestic militarism, though bolstering an attenuated self-conception, merely encases him in racially and historically prescribed and truncated roles.

Though Madam Treadway was initially reticent about hiring "colored help," Powther tempered this racially demeaning slight by summoning memories of working as a butler for "Old Copper" in Baltimore, whom he describes as "just about the richest man in the country." Thus, he perceives his proximity to an economically superior white family as currency to bolster his initially tenuous position with the race-leery Treadways: "A war of the kind that he was involved in had to be won quickly, and the ammunition consisted largely of a way of looking down one's nose, and, a good stock of stories about the tremendously rich, fabulously rich, families one had worked for" (163–64). This passage, coupled with the one in the previous paragraph, is particularly revelatory in its war metaphor; starkly exposed here is the gulf between real, "white" power and the feeble sense of "black" power Powther gleans from those same whites permitting him to *perform* blackness—that is, their allowing him to sate his chimerical sense of masculinity via "feminized" domestic roles of organizing and caretaking, which have historically fallen mostly on the shoulders of black women.

This dandified, effeminate masculinity reaches its apex in his busied preparations for "a high tea, in the afternoon, for three hundred young women from the plant" (335). Mrs. Treadway takes the time to commend him for punctiliously organizing the function—"It's perfect. Everything is perfect. Thank you, Powther" (351)—and afterward he surmises that "she was always thanking him for doing his job, as though he were an old friend who had done a favor for her." Mentally re-imagining himself as more peer than peon, Powther experiences a palpable adrenaline rush from Madam Treadway's approval: "There's a glow in me now, he thought, just as there is in these girls. She has restored my confidence, made me believe in myself again" (351). Thus, Petry vividly dramatizes

Powther's almost comically servile status, which engenders a revitalization of his anemic masculine disposition. Even the name *Powther* audibly gainsays his illusory sense of *power* (contrast Link's self-deprecating gloss on his own name as a "contraction of Lincoln," 67). Serving more of a menial grunt or foot-soldier role in his delusional "domestic war," Powther conjures images of archetypically American mammies such as Margaret Mitchell's obsequious Prissy and domineering Mammy from the thirties. As male mammy, Powther is totally oblivious to his own racial-economic derogation and how his labor merely bolsters puissant, war-profiteering colossi/families such as the Treadways, whose economic windfalls come through a military enterprise that exploits economically deprived whites and blacks while also reinforcing rigid class hierarchies. Within Feldman's dandy paradigm, one can see that Powther's "military bearing and discipline" almost parodically foreground his counterfeit male subjectivity: commanding a tea party for an "army" of white "girls," to whom he even compares himself, Powther achieves a Pyrrhic victory, one that can only temporarily forestall his gender- and race-based psychic implosion.

Though it might be tempting to presume Powther's dandyism as evidence of his asexuality, his fathering of three children problematizes this notion. On the surface, Powther's choice of Mamie Smith for a wife seems wildly improbable, given her voluptuous sensuality, in marked contradistinction to his own hyper-refinement; at one point, he reflects, "She was shaped almost like a violin, like the base of a violin, big beautiful curve, and as she turned toward the bed, he thought, If she were standing inside a frame, naked like that, with that look of expectancy on her face, all the museums in the world would sell their Da Vincis and their Manets and their Rubens in order to own this one woman" (193).[10] Particularly striking is not only the ostensibly androgynous Powther's psychosexual infrastructure, but that his attraction to Mamie is purely aesthetic—a different form of sexual objectification that situates women as the pinnacle of unrivaled, intoxicating beauty without accentuating their sexuality/sensuality.[11] From the purview of the aesthete/dandy, she exists more as *object d'art* than as a flesh-and-blood woman who might arouse him sexually. Such passages render Powther more a Prufrockian figure, given his own prudishness amidst Mamie's—and Bill Hod's—

flagrant eroticism. But his attraction makes sense within Feldman's theorization of this figure: "So crucial are female characteristics to the dandy's self-creation *that he defines himself by embracing women, seeking to share their characteristics.* I speak here not of a pseudoandrogyny, the male dandy improved or completed by taking on female characteristics in order to become a 'supermale.' Reconciliation, synthesis, complementarity are never the ways of dandyism" (6–7; emphasis added). Thus, one can see Powther's attraction to the hyperfeminine Mamie as a countervailing strategy: On the one hand, if he can't *be* female, he can at least attach himself to the most extreme incarnation of the feminine. On the other hand, and almost contradictorily, Powther's ability to woo and wed Mamie rescues him from the socially maligned status of feminine male, for in his gender-sexual calculus, only a "stud" could attract and maintain such a fiercely sensuous woman. Just as his proximity to the Treadways helps shore up an enervated masculinity, his ostensible "conquering" of Mamie elevates him on society's rigid gender/sexual totem, where patriarchal and phallocentric male identity is achieved by an ability to "tame," dominate, or possess women.

From more refracted gendered and sexualized angles, one could also envision Powther's asymmetrical male identity camouflaging a dialectical attraction to the book's two most prototypically masculine characters, Link and Hod. Powther's attraction might be borne out of both society's overdetermined somatization of blackness—that blacks exist as "pure body"—and out of these men's ability to wield agency as *men* in the external, nondomestic milieu. The former notion surfaces through Powther's physical fascination with them. At Mamie's initial introduction of Hod as—wink-wink—her "cousin," Powther reflects that Hod was "put together like a statue, no fat on him anywhere, tall, broad of shoulder, narrow of waist, a man with a quick graceful body" (202). Upon seeing a sleeping Hod and Mamie in bed, Powther cogitates, "Hod's body bore absolutely no relation to his face, his body was young and beautiful and with no knowledge of evil" (210). Petry deftly fashions this scene in ambiguous terms, as Powther could be said to admire Hod's Adamic, prelapsarian body as the apogee of physical male perfection, the antithesis of "Little Mr. Powther" (11). This physical (and perhaps latently homoerotic?) longing for the physical ideality that Hod embodies evinces itself in Powther's pathetically self-aggrandizing belief that he tolerates Mamie's adultery because his own lovemaking with her amounts to "defying Bill Hod, conquering Bill Hod" (194). In this classically Sedgwickian triangulation, Mamie's body becomes the mediating site of an unverbalized competition "between men" and a palliative for Powther's feelings of physical/sexual inferiority; or possibly, Powther redirects his latent same-sex attraction to Hod, the idealized male, to Hod's surrogate: Mamie, the idealized feminine. But Powther's phallic "conquest" of Hod through sex with Mamie is transitory at best, for he subsequently admits that her unwillingness to terminate the affair induces fear that "even that last vanishing traditional right of male ownership [is] gone" (211). And the ultimate display of fecklessness—his crying upon accidentally finding Mamie and Hod naked in bed (210) and Powther's eventual self-admission that he is "dreadfully aware of him, and afraid of him" (342)—only exacerbates his feeling of being testosterone-challenged. Lexically and euphonically insinuative of both god and "bod," Hod's unblemished physicality and carnal cocksureness trigger in Powther masculine panic on multiple levels.

A similar pattern of attraction-repulsion emerges through Powther's irrational jealousy of Link. Powther goes so far as manufacturing an adulterous relationship between Link and Mamie on the flimsiest of evidence. Barely concealing his deification of Link's superior physicality, Powther assesses his ersatz "rival" thus: "Link was the type they fell in love with, it was the way he was built, it was his height, and the breadth of his shoulders, and it was his face, he looked like a brute, and women, white and colored, loved men with faces like that" (172). Powther's white-inflected gaze, his sexualizing/bestializing of the black male body that reenacts a Euro-American Negrophilia-Negrophobia that underwrites such heinous violence as lynching, is particularly germane, given the legitimate claim that "in a white supremacist, patriarchal culture, the black man is thought to embody the essence of masculinity—masculinity in its purest, most unadulterated and therefore dangerous form" (Flannigan Saint-Aubin 1058). Far from cohering his fragmented masculine identity, Powther's alternating desire for/loathing of black men's bodies renders him all the more amorphous in terms of both gendered and sexual identities.

From this paradoxical perspective, Powther's vital role in Link's kidnapping and murder is all the more fitting. He agrees to accompany Mrs. Treadway and the cuckolded Captain Sheffield (with whom he identifies as a fellow victim of wifely treachery) to the Narrows at the behest of the unscrupulous "Madam," whom he reveres as a "great lady." He obsequiously submits to her sinister request: "I thought you might be willing to go into that area with us, and point him out to us" (387). Now firmly entrenched as a tool of the economically rapacious and militaristic "Treadway Gun People" (9), Powther facilitates their incursion into if not colonization of *dark* terra incognita—"that area"—to "prove he [Link] wasn't my brother. Prove to these people in this car, that all Negroes are not criminal"; he also resents Link's affair with Camilo, because it eventuates in "the face of this animal [being] permitted to enter my world" (386). As folklorist Patricia Turner notes in her analysis of the mammy prototype in *The Birth of a Nation*, "Early twentieth-century mammies did more than just cook for and clean up after white families. If necessary, they would raise their fists against other blacks in order to defend the sanctity of the white household" (52). But Petry's portrayal of a male mammy who willingly colludes with his conscienceless and supremacist white employers has far graver consequences than the verbal lashings the outraged mammy figure delivers to fellow blacks in deference to her white benefactors.

Powther's pivotal role in what amounts to a lynching—the ignoble Madam Treadway in true Lady Macbeth fashion choreographs Link's kidnapping and, in handing the jittery Bunny (a name befitting Powther's feminized white twin) the gun, does everything except pull the trigger herself—contains all of the elements of the Negrophilia-Negrophobia that Petry configures as a not-peculiarly-southern practice. Evoking the specter of the vile lynching bee, where black male genitalia are often severed and seized as "souvenirs," the Treadway kidnapping/murder dramatizes northern whites' ascription of a bestialized sexual superiority—and threat—to the dark Other; like their southern counterparts, Petry's white northerners harbor the same impulse to capture and exterminate the potentially sexually contaminative and destructive black male Other. Given that he is more prim than primitive and therefore unable to evoke the menacing though unfounded fear whites ascribe to Link, Powther predictably aligns himself with a white hegemonic superstructure and thereby experiences masculine domination by proxy.[12] But instead of stabilizing his sense of superiority as it does for its white male practitioners, antiblack violence unleashes in Powther guilt for having acted as a sort of racial Judas. His prominent albeit servile role in assassinating the far-from-frightening Link emotionally unnerves him, bringing about an emotional crisis.

Hence, the novel's last image of the thrice-depreciated Powther—as African American, as economic supplicant dependent upon moneyed whites, as cuckolded husband—is one of emotional disequilibrium and despair. Ironically enough, Powther's emotional death is announced by the child who Mamie suggests might be Hod's, J.C.: "He's just settin' around holdin' on his head. Mamie told him it would drive a body crazy if they had to keep lookin' at him settin' around holdin' on his head like that" (427).[13] Far from the cartoonish, fey marionette orchestrating tea parties for "Madam's" approbation, Powther severely trespasses by acting as a minion for the financially flush but morally bankrupt Treadways, who act as a northern lynch mob. Again, the previously naïve Abbie now epiphanically and sagaciously declares: "Perhaps it was his [Powther's] entry into my house which precipitated this, perhaps he was the one who out of some awful hideous weakness set the wheels in motion" (419). While it is Hod who is described as looking "evil as Satan" (299), Petry casts the pusillanimous Powther as more dangerous, his unstable masculine identity causing him to judge black brethren through the eyes of the unscrupulous and murderous whites whom he worships .

Thus, while *The Narrows* showcases the author's multi-scopic imaging of black male subjectivity, it is not unexpected that the two men most tormented on multiple levels—gendered, sexual, class, psychological—should experience some form of physical and psychospiritual death. Though so diametrically different on the surface, Link Williams and Malcolm Powther are disastrously tied nonetheless. Both worship at the altar of Bill Hod, the fools' god; or more specifically, they hold sacrosanct the antiquated, monocentric brand of masculinity he incarnates, one based on intimidation, violence, and phallic entitlement. As Arthur Flannigan Saint-Aubin observes, "If the black male body is the site of a testerical [phallic] obsession on the part of the dominant culture, it is also the locus of an acting out that obsession on the part of some black male subjects" (1059). Though he is acutely aware of Camilo Treadway's sexualization of him, Link nevertheless idolizes her, wrongheadedly seeing her as the conduit to a masculine status he assumes is withheld because of his race. In effect, his willing participation in the adulterous relationship amounts to a self-negating auto-eroticizing, which validates the very internalized Negrophobia that stepmother Abbie perpetuated.[14] Albeit in a slightly different register, Powther also accepts the dominant culture's abjectification of the black masculine, which accounts for his slavish devotion to the Treadways; consider the eerie parallel between Link's race-based attraction to Camilo and Powther's comparable—though nonsexual—apotheosizing of the woman on whom *he* bestows the honorific "Madam." In diametric opposition to Hod and Link's robust physicality, Powther's domesticized dandyism forecloses an ability to access the *corporeal currency* that, at least periodically, emboldens faux father and son—Hod in his sexual license and stranglehold over vice in the Narrows, Link in his ability to sexually enthrall Camilo. Buying into the dominant cultural episteme that conflates whiteness, masculinity, and power, the masculinely deficient Powther acts as willing accomplice to the Treadways' barbarity. Fictivizing both Link and Powther as suffering from whites' pathologizing of blackness and their attendant acceptance of this diagnosis, Petry dramatizes how black men themselves valorize stiflingly parochial constructions of male subjectivity that ultimately imperil them; even more, these men effectuate their own physical and emotional disintegration—a lamentable outcome that occurs not only in *The Street* and *The Narrows*, but also across the spectrum of black men who populate several of her short stories.

3

MASCULINE ANGST REVISITED

The Anguished Black Men of "Like a Winding Sheet," "Has Anybody Seen Miss Dora Dean?" and "Miss Muriel"

> The thought of her husband roused in her a deep and contemptuous hatred. At his every approach she had forcibly to subdue a furious inclination to scream out in protest. Shame, too, swept over her at every thought of her marriage. Marriage. This sacred thing of which parsons and other Christian folk ranted so sanctimoniously, how immoral—according to their own standards—it could be! But Helga felt also a modicum of pity for him, as for one already abandoned. She meant to leave him. And it was, she had to concede, all of her own doing, this marriage. Nevertheless, she hated him.
>
> —Nella Larsen, *Quicksand*

> Part of Janie's dilemma in *Their Eyes* is that she is both subject and object—both hero and heroine—and Hurston apparently could not retrieve her from that paradoxical position except in the frame story, where she is talking to her friend and equal, Phoeby Watson. As object in that text, Janie is often passive when she should be active, deprived of speech when she should be in command of language, made powerless by her three husbands and by Hurston's narrative strategies.
>
> —Mary Helen Washington, *Invented Lives: Narratives of Black Women, 1860–1960*

As novelists such as Nella Larsen and black feminist scholars such as Mary Helen Washington have contended, domesticity and its cherished institutions—marriage, motherhood—often short-circuited black female subjectivity, though occasionally affording women moderate degrees of fulfillment and occasional power. But in contradistinction to Harlem Renaissance luminaries like Larsen and Zora Neale Hurston, Ann Petry doesn't limit her critique of the home as a site that stymies women's quests for fulfillment or even as a bulwark against an impenetrably patriarchal external world; witness the mélange of horrors experienced by *The Street*'s denizens, regardless of gender or marital status. Complementarily, she hones in on the spatio-gendered role of the home space as it relates to black men's psychological evolution—or devolution. In essence Petry engages in something of a discursive reversal by interrogating black masculinity through the lens of the domestic. For instance, while marriage may severely hamstring black women's self-actualization (e.g., Hurston's Janie Crawford and Larsen's Helga Crane and Irene Redfield in *Quicksand* and *Passing*, respectively), in Petry's fictive universe, it can also psychologically destabilize black men. Her re-imaging of domestic place and black male psychic space lends credence to Maurice Wallace's claim that "for black masculine life as in black masculinist literature, the home would seem to constitute a tropic preoccupation" (120).

Analogously, men in a variety of enclosed spaces other than the home—bars, pharmacies, barbershops, factories—is a recurrent discursive situation, as these spaces facilitate Petry's explorations of black male interiority. While she often situates men in predominantly all-female milieus (most notably in the companionate short stories "Miss Muriel" and "The New Mirror," as well as in "In Darkness and Confusion"), she also scrutinizes male homosociality to explore myriad issues—sexuality and sexual liminality, transgressive or non-normative sexualities, gender roles as performative and unstable, the pitfalls of patriarchal/hegemonic ideals. Thus, her emphasis on the space–masculine identity nexus and her characters' challenges or adherences to univocal notions of gender and sexuality evince themselves in nuanced portrayals that, in retrospect, might be considered radical in scope and execution.

The spectrum of men who populate Petry's story-worlds includes recognizable figures: itinerant blues-singing, piano-playing Chink Johnson in "Miss Muriel," who bemoans that "all us black folks is lost" (18) and who isn't emotionally fulfilled until he terrorizes a feeble white shoe repairman; and Petry's most famous male protagonist, Johnson in "Like a Winding Sheet," whose racially toxic work environment and his failure to enjoy the benefits that naturally accrue to white men lead him to brutally beat his black wife to death. But as she does in *The Narrows*, Petry takes care to depict men who might be considered non-normative subjects, characters who inhabit unstable or non-orthodox positions as sexual and gendered subjects. One story features a tormented character who troubles the line separating male and female in his nurturing position as family retainer; another features a more stereotypically homosexual character who nevertheless retains a tenuous grasp on a particularly odious facet of hegemonic masculinity, in effect attempting to "pass" for straight though he's quintessentially queer. And given the cultural dictum that "assertive drive and contentious ambition were more fully accepted as official standards of manhood," and the accompanying maxim that "the softer, more feminine virtues became increasingly suspect" (Rotundo 282), Petry sketches these "feminine men" not as caricatures but as fleshed-out, multidimensional men disturbing society's rigid gender lines in unrelentingly heterocentric, effemiphobic contexts. Thus, John Forbes, the sexually enigmatic retainer in "Has Anybody Seen Miss Dora Dean?" whose agony over dwarfing racial and gender parameters results in his suicide, and Dottle Smith, the aesthete–southern dandy who is derided for being "kind of lady-like," elucidate Petry's commitment to simultaneously writing within and expanding the contours of black literary masculinity. Invariably, such pendulous portraitures witness against a static model for black male subjects, for Petry's characters might speak on the same frequencies as an Invisible Man or Bigger, but more often their unique wavelengths don't always register on the dogmatically narrow metronome of male ontology.

Androcentric Angst: "Like a Winding Sheet"

While perusing Mark Hussey's 2003 anthology *Masculinities: Interdisciplinary Readings*, I was a bit surprised to see "Like a Winding Sheet" (1945) included under the rubric "Black Masculinities: A Unique History." Not that I was startled to find the story anthologized—I would conjecture that it rivals Baldwin's "Sonny's Blues" as the most frequently published short story by an African American author. But, presumably, the story seems intended to represent a classic study of the degenerative impact of workplace racism and the domestic violence it catalyzes. Though I would not dispute this as the story's overarching theme, I think what is often elided in critical discussions is the protagonist Johnson's psychogender unraveling and Petry's dramatization of how his emotional infrastructure deteriorates not simply because of his niggerized status, but because of the interstitial space he inhabits between traditional patriarchal masculinity and an alternative, more temperate version. Only when he reverts to the socially orthodox masculine script do Johnson's emotional moorings become unloosened. I will focus here on the phases of Johnson's psychic deformation, which aren't only attributable to race but can be limned through the lenses of gender theory, folklore, and even sports history.

Petry deftly signals Johnson's fervent desire to go against the grain of the confrontational masculinity and spousal abuse more commonplace in the 1940s: "But he couldn't bring himself to talk to her [wife Mae] roughly or threaten to strike her like a lot of men might have done. He wasn't made that way" (200). To buttress her imaging of Johnson as almost a genetic anomaly vis-à-vis the hardwired aggressiveness of "a lot of men," she interweaves throughout the story the refrain "he couldn't bring himself to hit a woman." From the story's outset, Johnson is depicted as a man who resists the pitfalls of patriarchal domination: "He had planned to get up before Mae did and surprise her by fixing breakfast" (198). Though seemingly innocuous enough, Johnson's domestic impulse is exceptional given the story's time period, the mid-1940s. In a decade when World War II was raging and black men began solidifying their gendered-national identities by entering and abetting the hypermasculine endeavors of militarism and warfare, Petry cannily opens the story with a variation on the domestic masculinity Powther enacts in *The Narrows*. Johnson's emotional atrophying again harkens back to the writer Petry claims as a favorite: while *interracial* violence occasioned Frederick Douglass's sonorous lamentation that slave-breaker Covey's brutal regimen of backbreaking labor and concomitant physical and psychological violence brought about his bestialization—"a man transformed into a brute!" (105)—Petry chronicles the racially terrorized Johnson's transformation into an *intraracially* terrorizing, rampaging male.

True to the "southernness" underneath her ostensibly northern literary landscapes, Petry again employs a trope more prevalent in black southern literature: blacks' workplace as psychically and physically debilitating. The northern industrial plant that employs Johnson becomes an updated version of excruciating plantation slavery and its by-product, the mercenary and backbreaking sharecropping system. Though we usually think of southern writers such as Arna Bontemps, Ernest Gaines, and Alice Walker as depicting how blacks are given few options outside of economic peonage in glorified forms of re-enslavement, Petry is unfaltering in relocating this injurious system to the North, as she depicts a factory where the "whirr and the grinding [of the machines] made the building shake, made it impossible to hear conversations" and where the deafening noise obliterates communication, as the employees "appeared to be simply moving their lips because you couldn't hear what they were saying" (201–2).

Throughout the story, Petry vividly uses a tactile language to foreground physical pain as the hermeneutical prism through which we witness Johnson's psychic malaise. The story abounds with references to grinding physical discomfiture brought about by a job "that forced him to walk ten hours a night, pushing this little cart" (201) in automaton-like fashion. Frequently, he either complains to Mae or himself about how "all that standing beats the hell out of my legs" (199). A less-than-heroic relative of folk legend John Henry, Johnson's dehumanization metamorphoses the northern factory into a neo-plantation, where physical brutality and its attendant pain approximate economic incarceration and agencylessness. In fact, Petry buttresses the notion of black men's dependence on hyperphysicality as a form of self-actualization through the character's very name. Apropos her own interest in the folk icon John Henry, she draws Johnson—*John's son*—as the legendary black *Uebermensch*'s literary progeny, emphasizing his commitment to strenuous labor in spite of the exorbitant physical and emotional costs.[1] Marlon Ross's commentary on John Henry's spatial-racial-economic significance is instructive here: "Against the notion spread by plantation owners and white supremacists that African American men were *not* naturally predisposed to master industrial machinery . . . the John Henry legend spreads through popular song the word of black men's expertise and contribution in the industrial development spurred by the building of the intercontinental railroad. John Henry's tendency to die from hard labor, however, distinguishes him to the extent that these dominant values can seem futile in the face of an equally uncompromising economy of racial oppression" (*Manning the Race* 317).

As Petry's quasi-John Henry, Johnson inhabits a metaphorical no-man's-land vis-à-vis his folk forebear. Whereas the folkloric legend harnessed his incontrovertible physical strength as a creative counter-existence, Johnson's physical strength is defined by a type of dis-creativity given the mindlessness and monotony of his work, as Eva Tettenborn observes: "The conditions under which Johnson works underscore this social and racial displacement: forced to wander around, his work reinscribes his social position that makes it painful for him to uphold the integrity of his body and his self" (157). To be sure, pushing a cart and collecting spare parts is a precipitous drop on the masculine totem pole when compared to the physical acumen required to outmuscle a steel-powered hammer.

Compounding the physical hardships he endures is the emotional pain of racial oppression, which Petry twins with gender anxiety to mark Johnson's psychic deterioration. While James Green correctly notes that the changing labor landscape during World War II resulted in "more women workers than ever before, especially in the service and clerical sectors, and more black workingmen than ever before, especially in basic industry" (193), what Petry so perspicaciously dramatizes is an American workplace that does not seamlessly incorporate black men and white women; she accomplishes this by positioning a white woman as Johnson's boss. Mrs. Scott exacerbates his already palpable dis-ease, for "he never could remember to refer to her as the forelady even in his mind. It was funny to have a white woman for a boss in a plant like this one" (201). Johnson is vexed by the changing gender and workplace roles of the 1940s; clearly he adheres to a cult of true womanhood which disempowers women in the social sphere while equipping him with a putative genetically garnered power based on his anatomically "penised" status.

But just as his own name carries immense gender-sexual import, so too does his boss's: Her feminine appellation and male surname—*Mrs. Scott*—in effect blur the socially determined *gender* boundary that Johnson sees as demarcating male and female. Moreover, possibly to compensate for not being endowed with the de facto authority white men naturally enjoy, Mrs. Scott publicly humiliates Johnson with the vilest of racial epithets, fuming "the niggers is the worse" (202) when he implores her indulgence for being a few minutes late. Petry cleverly displays how both Johnson and Mrs. Scott compartmentalize in terms of race and gender, for both abstract and objectify each other synecdochically. His internal response to the anger she ignites is that he could never hit a woman, now meaning that he could never hit a *white* woman; and Mrs. Scott's opprobrious comments place Johnson in the unenviable position not of *Ueber*-nigger, but *Any*-nigger. Hence, Johnson's multiply attenuated status—as ersatz John Henry, as physically debilitated subject, as insufficiently masculine according to his socially calibrated gender barometer—renders the workplace not as a corrective site for his impaired masculinity, but one that bell hooks pointedly unpacks: "Most black males suffer psychologically in the world of work whether they make loads of money or low wages from overt and covert racially based psychological terrorism" (*We Real Cool* 24). Johnson's paroxysmal response to this "terrorism" provides him an ephemeral fulfillment, as he reverts to the most primal outlets for displaying male subjectivity through two socially sanctioned outlets: pugilism and phallocentrism.

As this story makes clear, nomenclature plays a pivotal role in all of Petry's works, as evidenced in the names Link and Hod—the former name inhering Miss Doris's claim that the entire community is "linked" in failing its prodigal black boy, the latter carrying religious and corporeal connotations. And while I will shortly discuss Petry's obvious insinuative appropriation of sexual slang as surname, I will first conjecture another reason informing her decision to use the name Johnson. To set up this point, however, I need to dissect Johnson's immediate mental response to Mrs. Scott's racial slur.

Though his mantra reverberates in his mind following their racially and sexually charged encounter—"he couldn't bring himself to hit a woman" (203)—Johnson's mind engages in a bit of physiological jujitsu, as he "felt a curious tingling in his fingers and he looked down at his hands. They were clenched tight, hard, ready to smash some of those small purple veins in her face" (203). Consciously or unconsciously, Petry appropriates the language of boxing to describe Johnson's spasmodic response to his racial humiliation. In fact, she envelops the entire section devoted to Johnson's mental response in the lexis of boxing; I will quote this section at length in order to elucidate this point:

> And he thought he should have hit her anyway, smacked her hard in the face, felt the soft flesh of her face give under the hardness of his hands. He tried to make his hands relax by offering them a description of what it would have been like to strike her because he had the queer feeling that his hands were not exactly a part of him anymore—they had developed a separate life of their own over which he had no control. So he dwelt on the pleasure his hands would have felt—both of them cracking at her, first one and then the other. If he had done that his hands would have felt good now—relaxed, rested. . . . The only trouble was he couldn't hit a woman. A woman couldn't hit back the same way a man did. But it would have been a deeply satisfying thing to have cracked her narrow lips wide open with just one blow, beautifully timed and with all his weight in back of it. That way he would have gotten rid of all the energy and tension his anger had created in him. (203–4)

This evocative passage strikes at the core of Johnson's almost pathological adherence to the tenets of masculine privilege and prerogative.

At its most rudimentary level, Johnson's reflexive response legitimizes the notion that "for many Black males who lack jobs, money, or status, the only real way to feel good about themselves or to truly gain respect is through the use of superior physical force—the only resource they feel truly works for them" (Noel Cazenave, qtd. in Majors et al. 251). Ineluctably, Johnson fashions a gratuitously masculinized response to Mrs. Scott's racial objectification as well as to the overall feminization he experiences at work; indeed, his job of pushing a cart and collecting spare parts conjures images of shopping which, in the 1940s at least, would have been deemed "women's work." While overtly expressive displays such as crying are not an option for any man in the 1940s regardless of race, boxing serves the dual function of permitting men to sublimate and express pain in a socially approved, albeit barbaric, manner. Concomitantly, it provides Johnson with a creative vehicle to offset his mind-numbingly uncreative work; clearly, the connection between the pugilistic sport and male creativity evinces itself in phrases such as "one blow, beautifully timed," marking a marriage of testosterone and stylized violence.

But Johnson's revitalization through his mental pummeling of Mrs. Scott via the incontrovertibly male ritual of fisticuffs is fleeting; boxing is only a placebo, for as literary and boxing scholar Gerald Early describes its evolution in the nineteenth century, "boxing was now ready to become the most metaphorical drama of male neurosis ever imagined in the modern bourgeois-dominated world" (10). While race is an unequivocal part of his psychic dis-ease, Johnson's gender neurosis lies in his vacillating adherence to two warring constructions of black male subjectivity, one alternatively moderated and nurturing, the other rigidly patriarchal and domineering.

An intriguing coincidence provides a possible temporal explanation for Petry's interjecting boxing as a trope for black male resistance and subjectivity: she was born in 1908, the very same year that marked the ascension of the first black heavyweight champion, Jack Johnson. Because "Johnson and [Joe] Louis are noted in the black communal psyche for having beaten white fighters, thus, having beaten white society" (Early 26), one can see why Petry's Johnson—advertently or not—would emulate the fighter who was able to defy and disrupt white patriarchal authority, albeit primarily in symbolic terms. What's more, Petry's description of Johnson's fantasy-battering of Mrs. Scott pulsates sexually: Language such as "soft flesh," "hardness of his hands," "pleasure," and "cracking at her" amount to an eroticized violence. Johnson might in fact harbor an unstated desire to subjugate Mrs. Scott by the only means to which he can avail himself: sexual domination. Since dark-skinned Jack Johnson came to embody a quasi-white masculinity through sanctioned violence, wealth, and very public dalliances with scores of white women, perhaps the character Johnson unconsciously imagined a reinvigorated subjectivity through these same hypermasculine though ultimately debasing means. In a perverted way, Johnson's desire to violate Mrs. Scott represents his acceptance of himself as the very embodiment of the salacious phallic referent that serves as his surname (see chapter 2's epigraphic quote from Fanon in which the black male body conjured images of "penis," "strong," "athletic," "boxer," and "Joe Louis" in the Anglo-Western imagination).

Correlatively, he also imagines her as a means to the ultimate end, the achievement of the hallowed state of white patriarchal domination. From this angle, his repressed rage might thinly camouflage a homosocial form of desire: Mrs. Scott is not so much the object of desire but "is rather a substitute, a deferral, the possession of which is (merely?) iconic or indexical. In this sense, the desire for the white woman *points:* it points to an absence, to a desired space; it is a screen that needs to be decoded" (Flannigan Saint-Aubin 1067). In this triangulation, Mrs. Scott's body becomes the site of mediation: through sexual and physical domination, he, like the boxer who shares his surname, can assume his genetically rightful place among the pantheon of "true" men, his Anglo-American counterparts who would deprive him of this status because of the stain of blackness. In decoding Petry's decision to name the story's protagonist as she does, one can discern multiple implications and connotations—racial, gendered, folkloric, athletic, sexual.

Abandoning his original commitment to a more measured masculine praxis, Johnson psychologically implodes/explodes in a convulsive rage when Mae playfully refers to him as "an old hungry nigger trying to act tough" (210). Losing his ability to lexically contextualize, he attacks his wife, presumably killing her. But his vicious attack on Mae as a sort of surrogate victim, as a stand-in for actual white women and the white men whom they represent, is only partially explained by race.[2] In dramatizing this sadistic denouement, Petry writes, "He couldn't drag his hands away from her face. He kept striking her and he thought with horror that something inside was holding him, binding him to this act, wrapping and twisting about him so that he had to continue it" (210). Thus, I would argue that this uncoiled violence is as much about masculine identity as it is about race.[3]

The specters of sexual and physical violence become default signifiers of male subjectivity in Johnson's gender epistemology, supplanting the blissful domesticity which engulfs the story's opening. The disjointedness he experiences when attacking Mae reflects a rupturing of mind and body, epitomizing the notion that "men have their masculine identity to gain by being estranged from their bodies and dominating the bodies of others" (Jane Gallop, qtd. in Calvin Thomas 12); hence, the gentle man falls back on the socially legitimized but psychically stunting and archaic emblems of manhood. Thus, Mae *androgynously* and paradoxically functions as a surrogate for the accordingly "true," exalted white woman *and* for the racially "castrating" white man. Petry coyly signals this gender dualism in terms of clothing: just before the fatal beating, Mae admonishes Johnson for wrinkling the overalls she wears to her own factory job; hence, Mae (*Man*?) becomes a viable and legitimate target for his repressed, pulsating raced, *and* gendered neuroses. Petry scrupulously stages the multiple anxieties that ignite Johnson's emotional dissolution, its source far more complicated than the omnipresent colorism usually identified as the sole culprit in so-called black naturalistic/protest fiction.

For Colored Wannabe Men Who Consider Suicide When Masculine Anxiety Is Too Much: "Has Anybody Seen Miss Dora Dean?"

Earlier, I noted Petry's citation of *The Autobiography of an Ex-Colored Man* (1912) as an admired text, a relevant claim given that so much of her own work explores not the oft- and overexamined issue of racial passing and miscegenation, but the more sub-rosa issue of gender liminality and sexual veiling.[4] Concomitantly, Nella Larsen's *Passing* (1929), like *Ex-Colored Man*, can be securely positioned under the rubric of "passing literature," a legitimized category given the surfeit of novels, poems, plays, and autobiographies that have dealt with this white-hot issue. More germane to the issues I'm foregrounding, Larsen's novel, like James Weldon Johnson's, dramatizes sexual passing as prominently as racial indeterminacy. I would position Petry's 1958 short story "Has Anybody Seen Miss Dora Dean?" alongside these fictions of sexual passing: While it does include an interracial male-female relationship, it is decidedly not a miscegenational one like that which Petry highlights in *The Narrows*. But its more shrouded agon traverses the terrain that Johnson embarked upon: the space of masculine otherness within a predominantly black, ostensibly heterosexual milieu. In fact, I would label *Ex-Colored Man* and *Passing* as *precursive* texts, given their authors' then pathbreaking explorations of nonconformist sexualities and gender performances. Published decades before "Dora Dean," these texts laid the groundwork for Petry's similarly screened but undeniably subversive interrogation of a sexually ambiguous black man and how this difference registers in a community already "othered" by the indelible stain of the mighty drop.

Certainly, miscegenation looms as both the sweetest and most pungent taboo in the American socioracial imagination. Consider the febrile responses generated by any number of names/episodes that are seared into the collective American un/conscious: T.J.-Sally Hemmings, the Scottsboro Boys, Emmett Till, the Lovings, O.J.-Nicole Brown Simpson. But other taboos capture our imaginations as well, though perhaps not eliciting as much fervor. For instance, suicide, especially in black culture and though much less so than in previous decades, remains a tender subject, as blacks have traditionally viewed it as an unpardonable transgression given the seemingly insoluble dangers, toils, and snares that the Harriet Tubmans and Frederick Douglasses overcame; white racism was no match for the moral and physical fortitude of Aunt Hagar's children. Moreover, putative Christian prohibitions against taking one's own life make it an even more maligned option for a black community that has always been socially conservative despite its protracted struggle to disassemble the citadel of segregation.

In addition to addressing the intraracial response to suicide, Petry revisits the notion of male sexual otherness—and implicitly the Douglasian "love that dare not speak its name"—through her male protagonist, who straddles the balkanizing fence separating sanctioned male-female behavior. Though homosexuality may or may not be one of the contraventions explored in "Has Anybody Seen Miss Dora Dean?" she masterfully intertwines the specter of gendered difference with nonsexual interracial relationships and suicide in dissecting multiple forms of difference and deviation.

That Petry would craft a story in the late 1950s about a black suicide may not seem necessarily groundbreaking, given that William Wells Brown's *Clotel* (1853) and Arna Bontemps's frequently anthologized short story "A Summer Tragedy" (1933) previously portrayed black lives that were so besieged by racial hardships that self-immolation became the final solution. And, to be sure, scores of black writers would more explicitly explore what the African American community has traditionally judged a sacrilegious act rooted in psychological and moral cravenness: Baldwin's work alone contains three suicides, and a mix of novelists and playwrights from the 1960s through the 1980s—Adrienne Kennedy, Charles Fuller, Toni Cade Bambara, and Randall Kenan—would tackle the heretofore profane act.[5] But in another of many interesting ironies that link Petry with literary contemporaries other than Wright, "Dora Dean" appeared four years before Baldwin's more sensational *Another Country*, a work whose sexual pyrotechnics—its multivalent couplings across lines of race, gender, and nationality—earned it a popularity and acclaim that Petry's post-*Street* publications would never enjoy. Like *Another Country*'s Rufus Scott, Petry's John Forbes is an apparitional palimpsest—both are dead for much if not the entirety of each text—for an array of characters will posthumously inscribe and reinscribe not his epitaph, but their individual interpretations of his life and death in terms of their own racial, sexual, and gendered epistemologies.[6]

De-emphasizing emplotment, Petry constructs "Dora Dean" retrospectively as a series of remembrances about Forbes and his relationships with two women—his black wife, Sarah, and his white employer, Mrs. Wingate. Employing the framed narrative as her technical scaffolding, Petry opens the story in the present, as Sarah's grandson Peter informs the unnamed narrator that his grandmother requests that she come to Bridgeport, Connecticut, to receive some valuable china, "a tall chocolate pot" with "matching cups and saucers" (107) that the dying Sarah would like her to have. More associational than sequential, the action revolves around not so much Forbes's death but possible motives given the composite profile that different characters retrospectively construct of him. Indeed, his death is a conundrum: though it occurred when the narrator was only nine years old, its mysteriousness and inexplicability cast a long shadow, given that he stood out as a "tall, slender, and graceful" (99) man who worked as a butler for the "enormously wealthy" white Wingates, whose summer "cottage" in Wheeling was "an exact replica of an old Southern mansion—white columns, long graveled driveways, carefully maintained lawns, brick stables, and all within six hundred feet of Long Island Sound" (95).

Upon Mr. Wingate's death and at Mrs. Wingate's behest, Forbes moves into the Wingates' Bridgeport mansion (their winter home), appropriately located "at the south end of the city" (103); Forbes's relocation separates him from Sarah, with whom he lived for only three weeks after their marriage. For what she perceives as a relatively minor intrusion upon the newly married couple, Mrs. Wingate "increased Forbes' wages and promised to remember him most generously in her will" (103). Given the solemn truth that as the "loneliest of our deaths," suicide has "the ironic potential of revealing the private and quiet storms of publicly well-managed lives" (Holloway, *Passed On* 89), the reader is left to extrapolate, through the filtering perspectives of the community, why such an apparently "well-managed" life as Forbes's would culminate in self-annihilation.

In fact, it is the characters' and community's interpretation of Forbes's death which is as much the narrative's centered subject as the reasons underlying the collapse of his internal bearings. What is so technically deft about the story is its self-reflexivity, its meta-discursive components. While the horrific act of suicide provides the narrative's raison d'être, Petry painstakingly cloaks this action within layers of often disparate memories, often transmitted via letters, rumors, innuendo, and gossip. She exposes the very flawed hermeneutical processes of those who survive Forbes, revealing as much about them as she does about the actual subject of interpretation. We as readers are thus cast in the same role as the community—trying to reassemble shards of information in assessing not just why someone would take his own life, but what the reactions to this act reveal about those within the character's spatial and emotional orbit. Thus, the story is as much about the inexact "science" of interpretation—the imperfect personal and collective hermeneutical strategies—as it is about racial, sexual, or gendered anxieties. But inexorably, the question of extra- and intratextual interpretive frameworks is symbiotically bound to another central narrative question: What happens to the black male subject who veers from socially sanctioned masculine ontological praxes? Forbes, ultimately, doesn't so much dry up as psychologically explode.

Echoing her portraiture of the effete butler Malcolm Powther of *The Narrows*, Petry reimages another black male who disrupts the boundaries between male and female. Forbes's very physical appearance ("tall, slender, graceful") evokes *bisexuality* not necessarily in terms of sexual orientation, but in terms of social constructions of male and female. He is alternatively described as "wiry and tremendously strong" (97) and as a "highly stylized figure in a marionette show—black, erect, elegantly dressed, effeminate, temperamental as a cat" (99). The narrator fills out what becomes the community's collective profile of Forbes's essential self:

> He was a tall, slender black man. He was butler, social secretary, gentleman's gentleman. When Mr. Wingate became ill, he played the role of male nurse. Then, after Mr. Wingate's death, he ran the house for Mrs. Wingate. He could cook, he could sew, he could act as coachman if necessary; he did all the buying and all the hiring. (95)

Fulfilling a multiplicity of cross-gender servile roles within the white household, Forbes embodies the black retainers who populate plantation lore and southern fiction—hence, the Wingates' Wheeling cottage resembling a transplanted, northern "old southern mansion" (95). While the roles tilt more toward the traditionally female than to the male, Forbes's seemingly incongruous physical attributes and domestic talents render him the epitome of what Jessica Feldman describes as the dandy, who exists "neither wholly male nor wholly female, but as the figure who blurs these distinctions, irrevocably" (11). But Forbes, like Malcolm Powther, lives in an American society generally and in an *African* American society specifically that mandates gender roles be governed by rigid distinctions between the masculine and the feminine. Therefore, Forbes's fundamental gender transgressivity delineates him as irrevocably othered, thereby stoking rumors about his sexuality based on society's intractably prescribed gender roles.

Indeed, the fact that this "gentleman's gentleman" inhabits a "no-man's-land" regarding gender *performativity* dooms him to the proscribed status of *sexual* outlaw, a position he may or may not genuinely occupy. I think Petry purposefully fashions Forbes as sexually indeterminable, though I am inclined to conjecture that he may have been more homo- than heterosexual. Not falling into the very gender-sexual "slippage" that colors the characters' interpretations of his death is a tall order; given that our culture routinely and facilely equates effeminacy with homosexuality, it would be more than plausible to argue that Forbes is a feminine gay man who finds his true niche performing women's tasks. This view is articulated at least twice, first through the narrator's recollection that "his voice was slightly effeminate, his speech very precise" (95), and second by the narrator's father, who deems him "so ladylike" (100). This is where the meta-fictive dimension of the text emerges, for Petry exposes how we as readers are subject to the very same gender/sexual biases that color the survivors' (mis)interpretations of the living and the death-in-life Forbes. But given the very unspeakableness of homosexuality in African American literature historically—critic J. Lee Greene accurately observes that African American novelists before the 1960s "were reticent about discussing homosexuality" (187)—I would argue analogically/circumstantially that Petry too makes the character's sexuality relatively enigmatic, thereby potentially buttressing the possibility of sexual difference—and in the community's eye, *deviance.*

Just as slave narratives such as Harriet Jacobs's *Incidents in the Life of a Slave Girl* require us to read the silences, to scrutinize what is unsaid in deference to the sexual proprieties of a puritanical nineteenth-century America, "Dora Dean" requires a comparable assiduous probing of the elisions not around rape and concubinage, but the textually unutterable sexual orientation. Taken cumulatively, several details about Forbes point to a sexually disguised, concealed, and repressed life; moreover, Forbes's actions prototypically replicate those of scores of gay men in the 1950s, who sought refuge in marriage and/or institutions such as the ministry that would quell suspicions about their sexuality. The narrator recalls Forbes whistling the eponymous tune, which refers to the 1896 "Creole Show," a brown-and-tan revue "notable for a chorus of sixteen beautiful brown girls" (96); specifically, the narrator recalls her father's derisive laughter at Forbes whistling a tune so unabashedly (hetero)sexual, given the butler's surface primness: "I suppose it amused my father to think that Forbes, who seemed to have silver polish in his veins instead of good red blood, should be whistling a tune that suggested cakewalks, beautiful brown girls, and ragtime" (96).[7] The narrator elaborates on Forbes's attraction to the jazz-piano-playing, twenty-year-old Sarah Trumbull, who is a "facsimile" of the ravishing Dora Dean:

> He fell in love with her when he was forty years old. That was in 1900. He was so completely the perfect servant, with no emotional ties of his own and no life of his own, that my family seemed to think it was almost shocking that his attention should have been diverted from his job long enough to let him fall in love.
>
> But it must have been inevitable from the first moment he saw Sarah Trumbull. I [the narrator] have a full-length photograph of her taken before she was married. She might well have been one of those beautiful girls in "The Creole Show." In the photograph, she has a young, innocent face—lovely eyes, and a pointed chin, and a very pretty mouth with a quirk at the corner that suggests a sense of humor. (97–98)

Particularly relevant in terms of Forbes's possibly latent homosexuality is that he seems to desire an idealized, hyperfeminine "facsimile" of a woman—almost an *idea* of woman as aestheticized object and not as flesh-and-blood person. Additionally, the disparity in Forbes's and Sarah's ages suggests not so much a love interest as it does a fatherly one in someone over whom he can wield control.

Finally, Forbes's lack of an "emotional life" connotes a certain self-compartmentalizing, as he might have been inclined to cordon off the socially unsavory aspects of his own sexuality. In effect, Forbes "married" his role as butler because it allowed him to toggle between the heteronormative, socially sanctioned role of "husband" and the more preferable feminized though potentially racially demeaning one of male mammy. By subsuming his private and socially proscribed sexual life underneath the socially acceptable role of "gentleman's gentleman"—the phrase itself unintentionally lexically-sexually homocentric—Forbes was able to avoid having to actively fulfill the socially decreed role of husband. Given both the time—1900—and his age—forty—perhaps the social pressures on Forbes to assume his gender-mandated role (though, of course, there's no comparable status of "old maid" or "spinster" for men of a certain age, notwithstanding these words' pejorative connotations) required him to act less "ladylike" and "man up" by marrying.

Given this sexually mottled personal history, it is not surprising that Forbes should so willingly accede to Mrs. Wingate's request that he reside with her because, she avers, "he was her mind, her heart, her hands" (96). And given Forbes's—at the very least—disinterest in sex, Mrs. Wingate's mansion becomes the antithesis of the southern plantation, where sexual encounters between blacks and whites were fairly commonplace. In effect, the Wingate mansion is a veritable nunnery, an asexual *cordon sanitaire* where Forbes is spared the burden of compulsory heterosexuality while still appearing to fulfill that role as Sarah's titular "husband" (aided by the fact that they do bear a son, the aforementioned Peter). Forbes's racial-sexual anxieties render another recollection both comically absurd and disconcerting. When the narrator recalls her father describing that Forbes "could get Mrs. Wingate in and out of a carriage or a car without effort" (97), the narrator conjures up a "curious mental picture of Forbes—a lean, wiry black man carrying an enormously fat pink and white woman piggyback. . . . He stood straight, back unbent, so that she kept sliding down, down, down, and as he carried this quivering, soft-fleshed Mrs. Wingate, he was whistling 'Has Anybody Seen Miss Dora Dean?'" This darkly amusing, mildly lewd tableau becomes a parody of the carnally sensuous images that usually accompany thoughts of always-taboo interracial sex—no confusing this relatively sexless pair with the black "plantation buck"/white, sex-starved mistress who would populate lurid period melodramas such as the 1970s *Mandingo*.

Continuing in their roles as talebearers regarding personal information about the chimerical Forbes, the narrator's parents continue to "undress" him sexually, serving something of a choral function in their conflicting interpretations of his non-normative gender identity, interpretations that *slip* into speculations about his sexuality. When the narrator's father remarks that "maybe he was the type that never should have married" (100), his wife presses him to elaborate on this provocatively elliptical observation, which gives way to more candid opinions:

> "But what did you mean when you said he was a type that never should have married?"
>
> "Well, if he'd been another type of man, I would have said there was more than met the eye between him and Mrs. Wingate. But he was so ladylike there couldn't have been. Mrs. Wingate thought a lot of him, and he thought a lot of Mrs. Wingate. That's all there was to it—it was just like one of those lifetime friendships between two ladies."
>
> "Between two ladies!" my mother said indignantly. "Why, what a wicked thing to say! Forbes was—Well, I've never seen another man, white or black, with manners like his. He was a perfect gentleman."
>
> "Too perfect," my father said dryly. "That type don't make good husbands." (100–101)

This conversation exposes a general suspicion on the part of American/African American culture regarding sexually ambiguous male subjects. On the one hand, the father's designation of Forbes as female coincides with what gender historian E. Anthony Rotundo adduces in his observations about nineteenth-century American masculinity: "Some unmanly men, instead of being compared to women, were now *called* women" (272). As well, Rotundo finds that this designation coincided with a broader lexical shift, since "in the last two decades of the nineteenth century, a whole new set of words came into being (degenerate, pervert, invert, fairy, homosexual) which labeled the person as the essence of the homoerotic" (275). Thus, one can see the conflation of similar but distinct non-normative sexual desires and gendered behaviors, which at the very least hint at the possibility of Forbes's unacknowledged same-sex desires.

Thus, given the conjoining of effeminacy and homosexuality at the fin de siècle, I think it neither implausible nor stereotypical to hypothesize that Forbes was a closeted gay man. Perhaps not coincidentally, *The Narrows*' Abbie Crunch describes a wealthy white male, Mr. Valkill, as also possessing "perfect manners" like Forbes; furthermore, the novel unambiguously portrays Mr. Valkill as a married homosexual who seeks to, in Frances Jackson's words, "corrupt" the adolescent Link, who briefly works as the Valkills' "houseboy" (392–95). Though Forbes is never shown engaging in same-gender sexual encounters and acting "against nature"—

a phrase Weak Knees uses to warn young Link about the peril involved when "any man who starts sweet talkin' to you" (394); and not surprisingly, Mr. Valkill does make overtures toward young Link when Mrs. Valkill is away—the narrator's mother's vehement response to her husband's "gender reassignment" of Forbes speaks to our culture's general and enduring antipathy to even the hint of both effeminacy and same-sex desire. The mother's application of the term "wicked," like Weak Knees and Frances's invocation of code words/phrases "against nature," "corrupt," "abnormal," and "sexual pervert" as synonyms for homosexuality, inheres the omnipresent biblical prohibitions that many black Americans summon when condemning homosexuality as an "abomination."[8] Petry even signals homosexuality's unspeakableness syntactically: note the dash—a gaping grammatical gay hole—when the mother attempts to complete the sentence "Forbes was—." The very whiff of homosexuality turns the speaker speechless, marking an ontological absence that stymies attempts to *name* Forbes, the subject of her declarative sentence for whom no proper, *speakable* compliment exists. While it is inarguably true that "given the constant surveillance by whites of black bodies within the institution of the family, black heterosexual men in particular have a vested interest in disavowing any dissident sexuality in their quarters" (E. Patrick Johnson 37), Petry clearly suggests that this disavowal can be as ardent in heterocentric black women as it is in homophobic black men. In effect Petry almost hieroglyphically inscribes the plight of what the black community deems as sexually dissonant, defiled, and deviant—*wicked*—through a miasma of innuendo and wordlessness.

If Forbes's position as butler for the widowed Mrs. Wingate represented something of a safe space where he could experientially forge an alternative to hypermasculine orthodoxy while sublimating his socially abhorrent (possible) same-sex desires, then her death is a stunning blow to the alternative, more temperate manhood his position made possible. Note his psychophysical dissolution upon her death:

> He was still immaculate, but he was now too thin—bony—and his movements were jerky. He seemed to have a dreadful, almost maniacal urge to keep moving, and he would sit down, stand up, walk about

> the room, sit down again, get up, walk about again. At first she [Sarah] used to say that he was nervous, and then she amended this and enlarged it by saying he was distraught.
>
> Mrs. Wingate had been dead exactly two years when Forbes committed suicide. (108)

One could certainly affix a racial component to Forbes's mental and physical undoing.[9] However, given Forbes's attempts to negotiate a society that is simultaneously heterocentric, homophobic, and effemiphobic, I would ultimately posit a symbiotic relationship between her physical death and his psychic one.

Whereas Johnson in "Like a Winding Sheet" channeled his socially aborted attempts to fulfill society's mandated masculine roles into spousal violence, Forbes turns his distress inward. The source of Forbes's emotional pain might stem from his inability to fulfill the normative functions of heterosexual and husband, roles which his sexless "marriage" to Mrs. Wingate allowed him to obviate. Given that "homosexuals are far more likely than are heterosexuals to have attempted or seriously considered suicide" (Ruse 213), and finding the pressure to conform to these socially mandated roles too much to bear in the wake of Mrs. Wingate's death, Forbes did what many gay or sexually questioning people in our virulently homophobic culture did. In essence, Mrs. Wingate's "southern" mansion functioned as a veritable gender-sexual closet; with her demise came also the collapse of Forbes's psychosexual infrastructure, for her home shielded him from the opprobrious gaze that black (and, of course, white) society trains on its male members who fail to abide by acceptable masculine protocols.

Finally, the fact that he kills himself literally on the other side of the railroad tracks in "Shacktown," described as a sexually squalid locale where "all those barefooted foreign women live, and practically every one of those orange-crate houses they live in has a red light in the window" (101), is spatially-sexually resonant. Forbes's death in the sexually seedy and peripheral "Shacktown" coarsely mocks his own unseemly attempts to live a sexually and gender-normative life; in essence, the spectacle of his suicide is a grotesque parody of the de-limiting social spectacle that would require him to "shack up" with his wife following the death of the white "mistress" who had no sexual designs on him. Sarah's bitter epitaph further buttresses the notion of Forbes as sexually frustrated and irrevocably Other: she denounces her grandsons because "they will run with whores. . . . Just like Peter [their father] does. Just like Forbes kept trying to do, only he couldn't. That's what he was after in Shacktown that time, and when he couldn't—just wasn't able to—he laid himself down on the railroad track" (110). This stark passage reveals not only Sarah's palpable hatred of the men in her family but, significantly, it echoes the narrator's mother's flustered attempts to (not) name Forbes's sexual difference (note the dashes signaling that both passages are freighted with the unspeakable), a difference which both women, like the society in which the tormented Forbes resides, found utterly unutterable. In a circumlocutory narratological tour de force reminiscent of both James Weldon Johnson and Nella Larsen, Petry names without naming, condemning a black community that menaces its sexual/gendered dissidents while oblivious to how its own self-devaluation perpetuates a pattern of othering and expulsion.

From Sissyism to Vigilantism: "Miss Muriel"

It is historically and discursively appropriate that Petry published the volume's title story in 1963 (e.g., the bombing of the Sixteenth Street Baptist Church in Birmingham),[10] a red-letter year not only for the many racial standoffs being waged but also for the conflicting definitions of black masculinity being argued in intraracial quarters. Indeed, the sixties' cavalcade of prominent black men—Martin, Malcolm, Bayard, Eldridge—speaks to often competing and irresoluble masculine subjectivities. Foregrounding the core gender issues that pervade Petry's entire corpus, "Miss Muriel" exhibits the author's ability to commingle the various masculine anxieties I've addressed throughout this chapter: *homoracial* angst emerges in the black male characters' ill-conceived attempts to define themselves as autonomous masculine subjects in the most socially anachronistic senses; *homosocial* tensions flare up in various all-male formations when they attempt to forge alliances to combat their feelings of inequality, inadequacy, and alienation; and *homosexuality*, in the thinnest of thematic guises, figures centrally as alternatively socially viable and incompatible with the sixties' cult of true black manhood.[11] Centering a series of triangulations *between men* who objectify women solely to achieve a pathetically outmoded masculine ideal, Petry episodically constructs "Miss Muriel" as a tale that lays bare black men's woefully misguided attempts to claim the mantle of masculine sovereignty on the backs of those whose identities they deem abject—not only women, but white men and, most regrettably, each other.

"Miss Muriel" is Petry's most autobiographical work, emanating from the drugstore environment in which she was reared.[12] Sketched from the cultural and racial spaces of her youth, the story is set in a building that doubles as the family's homeplace and workspace, with the drugstore abutting the family's domestic refuge from their duties as the black pharmacists in the predominantly white hamlet of Wheeling, New York (another fictional Old Saybrook). Invariably, the borders separating these respective spaces are more perforated than concrete, and conflict emerges when various boundaries—work/home, male/female, black/white, homosexual/heterosexual—become blurred and enmeshed. More character-driven than plot-centered, most of the action revolves around the day-to-day lives of the narrator's black pharmacist family—her father, Samuel; her unnamed mother; the mother's sister Sophronia (also a pharmacist); and three male interlopers: black Chink Johnson and Dottle Smith, and white Mr. Bemish. Petry filters the narrative through the precocious but unnamed twelve-year-old daughter; though the story can be read as a classic *Bildung* tracing her initiation into an adult world besieged by multiple isms—classism, sexism, heterosexism, even ageism—I will foreground the men's unsettling attempts to adhere to an austerely and impenetrably monocentric narrative of masculine subjectivity, which culminates in their own self-debasement through scapegoating and the specter of violence.

The title itself signals Petry's adroit utilization of the story-within-a-story device. Providing the text its thematic and structural grounding, the "Miss Muriel" tale proper is told by Dottle Smith, a southern friend who routinely visits the family while being hosted by his former college classmate and Wheeling denizen Johno Ecckles. The two men take the narrator on a crabbing excursion that mainly involves improvisatory telling of richly layered and complex stories about the South, race, and black folk culture. The narrator recollects,

> Dottle almost always tells the story about the black man who goes in a store in a small town in the South and asks for Muriel cigars. The white man who owns the store says (and here Johno becomes an outraged Southern white man), "Nigger, what's the matter with you? Don't you see that picture of that beautiful white woman on the front of this box? When you ask for them cigars, you say *Miss* Muriel cigars!" (34)

Ostensibly, this thumbnail sketch of *the* southern taboo—the region's interminable fear of a white woman–black male coupling—serves as the master narrative in terms of the black male characters' sense of self-worth and self-actualization. Dottle's less-than-folksy parable functions on an array of levels: clearly, it serves as a cautionary tale for black men to "stay in their places" lest the full force of the lynch mob be unleashed; but for black men it also represents the dominant masculine ontological base on which they should structure their own subjectivity. Throughout the story, black men, both directly and indirectly, inculcate and replicate this univocal narrative of masculine authority which fetishizes male competition and exploits women's bodies as the battleground on which their testosterone-sodden wars are fought. In effect, their multiple anxieties appear to stem from living in a hermetically sealed and predominantly white northern milieu where they are still deprived of their presumed masculine privilege that is abrogated in the unabashedly Jim Crow South.

Upholding the idea that black masculinity "is often emblematic of an intersection of deficiency and effaceable power, which takes on numerous formations (e.g., power over women, other men, nature)" (Beavers 256), the story exposes the vagaries of black men's embracing the epistemic masculine ideal and their inexorable attempts to satisfy its requirements. To this end, Petry foregrounds a constellation of men vying for sexual and racial power, with Chink serving as the lightning rod for the various competitions. Petry grounds her portrait of him in the mythology surrounding the itinerant black bluesman. Entering the town as a wayfarer, Chink has been hired to play piano at the local inn, and his appearance immediately evokes a range of responses. The narrator provides the first glimpse, describing him as a "dark-colored man" who "wear[s] a white suit, the pants quite tight in the leg"; she is also "alarmed" by his eyes, which "are reddish brown and they look hot, and having looked into them, I cannot seem to look away" (17). And eventually, like scores of fictivized blues heroes and sheroes, he will emerge as the collective voice for black disempowerment, proclaiming in impeccable black English "All us black folks is lost" (18). Chink embodies what novelist/critic Albert Murray might classify as the blues hero, who combines his artistic talent and a homespun folk wisdom to comment on any number of issues, primarily racial and sexual ones.

If the narrator's description leaves any doubt about Chink's potent carnality—the sexual aura to which the prepubescent narrator herself responds—then her father Samuel's summation of Chink makes it incontrovertible. When his wife inquires further about the stranger who entered the drugstore to purchase hand lotion, the normally reserved Samuel breaks into some bawdy sexual signifyin' in a blues-tinged word-riff:

> "I'm talkin' about Tremblin' Shakefoot Jones. The piano player. The piano player. The piano player who can't sit still and comes in here lookin' around and lookin' around, prancin' and stampin' his hoofs, and sniffin' the air. Just like a stallion who smells a mare—a stallion who—"
>
> "Samuel! How can you talk that way in front of this child?"
>
> My father was silent. (21)

Samuel's blues outburst is just that, however; as the narrator reveals, "He sings in the Congregational church choir," where such earthiness would warrant censure. To be sure, this passage portrays Samuel as the antithesis of what Gladys Washington calls "a man of principles and character" (G. Washington 27). Primarily sacred rather than secular, Samuel clearly inhabits a socially sanctioned but stifling version of moderated masculinity, in direct contradistinction to the profane Chink, who "is not a gentleman" (27) in the narrator's and community's eyes.

Along with the narrator's descriptions of him, Samuel's crude appraisal of Chink provides crucial information about the multiple masculine anxieties the text vivifies. Foremost, Samuel's blues-profile buttresses the notion of Chink's near-aromatic virility as threatening, as his unbridled sexual energy pulsates throughout the story. In a particularly illustrative, even graphic example, the narrator describes his weekly carriage ride in which he chauffeurs a group of black maids to the drugstore to purchase supplies: They pile into Chink's wagon, "long full skirts in disarray. One of them sat in Chink's lap, laughing" (43). After fulfilling the maids' request to "go in the woods," Chink drives them past the drugstore on the way home, all the while "singing a ribald song, about 'Strollin' and Strollin'.'" The sexually magnetic Chink later brazenly courts Samuel's sister-in-law Sophronia—going so far as entering the family's home uninvited and serenading them with a raw "talkin' blues" (28–29)—raising the possibility that Samuel views him as an unwanted rival for his unstated desire for his sister-in-law. Finally, Samuel's own aforementioned blues spasm and his wife's admonition portray him as the stereotypically "henpecked husband"; she even intervenes upon his attempt "to explain to Sophy how I feel about that piano player," derisively quipping, "Has Sophronia asked you how you feel about Mr. Johnson?" (48). Thus, while Samuel and Chink might seem diametrically opposed, with Samuel as a put-upon patriarch who is sexually and verbally frustrated on every level, Petry configures them as mirror opposites, as both subscribe to the notion that male subjectivity is founded upon the ability to control and dominate the "fairer sex" as well as each other.

If "Miss Muriel" reflects Petry's long-standing interest in assailing the excesses of patriarchal privilege and black men's misdirected exultation of it, the story also foregrounds another of her prominent thematic concerns: sexual dissonance and the community's response to those who appear to flout its mores. I will preface my discussion here by expressing a personal coterminous feeling of admiration *and* discomfiture with Petry's portrayal of black male subjects who don't toe the parochial gender/sexuality line. On the one hand, I applaud her for peopling her fictive communities with a mosaic of sexually diverse black men, which few writers at the time did. On the other, I think Charles Nero's denunciation of many black writers' tendency to portray gay men as "effeminate, sarcastic males who lead meaningless lives; they disrupt families, are misogynists, and are marginal to black communities and institutions" (312) has some merit, even in a writer who routinely challenges encasing gender and sexual boundaries. Take, as evidence, the effeminately caricatured minor character from *The Narrows*, undertaker Frances Jackson's assistant Howard Thomas, whom Abbie sizes up as being "built like a eunuch, or what she [Abbie] thought a eunuch would be built like, very tall, very fat, soft fat, too broad across the hips, and he had a waddling kind of walk," all of which complement his "woman's mouth" (224–25); at one point, Abbie even slips and calls him "Mrs. Thomas" (232). This exaggerated, pejorative profile makes the characters'—if not the author's—effemiphobia irrefutable. But unlike her practice with this tangential character, Petry centers the sexually transgressive Dottle Smith in terms of narrative action, for he plays a prominent role as one of the narrator's male role models and as another character who is paradoxically menaced by and enamored with an anachronistic brand of male subjectivity that extols competition, chauvinism, and violence.

Rehashing the bathetically fey demeanor that shaped her snapshot of Howard Thomas, Petry leaves nothing to the reader's imagination in her depiction of Dottle, whose androgynous name telegraphs difference and possible deviance.[13] He openly flouts normative behavior in terms of both appearance and sexual orientation. At various times, the narrator describes him thus: "He smelled faintly of *lavender*" (32; emphasis added), a color synonymous with homosexuality and later gay liberation; "he had on a starched white shirt, and a flowing Byronic kind of black tie" (32), noteworthy given Byron's reputed homosexuality; and Dottle "has a very fat bottom and he sort of sways from side to side as he walks" (36).[14] As if Petry hasn't sissified him enough, Dottle recites Shakespeare's sonnets—contemporary literary scholars have speculated that the Bard reputedly addressed them to a young man—"in a rich, buttery voice"; and in the denouement, when the drugstore is deluged with bats, the rich, buttery voice gives way to "a high-pitched squealing" (50). This final trait iterates Marlon Ross's observation about how writers cued sexual difference in the 1930s: "One of the ways in which men of this period signal their desire for other men is through the assumption of a queer voice, the falsetto of the castrato, whose muted larynx comes to represent the sexual mutilation of homosexual deviance" (272).[15] But as if vocal timbre, a customary indicator of sexual difference/deviance, doesn't adequately convey Dottle's effeminacy, Petry fills out his profile with incontrovertible details about his sexual *proclivities.*

Though the DuBoisian trope of veiling has come to signify racial misperception and invisibility, on "Miss Muriel's" sexual gauge, it literally and figuratively registers sexual difference. Having attached a piece of mosquito netting to his wide-brimmed Panama hat, Dottle "looked like a woman who was wearing a veil" (36). But prior to noticing his flamboyant picnic accessories—more than hinting at transvestitism—the naïve narrator makes his sexual orientation plain. She casually divulges that during his annual summer visits "sometimes he brings a young man with him. These young men look very much alike—they are always slender, rather shy, have big dark eyes and very smooth skin just about the color of bamboo"; the narrator also refers to them as "pretty boys" (31–32). Petry masterfully puts these observations in the mouths of babes, permitting the author to stereotypically "mark" the character under the guise of painting an unmediated, "innocent" portrait of him. In fact, the observant narrator even unknowingly outs Dottle and the narrator's married uncle Johno's "down-low" relationship: her harmless query, "Why does Aunt Ellen [Johno's wife] always go on vacation when Dottle comes?" (32), followed by a telltale silence from her father, unclosets the closeted, for we can infer that the former college roommates are merely continuing a less-than-clandestine relationship that had its genesis in their undergraduate days. Worth noting is that Petry drew upon actual persons she recollects from childhood as models for Dottle and Johno: she based the latter on an uncle, the former on one of his friends who visited every summer; she doesn't, however, comment on these men's sexual orientation (As well, "John Eccles"—known or unbeknownst to Petry—was a figure active in LGBT causes in the late 1950s/early 1960s).[16] Within the story itself, the gay die is finally cast when our prepubescent sexual informant discloses that Dottle "teaches English and elocution and dramatics at a school for black people in Georgia" (30). Though there's no evidence that Petry read or viewed Tennessee Williams's *A Streetcar Named Desire* (staged sixteen years before she published "Miss Muriel"), Dottle emerges as an ebony, anatomically male Blanche DuBois, another English-teaching southern belle whose "proclivities" for young men, excessively frilly, hyperfeminine costumes, and alcohol—and most notably, her hyperfeminine performance—barely camouflaged her embodiment as the stereotypical gay male.

The preponderance of such details would position Dottle as a literary precursor to more recent extravagant black sissies who've dotted the American/African American popular landscape—think here of the fey film reviewers "Blaine and Antoine" on Fox's 1990s comic variety hit *In Living Color;* "Melvin the hairdresser" from the wildly popular, nationally syndicated *Tom Joyner Morning Show* radio program; and, most recently, drag queen extraordinaire RuPaul of "Supermodel" and LOGO (gay) cable television network fame. Prefiguring these widely circulated and sanctioned portraitures/caricatures, Petry ostensibly exploits her effeminate characters in a manner that replicates how gay men/sissies have functioned in the popular and literary imagination: as barometers against which "true black men" can measure and mentally bolster their own possible deficient testosterone levels.[17]

Congruently, both Samuel and Chink can enhance what they consider their enfeebled or insufficiently masculine selves. By trashing Dottle as deficiently masculine, Samuel can relieve his feelings of sexual inadequacy (vis-à-vis Chink) and ineffectuality (vis-à-vis his wife's rebukes within his hyper-estrogenized household): Note Samuel's deliciously (and unintentionally) bitchy aspersion of Dottle: "All he needs are some starched petticoats and a bonnet and he'd make a woman—he's practically one now—and he's tee-heein' around" (47). Likewise, Chink can ease his sense of racial-gender disempowerment, most explicitly revealed when he upbraids the narrator for repeating the "Miss Muriel" folktale—"It ought to be told the other way around. A black man should be tellin' a white man, 'White man, you see this picture of this beautiful black woman? *White* man, you say *Miss* Muriel!'" (37).[18] Chink's derisive, off-the-cuff remark that Dottle "seems kind of ladylike" is another verbal—if not tangible—recuperation of the white patriarchal authority he's been denied and that feminized men such as Dottle pervert. Though he was expounding upon black gay men generally, remarks by the late filmmaker Marlon Riggs (*Tongues Untied; Black Is . . . Black Ain't*) carry especial currency regarding gay men's essential role in fortifying heterosexual African American men's unstable sense of "true manhood":

> What lies at the heart, I believe, of black America's pervasive cultural homophobia is the desperate need for a convenient Other *within* the community, yet not truly *of* the community, an Other to which blame for the chronic identity crises afflicting the black male psyche can be readily displaced, an indispensable Other which functions as the lowest common denominator of the abject, the base line of transgression beyond which a Black Man is no longer a man, no longer black, an essential Other against which men and boys maturing, struggling with self-doubt, anxiety, feelings of political, economic, social, and sexual inadequacy—even impotence—can always measure themselves and by comparison seem strong, adept, empowered, superior. (293)

Therefore, both Chink and Samuel's puerile but racially/culturally sanctioned putdowns of Dottle emanate from American/African American homophobia, effemiphobia, and overwhelmingly inelastic economies of masculinity. In terms of the black masculinity stratum Riggs outlines, Samuel and Chink are elevated simply by *not* occupying the lowest rung, reserved for flamboyant (though *fabulous*) non-men like Dottle, a discredit to his gender, and, by extension, race.

Given this seeming inviolable male caste structure, the story's denouement is at once confounding and, paradoxically, wholly fathomable. It concludes with a gathering of Sophronia's suitors in the drugstore. Along with Dottle, a faux suitor merely playing at heterosexual courtship, and Chink, the libidinous bluesman to whom she seems attracted, is Mr. Bemish, the shoemaker who resides on "Petticoat Lane" and is described as "a little white man with gray hair" (2). Petry clearly intends for him to be a parodic opposite of the more notorious and threatening southern male who assaults black women with impunity and whom men like Chink and Dottle therefore loathe. During his quasi-courtship of

Sophronia, Mr. Bemish—Blemish?—"jumped straight up in the air, like a dancer, and clicked his heels together three times" (46). However, when a flock of bats floods the store, it is Bemish, rather than Dottle and Chink, who is genuinely concerned for Sophronia's welfare, as he "clasped Aunt Sophronia to his bosom, covering her head with his hands and arms and he kept murmuring comforting words" (50); and though she is not necessarily sexually interested in him, she "seemed to nestle in his arms, to cuddle closer to him, to lean harder every time a bat swooped past them." This act humiliates and emasculates Chink mostly and, by association, Dottle, at least in their hidebound conceptualization of masculinity. They perceive the valiant behavior of the dreaded (white) *Man* as an encroachment upon their "territory"—Aunt Sophronia, the embodiment of the black "Miss Muriel" in Chink's rendition of the story first related by Dottle; consequently, Chink and Dottle hastily form an ad hoc posse: "[Dottle] and Chink headed straight toward Mr. Bemish. They are very tall men and Mr. Bemish is short and slender, and they converged on him, one from the rear and the other from the side, he looked smaller and older than ever" (51). Their malicious threat to "sew up" Mr. Bemish occasions the pitiful man's flight to Massachusetts, as Petry inverts the migratory trope of blacks fleeing a dystopic, racially hostile South by having a white man take flight for the North lest his life be snuffed out by a quasi-black lynch mob. In contradistinction to the dominant discursive situation in which black male desire is contained and regulated, Chink and Dottle police what they see as white men's historical sexual license with respect to black women.

Prefiguring novelists John Edgar Wideman and Toni Morrison, who depicted the inefficacy of black male vigilantism in *The Lynchers* (1973) and *Song of Solomon* (1977), respectively, Petry unblinkingly assails black men blindly mimicking the very venomous white patriarchal terrorizing tactics responsible for exterminating black individuals and entire communities, both real and literary—think of Tulsa's "Black Wall Street" in the 1920s or the marauding white mobs portrayed in works such as Charles Chesnutt's *The Marrow of Tradition* (1901). On the one hand, the threat lodged against Mr. Bemish epitomizes what John Stoltenberg ironically calls the "ethics of the 'manhood act'" which, in order to "work effectively, there must be a point of reference who is treated unjustly (be it disparagingly or violently—it's a continuum), and the mere fact of male genitalia does not exempt one from being this point of reference over and against which certain other male humans mark their 'manhood' status" (382). Within this schematization, Bemish (like Dottle earlier) functions as the "point of reference," the touchstone for black men's tenuous grasp of the most baleful components of unencumbered patriarchal masculinity. But in portraying Bemish as the object of the black male vigilantes' vitriol, Petry underscores the absurdity and irrationality of their selection of Bemish as synecdoche for white hegemonic aggression, since he is clearly a denuded, even feminized version of the narrow-minded patriarchy that Chink and Dottle valorize. Even their threat to "sew up" Bemish undermines their attempted hypermasculinized punishment, as they lexically invoke a stereotypically feminine activity to describe their impending vigilante justice.

Certainly, Chink's role in and rationale for this shameful enterprise are obvious enough: They allow him to recuperate the anachronistic male subjectivity he believes has been withheld because of his race. In addition to re-envisioning the "Miss Muriel" story as a paean to black male power over black women and white men, he replies to the narrator's question regarding his familiarity with Atlanta by reciting a particularly ugly southern folk aphorism: "Nigger, read this. Nigger, don't let sundown catch you here. Nigger, if you can't read this, run away" (36). But I think the more critically compelling issue concerns Dottle's role in Bemish's persecution and expulsion: Dottle now exchanges his effete, dandyish persona for that of a "race man" who willfully torments nonthreatening whites.

I would posit several motivations for Dottle's transformation from sissy to vigilante, related to his discrepant identities as *gay* man and *black* man. On the most basic level, he perhaps sees in the genteel Bemish a mirror of his own anemic masculinity; Dottle thus projects—and thereby deflects and dilutes—his own masculine anxiety onto his white counterpart. Hence, his allegiance to Chink represents something of a quasi "same-sex" marriage, since violence has typically been a vehicle through which men have sublimated and enacted forbidden same-sex desires. Petry hints at Dottle's attraction to him when Chink serenades the black maids during their outing: "Dottle lit a cigar and puffed out clouds of bluish smoke and said, 'I never heard the mating call of the male so clearly sounded on a summer's night'" (44); at another time, we see Dottle "standing near the back of the store, watching Chink" (49).[19] These passages, alternatively suggesting phallicism and gay cruising, accentuate Dottle's sexual longing for the more demonstrably masculine male who, in his mind's eye, perfectly complements—and compensates for—his irrepressibly more feminine mien. But Dottle's actions, though not as self-destructive as Forbes's, also dramatize the plight of the black gay man whose contaminated sexuality compromises his affiliation with the black community. If rapper Ice Cube's exclamation that "true niggers ain't gay" (qtd. in Kendall Thomas 59) holds socioracial currency, then Dottle must negotiate not only his sexual difference, but also his racial "disloyalty" to a community that abjures homosexuality in the name of racial solidarity and black authenticity.

In writing about the limited options of black gays prior to the 1960s in terms of "embracing" their sexuality at the risk of being estranged from their "home" African American community, Marlon Ross asks a pointed and germane question: "If a black homosexual were to be ostracized from his community, where on earth could he go?" ("Glances" 502). Indeed, Dottle culls an exaggerated racial stance vis-à-vis whites to curry favor with a community that, while looking askance at his overt femininity, countenances him because of unimpeachable racial loyalty. Significantly, we learn upon Dottle's arrival that he and Johno are "so light in color they look like white men" (30). Given darker-skinned blacks' historical ambivalence and occasional hostility toward those of lighter hue, Dottle atones for this epidermal "shortcoming" by rabidly repudiating whiteness: he himself describes his repulsion as a "cultivated and developed and carefully nourished hatred of white men" (30), suggesting that this hatred is not so much genuine as it is rehearsed. Replicating Chink's ardent Anglophobia, which of course camouflages an attendant Anglophilia, Dottle engages in a type of hyper-racism whose function is twofold: it solidifies his fragile place as "race man"; and it shrouds his homoerotic desires, which might be cause for racial exile. In effect, Dottle adopts what Mark Anthony Neal deems a "homo-thug" persona, which black gay men don to "mask their homosexual identities or to reinforce the image of a black masculinity that challenges the prevailing images of 'faggotized' gay men" (82). Racial authenticity becomes the "cure" for the pestilence of homosexuality, though in reality it is a bogus one. I would conjecture that Dottle's participation in ritualized racial violence is only a stopgap measure, one that will not exorcise his faggotry—his desire for Chink or the "young men" who often accompany him on his annual northern sabbatical.

Finally, in anticipation of my discussion of the gothic themes and conventions that permeate much of Petry's work, I would be remiss in not discussing the narrator's epiphanic denunciation of Chink and Dottle's unbridled callousness and the image her repudiation conjures up. When they try to explain their inexplicably mercenary treatment of Bemish, she spews the story's final epithet: "You both stink. You stink like dead bats. You and your goddamn Miss Muriel" (57). Quite clearly, the narrator "rejects not only Chink and Dottle's expulsion of Bemish but also the [Muriel cigar] narrative that seemingly motivates their action" (Wiebe 70). While both men might be criticized for "teaching" the narrator to curse, she is Petry's spokesperson for a more enlightened, inclusive form of community that does not "reversely" race—does not exclude on the basis of one's presumed melanin deficiency. But even more so, Petry perhaps unwittingly makes a gay-positive statement if one looks at the narrator's comment in terms of the tropological and colloquial-cultural significance of bats and "battiness."

On the surface, the young narrator's remonstrations hearken back to chestnuts about bats. Since they are routinely associated with blindness, fear, disease, and insanity, their symbolic import is fairly plain. Indeed, Chink and Dottle's jaundiced actions emanate from the same virus that courses through the racist and patriarchal white male psyche that conflates blackness, otherness, disease, bestiality, and powerlessness. But bats also carry a cultural-etymological weight if we consider the notion of the "batty man" in musical and nationalistic discourses over the past twenty years. This Jamaican slang is defined as a "term for one who is a male homosexual. A concentration of the Jamaican words for the human posterior (batty) and man; a derogatory term for a male who is homosexual . . . also known as chi chi man" ("batty man," *urbandictionary.com*). Judging by the alacrity with which he joins Chink's crusade against the white, faux patriarchal Bemish, Dottle internalizes his own community's repulsion with him as the African American incarnation of the "batty man"/sissy. Just as Johnson's eroticized fantasy violence against his white female boss in "Like a Winding Sheet" reflected his acceptance of himself as the sexual derogative his name denotes, so too does Dottle ultimately conceptualize himself as a slur, as a sullied version of masculinity that can be recuperated only through an engagement of virulent antiwhite violence in the name of racial solidarity. Having expunged Bemish, Dottle deludes himself into believing that he can be granted membership in the vaunted black masculinist hegemony. Unbeknownst to her, of course, and from a more contemporary interpretive framework, the precocious young narrator, in denouncing Dottle as a dead bat, also speaks for many who'd just as soon have the "stink" of deformed, aberrant "batty men" like Dottle eradicated from society. Ultimately, Dottle fails to realize that no amount of reverse gay bashing or reverse racism can compensate for the "unnaturalness" that he cannot purge, regardless of whether he dare speak its name. Thus, via the narrator's malediction, the story intimates that Dottle might not be immune from the very violently eradicative "solutions" he himself helped enact against his white br/other, Bemish.

With a constellation of dizzyingly complex and compelling characters, Petry's canon rivals that of other authors who interrogate and problematize black literary masculinity. The breadth of her narrative subjects, ranging from the hyper- to moderately masculine and from the macho to the sissy to the "DL" brother, positions her as a writer ahead of her time, paving the way for contemporary literary kinswomen like Toni Morrison and Gloria Naylor, authors who also envision and inscribe black men beyond the confining, monoscopic notions of heterocentric masculine subjectivity. As African American writer/activist Cheryl Clarke so succinctly concludes, "Petry's male characters are startling, heroic, and tragic. . . . Petry gives us sentient, complex, vulnerable Black men" (36). Painstakingly, Petry showcases the diversity within the subsuming and reductive shibboleth "black masculinity," positing alternative ontological praxes with respect to one's gendered self.

4

"OPPOSITIONAL GOTHIC"

The Street *and Ann Petry's Place in the Literature of Terror*

> Insofar as *Gordon Pym* is finally a social document as well as a fantasy, its subject is slavery; and its scene, however disguised, is the section of America which was to destroy itself defending that institution. It is, indeed, to be expected that our first eminent Southern author discover that the proper subject for American gothic is the black man, from whose shadow we have not yet emerged.
>
> —Leslie Fiedler, *Love and Death in the American Novel*

> The Gothic is used as an answer to this patriarchal paradigm. It seems that whenever women reach back to find a literary form to convey protest, or rage, or terror, or even humor, they find the Gothic. It seems that the Gothic form allows us—as readers and as writers—to express the conflict for which patriarchy has had no name.
>
> —Juliann Fleenor, introduction to *The Female Gothic*

Viewed collectively, the titles of canonical and lesser-known African American texts project a long-standing—if unintentional—concern with the nexus between blackness, fear, and terror. *Our Nig; or, Sketches from the Life of a Free Black, in a Two-Story House, North. Showing that Slavery's Shadows Fall Even There;* "Mars Jeems's Nightmare"; *Of One Blood; Or, The Hidden Self; Invisible Man; Shadow and Act; The Spook Who Sat by the Door; A Visitation of Spirits; Let the Dead Bury Their Dead*—these titles' common bloodline is that they pulsate with gothic traits: the split or divided self, a theme which has epidermal, psychological, spatial, and national implications; the preternatural concern with blackness as the unconscious horror haunting the personal and collective white American psyche; the omnipresence of blackness as a befouling but ineradicable presence in the American psychic landscape; and the irrepressible materiality of those things designated alien and grotesque—the black, the female, the homosexual, the nationally dispossessed, all of which constitute an abject morass sullying America's mythic sense of innocence, equality, and opportunity. If the "unspeakable" is "one of the most distinctive of Gothic tropes" (Sedgwick, *Between Men* 94)—not "unspeakable" simply in the Morrisonian sense of enslavement and its interminably malignant physical and psychological legacy—then the gothic is and has been securely implanted in the black literary imagination, from Phillis Wheatley's eighteenth-century entreaties on behalf of her "benighted" race in "On Being Brought from Africa to America" to Randall Kenan's *A Visitation of Spirits*, a contemporary exhumation of the black gay experience from the canonical burial ground in which forebear James Baldwin's homocentric narratives are too often interred.

Incontrovertibly, "certain aspects of the American experience may be understood as inherently Gothic: religious intensities, frontier immensities, isolation, and violence; above all, perhaps, the shadows cast by slavery and racial attitudes" (Lloyd-Smith 25). The central irony, of course, is that the gothic in America has been traditionally viewed as the purview of canonical white male authors, as Fiedler's fulsome claim attests. While Poe may have "colonized" the form for literary descendants Twain, James, Faulkner, et al., *Gordon Pym* preceded the most gothic of American autobiographies, Douglass's 1845 *Narrative*, by a mere seven years. Unacknowledged in Fiedler's somewhat myopic comment is, then, that the generative genre of African American literature, the slave narrative, is suffused in gothic imagery and tropes. And since the crucible of the African American novel is the slave narrative, it follows that writers as diverse and as temporally vast as Harriet Wilson, Pauline Hopkins, Charles Chesnutt, Richard Wright, and Gloria Naylor, whether they acknowledge it or not, find the *black* gothic an apposite and effective mode of discourse for articulating the dis-ease of different forms of dispossession and alienation in the Anglo-American historical and cultural consciousness.

"I Am a Conjure Woman": Toward a Theory of Petry's Hybridized Gothic

The historical atrocities visited upon black bodies render gothic a fertile discursive landscape for the African American literary imagination.[1]

Given the scores of African American texts that could be placed under the gothic rubric, the terror inflicted on African Americans provides the mise-en-scène for the black literary imagination: Though it is a contestable point, one could nonetheless make the case that, at least through the 1960s, the preponderance of black literature might be considered a "literature of terror," with slavery of course standing as the "original sin" which provided the artistic matrix for subsequent black authors. Before discussing the aesthetic and thematic concerns underlying Petry's gothic poetics, it is important to particularize the parameters of the genre itself. Though Teresa Goddu legitimately concludes that "despite its formulaic and conventional nature, despite its easily listed elements and effects—haunted houses, evil villains, ghosts, gloomy landscapes, madness, terror, suspense, horror—the gothic's parameters and 'essence' remain unclear" (5), it is still necessary to conceptualize a template for discussing the gothic's core elements and how Petry's work both invokes and subverts the form.

To fashion an aesthetic blueprint for interpreting Petry's fiction from a gothic perspective, I turn to the indispensable work of the late Eve Kosofsky Sedgwick and Jerrold Hogle. Focusing primarily on British literature, Sedgwick in *The Coherence of Gothic Conventions* identifies some "characteristic preoccupations": "These include the priesthood and monastic institutions; sleeplike and deathlike states; subterranean spaces and live burial; doubles; the discovery of obscured family ties; affinities between narrative and pictorial art; possibilities of incest; unnatural echoes or silences, unintelligible writings, and the unspeakable; garrulous retainers; the poisonous effects of guilt and shame; nocturnal landscapes and dreams; apparitions from the past" (9–10). Hogle provides the following numerical schema, the dimensions of which both intersect with and augment Sedgwick's:

1. the haunting of an antiquated, often *falsely* antiquated, space by the monstrous specter(s) of a hidden primal crime, which can be discovered only by probing through layers of memory, documentation, or buried physical evidence;
2. the connection of both that setting and the crime to class-climbing and property-seeking drives in the major characters and their middle-class readers . . .

3. the repression of primordial feminine origins—often in the form of a sequestered or distanced mother figure—to shore up a patriarchal hierarchy whose counterfeit grounding is increasingly exposed;
4. the employment of such repression in the fabrication of a rising middle-class suburban community caught between the receding past of the country estate and a capitalist future of individual, though actually city-based . . .
5. the middle-class throwing off or throwing under—the psychological and cultural "abjection" in Julia Kristeva's *Powers of Horror*—whereby all that class climbers strive to free themselves of (dependency on the feminine, connections to working-class hard labor, desires for aristocratic decadence, mixed racial origins, nonstandard sexual longings, roots in supposedly less evolved conditions, great economic uncertainty, dysfunctional families, etc.) is projected onto spectral or monstrous others. (215–16)

Just as black writers have traditionally "bent" forms to suit their larger aesthetic agenda—for instance, Chesnutt's reconfiguring of the racially nostalgic but demeaning "Plantation Tradition"—Petry too foregrounds some of the elements Sedgwick and Hogle delineate: how obsessive class climbing is externalized through frigidly cold and foreboding landscapes in *The Street* and "The Witness"; or how "retainers" such as Louella Brown "haunt b(l)ack" to avenge the iniquities of racist, patriarchal profligacy. However, given that "the gothic genre is extremely mutable" (Goddu 5), Petry expands the boundaries to dramatize, for instance, how blacks' own psychoracial and psychosexual fragmentation can be as self-destructive as the "patriarchal world" which Juliann Fleenor in this chapter's second epigraph positions as the "center" of (white) women's gothic writing.

Thus, the frequent gothic eruptions that permeate *The Street* (and several short stories, which are examined in the following chapter) dramatize Petry's reconceptualizing of gothic conventions to "Africanize" what has been narrowly conceived as a Euro-American form to convey darker truths about an amalgam of terrors—including but by no means limited to racial ones—that befall the black subject. Petry's formulation of a counter-gothic emanates from her self-assessment that, like those in her lineal bloodline, "I am a conjure woman" (Petry, "Ann Petry" 268).[2] Whether it be internecine, intraracial gender conflict or cross-racial antagonisms which manifest themselves psychically and spiritually, Petry's counter *Afro-Gothic* defies such jejune categories as protest gothic or feminist gothic or Afrocentric gothic. While critic Evie Shockley in her insightful essay "Buried Alive: Gothic Homelessness, Black Women's Sexuality, and (Living) Death in Ann Petry's *The Street*" is warranted in performing what she calls a "reconsideration" of the novel "that reckons with the extent to which social terror is constructed as a way of life for the mostly poor, African American residents of Harlem" (439), I would add that the scope of Petry's narrative concerns—horror; sexual and racial neuroses; unquenchable materialism and the dis-ease it engenders; spatial confinement; commodity, racial, and gender fetishisms—moves *The Street* beyond the realm of "social" terror. The novel's catholicity marks Petry's as a malleable gothic architectonics, the framework of which she manipulates and alters for manifold rhetorical ends.

A "Deranged and Degenerate Utopia": Images of Enslavement, Monstrosity, and Cannibalism in The Street

Though literary scholar/historian Eric Sundquist did not envision Ann Petry when he used this phrase to characterize Faulkner's *Sanctuary* as a "modernist Blithdale" (56), it nevertheless encapsulates the thematic and geo-spatial underpinnings of her best-known work, *The Street.* While critics have often concentrated on issues related to environmental determinism, economic racism, and inviolable sexism, my interpretation of the text goes beyond these concerns in deconstructing Petry's visually gut-wrenching images which render black life as a bleak, unstinting horror from which there is little respite.[3] Petry saturates the text with images that are uniquely gothic—catatonia; paroxysmal, blood-curdling violence; confinement and entombment; psychosexual neuroses; villainous and shape-shifting characters who worry and dislocate the line separating "good" and "evil"; and an omnipresent and palpable specter of impending death. To be sure, these pervasive images collectively create an "excess," which critics such as Susanne Becker describe as a staple of the gothic. In the opening chapter alone, Petry concocts a terrifying atmosphere with her unsparing descriptions of both places and persons: "On Eighth Avenue it meant tenements—ghastly places"; "the hallways here would be dark and narrow" (4); the "woman's eyes" were "as still and as malignant as the eyes of a snake"; "The stairs went up steeply—dark high narrow steps" (6); "As she [protagonist Lutie Johnson] climbed up the last flight of stairs, she was aware that the skin on her back was crawling with fear. Fear of what? she asked herself. Fear of him [Jones, the building superintendent], fear of the dark, of the smells in the halls, the high steep stairs, of yourself?" (13). Even before Lutie enters the building, Petry portends the impending dread in her description of the sign advertising apartments: "Its original coat of white paint was streaked with rust where years of rain and snow had finally eaten the paint off down to the metal and the metal had slowly rusted, making a dark red stain like blood" (3). Cumulatively, such descriptions provide the narrative scaffolding for the entire text's unpacking of physical, psychological, racial, and sexual monstrousness.

Obviously Morrison's *Beloved* (1987) can be read as the pinnacle of racial, sexual, and physical barbarism and emotional terror: its emphasis on ghosts and hauntings, the burial of and visitation by the murdered baby, the repression of the "unspeakable" and the irrepressibleness of memory, the necessity of confronting the ghastly trauma of enslavement in order to make the black self psychically if not physically whole. As Hogle points out, the eponymous apparition stands for the "abjection and embodiment of an extensive collective memory among African Americans, ranging from the loading onto women of greater subjugations in slavery itself all the way back to the original loss of Mother Africa in the voyage across the Atlantic in the bowels of the ships that first brought black captives to the New World" (221). Morrison's ingenious narratological strategy is to return not only to slavery, which so many critics have identified as the *autochthonous* American gothic event, but to journey back further by invoking the Middle Passage as the primordial moment of black terror. As part of her *re-memorying*, Sethe Suggs recalls the transmission of her family history via one of her mother's companions, Nan, who'd also been ripped from Mother Africa and debased as sexual cargo: "'Telling you. I am telling you, small girl Sethe,' and she did that. She told Sethe that her mother and Nan were together from the sea. Both were taken up many times by the crew" (62). Though this may in fact be one of a scant number of references to the harrowing transatlantic journey, Morrison's inclusion of it speaks to the racial-architectural concerns which reverberate throughout *The Street:* the constant emphasis on tight or enclosed spaces harkens back to this *ur*-gothic black experience.

Petry draws upon this primal moment of terror to heighten readers' awareness of the post-nautical, post-slavery confinement of blacks in geo-racial and spatial terms. Incontestably, "the dominant images of the novel are claustral and suffocating—walls, cages, cellars, even those people's stares" (Andrews 195). The Harlem tenement, where "buildings were old with small slit-like windows, which meant the rooms were small and dark" (*The Street* 4), epitomizes the cloisters into which blacks were/are "tight-packed" in northern cities from New York to Detroit to Chicago. Note how Petry describes the edifice where many of the protagonists reside—here she concentrates on Lutie's own cramped hovel—and how this description strikingly approximates the revolting conditions of the slave ship: "All through Harlem there were apartments just like this one, she thought, and they're nothing but traps. Dirty, dark, filthy traps. Upstairs. Downstairs. In my lady's chamber. Click goes the trap when you pay the first month's rent. Walk right in. It's a free country. Dark little hallways. Stinking toilets" (73). And expanding the contours of the Harlem dystopia to which blacks are confined, Petry later writes: "And it wasn't just this city. It was any city where they set up a line and say black folks stay on this side and white folks on this side, so that the black folks were crammed on top of each other—jammed and packed and forced into the smallest possible space until they were completely cut off from light and air" (206). Such malodorous, stultifying conditions demonstrate how standard gothic tropes can be used to evoke different forms of historical violence; such passages thereby concretize how the indignities suffered on the slave ship are chronic, reincarnated in squalid enclosures to which black bodies are restricted. Its modern-day counterpart, the tenement, is a "bowel"-like tomb that also "holds" blacks—not with chains and other torturous appurtenances, obviously; instead, blacks at midcentury are now geographically tethered to Bantustan-like quarters in a nominally "free country."

Subsequently, the claustrophobia and effluvia induce in Lutie a nightmare in which she

> screamed and screamed and windows opened and the people poured out of the buildings—thousands of them, millions of them. She saw that they had turned to rats. The street was so full of them that she could hardly walk. They swarmed around her, jumping up and down. Each one had a building chained to its back, and they were all crying, "Unloose me! Unloose me!"
>
> She woke up and got out of bed. She couldn't shake loose the terror of the dream. . . . Yet she was so filled with fright from the nightmare memory of the dream that she stood motionless by the bed, unable to move for a long moment. (193)

Petry expertly mines the lexis of terror for racial ends, as Lutie's nightmare directly links the quasi-enslaved Harlemites with their innumerable spiritual ancestors who perished during the execrable transcontinental voyage of death. Inarguably, the apartment building "is the very antithesis of 'home': rather than being a safe haven, this building quite evidently houses the kinds of evil that the domestic space is purported to exclude" (Shockley 447). At another point in the text, Petry evokes images not only of blacks' historical catastrophe but also of the twentieth century's most haunting genocide, the Holocaust: "The inside of the houses fairly steamed; the dark hallways were like ovens" (142). Here, history's most wretched victims are wedded; whether they be the ghosts of African or Jewish ancestors exterminated by water or fire, in Petry's gothic syntax, the "millions" who perished during the kidnapping and forced dislocation inhabit the bodies of the walking dead who inhabit her sepulcher-like Harlem. Such passages underscore what Goddu deems gothic's ability to "rematerialize the ghosts of America's racial history and enable African-American writers to haunt back" (132)—or, I would insist, "haunt *black*." Petry inscribes Harlem metonymically as a modern-day slave ship, while simultaneously limning the psychically debilitating effects such spaces have on individual characters; thus, she spotlights the nexus between such physically degenerating spaces and their inhabitants' eroding psychic foundations.

Whereas the haunted abbey, house, and plantation are stock settings in pre-twentieth-century Euro-American gothic, these edifices have been "modernized": "the house, not the castle, becomes the site of trauma" (Lloyd-Smith 75). That Petry chooses the drearily mundane setting of the apartment slum as the novel's dramatic locus concretizes her adaptation of conventions deemed unique to the female gothic genre, which Lynette Carpenter and Wendy Kolmar assert centers "women victimized by violence in their own homes" and "women dispossessed of homes and property" (10). While the tenement is obviously not a homo-gendered space, such decrepit environs have been the residue of an economic system that destabilizes black families: in a nation that deifies the family, securing affordable housing has been historically contingent on black women and children subsisting on one income—meaning that black men must be either invisible or amputated from the family altogether. And if contemporary critics' insistence that the prisons that warehouse black men represent newfangled plantations holds sway, then one can comparably conceptualize the squalid tenement as an updated, predominantly female version of the slave ship.

The Street's shanty is occupied predominantly though not exclusively by a mélange of manless women: Lutie, who winds up there with her son Bub after the dissolution of her marriage; Mrs. Hedges, referenced always by a marital appellation though a husband is never mentioned, who runs a brothel from her apartment and gives shelter to the despondent young women whose bodies and labor she exploits; and the woebegone Min, who, though the live-in companion of the building superintendent Jones, spends most of her waking hours alternatively alone, physically and emotionally assaulted by Jones or plotting to keep him from evicting her. This potpourri of women, buffeted economically, sexually, psychically, racially, is unable to experience the home as a safe and nurturing space. Structurally, though Petry foregrounds Lutie's catalog of menacing experiences, she carefully positions other women's stories within Lutie's narrative arc, thereby giving the novel a verbally layered, polyphonic effect; in this way, the text approximates a discursive convention Becker associates with what she calls "early feminist fiction" in which "gothic 'excess' marks the form with its multiple female stories and with the gothic emotions of horror and fear, only to heighten its realism" (32). Stitching this unnerving and unrelenting tapestry of women's dreadful *her*stories, Petry demythologizes the American home as a protected, "safe" domain for African American women, conjuring images of the "cottage" that Dr. Flint threatened to erect to facilitate the sexual subjugation of his "property," Linda Brent/Harriet Jacobs. So while the American gothic departs from its European precursor—"Rural towns and plantations replaced castles and abbeys" (Liggins 359)—Petry further Africanizes the form by imaging the spectral urban slum as an updated version of such spaces as were previously the sine qua non in gothic literary discourse.

Lutie Johnson

An amalgam of both quotidian and ego-driven desires, and a radiant black beauty, Petry's Lutie complicates any prescribed fictive agenda that vilifies one gender while romanticizing the other. Ostensibly, Lutie epitomizes the anachronistic gothic damsel-in-distress, as the novel opens with her desperate search for a home. Further, Petry spatializes the voluminous psychic, racial, and sexual menaces and anxieties—real and imagined—that beset Lutie throughout the text, thereby illustrating the novel's integration of classic gothic tropes. During a drive through the mountains with the sexually aggressive bandleader Boots Smith, Lutie openly fears that "'I get the feeling they're closing in on me. Just a crazy notion,' she added hastily, because she was reluctant to have him get the slightest inkling of the trapped feeling she got when there wasn't a lot of unfilled space around her" (160); and in a fleeting but thematically consequential moment, her recollections are described thusly: "From the time she was born, she had been hemmed into an ever-narrowing space, until now she was nearly walled in and the wall had been built brick by brick by eager white hands" (323–24). These images, clearly intertextually reminiscent of Dr. Flint's threatened encaging of Jacobs and Poe's pervasive walling off of the feminine ("Usher," "The Black Cat"), show Petry incorporating the leitmotifs of entombment and sequestration to convey Lutie's unceasing feelings of despair and dread—what in Freudian psychoanalytic theory would be considered *Todestrieb* or the death drive (literally and figuratively embodied in the trek through the mountains).

Petry, too, renders Lutie's sexual persecution in real terms, the character's extraordinary attractiveness marking her as a perpetual target. Repeatedly, all of the major (and minor) characters—male and female—designate Lutie a prize for her beauty and harbor salaciously "dark designs" (19) because of what one character deems her "unusual" allurement (45); another character who hopes to sleep with her is mesmerized by her "long legs, straight back, smooth brown skin, and smiling eyes" (263). Perhaps this protracted emphasis on Lutie's physical attributes marks Petry's parodying of the gothic heroine, another form of what Becker delineated as gothic "excess"; this signifying might even be reflected in the character's name: Lutie suggesting "Beauty" or "Booty," the latter carrying denotations of treasure as well as colloquial/vernacular suggestiveness of black women's physical "assets." To be sure, Petry aims to particularize the unrelenting perils black women face in a fiercely and predatory patriarchal environment. But just as significantly, her oppositional gothic challenges the schematization Becker outlines as standard in the genre: instead of Lutie singularly representing a moral touchstone for the depth of different characters' "sinister" natures, she also possesses what Fiedler would call the maiden's "darker impulses" (qtd. in Sonser 60), behaviors that might be classified as odious if not monstrous, akin to the very racist, classist, and sexist treatment that is routinely inflicted upon her. In this way, Petry makes vicious and appetitive impulses less male-specific and thereby explodes notions of the "proper" feminine subject of black women's literary creations—the disempowered, infallible, eternally victimized black woman.

Ostensibly, the novel sets up a dyadic "good versus evil" scenario in its portrayal of the preyed-upon Lutie and the predatory William Jones, the lecherous building superintendent who's described in carnivorous, malevolent terms throughout the novel: "Nothin' but evil" (20); "eating her up with his eyes"; "snuffing on my trail, slathering, slobbering after me like some dark hound of hell seeking me out" (25); "lickin' [his] chops" (90).[4] However, Petry deviates from this binaristic model in exposing Lutie's own "heart of darkness," her obsession with all things *white*—the dominant Anglo-American episteme—and *green*—an insatiable desire to amass money—to the point that her own behavior becomes a direct variation of Jones's ravenous desires.[5] This is perhaps most evident during her stint as maid for the "filthy rich" white Chandlers, whose commitment to greed and opulence Lutie initially deems "a world of strange values," but later "absorb[s] some of the same spirit" (43). Petry again employs the trope of space to delineate and concretize Lutie's Anglocentrism. Consider her response to Jones's question regarding the color she desires he paint her apartment's rooms—"White. Make all the rooms white" (24). This might at first glance seem an innocuous wish to have the cloistral space appear larger. However, given how she apotheosizes the previously "strange" Chandler-type values, even such a request becomes suspect. This episode precedes the one in which the mountains, instead of signifying boundlessness, appear to be "closing in" on her; analogically, one could anticipate that the apartment's deceptively larger white space—an objective correlative for the white ontology and ethos she worships—will similarly encase her as well. Hence, her desire for white space evinces not an expansion of space but its recession—even a type of entombment.[6] Just as Melville's white leviathan became an existential synecdoche for the cavernous void, for nothingness, for death itself, Lutie's own amplification and exaltation of all things white will hasten her own psychic-spiritual interment as well.

Further, while Jones's devious and deviant bearing may mark him in Fanonian terms as the apogee of physical and moral "dirtiness," Lutie's own economically lecherous actions make these characters less polar opposites and more *mirror* opposites, only separated by the accident of biology. Petry's counterbalancing of these seemingly antipodal characters is most evident when Lutie concocts her own schemes to reap financial gains. While bandleader Boots Smith may appear to be a younger incarnation of the bestial Jones (upon first meeting Boots—a common moniker for pets—Lutie compares him to the Chandlers' cat, "lean, stretched out full length, drawing itself along on its belly, intent on its prey" 150), and while he will in fact reenact Jones's sexual rapaciousness when he tries to rape Lutie in the novel's climax, her own obsession with exploiting *him* financially positions her more closely to Jones as someone guided by wolfish impulses. As well, Boots's name hints that Lutie envisions him as *her* "booty," albeit not in the carnally suggestive sense but in a monetary one. Imagining the invitation he extends to her to sing with his band as a financial lifeline, she carnivorously fantasizes: "He had probably tossed out this sudden offer with the hope that she just might nibble at it. Only she wasn't going to nibble. She was going to swallow it whole and come back for more" (151). Moreover, her monetary voraciousness is every bit as calculated as her nemeses' sexual designs: "It wouldn't be easy to use him. But what she wanted she wanted so badly that she decided to gamble to get it" (152). And though she is not naïve enough to believe that Boots's offer stems from her singing ability rather than from his phallic exigencies, she nevertheless admits that she ran "headlong" into the mutually exploitive relationship, "snatching greedily at the bait he had dangled in front of her" (161). In effect, something of a transmogrification has occurred: Lutie—the perpetually objectified beauty/booty—degenerates morally and spiritually and replicates the gluttonous behaviors which stymie her own progress/evolution. Regrettably, she mimics the outlaw behavior of the very systems which otherize her, most dramatically in the scheme she hatches to take advantage of economically deprived and displaced black orphans.

With a name as richly denotative as Lutie—*loot* suggesting both ill-gotten monetary spoils and material pillaging—her next money grab illuminates the canniness of Petry's nomenclature. Upon the suggestion of her (appropriately enough) bootlegger father, "Pop," Lutie *super*intends a venture in which she and her husband Jim agree to provide housing for "State chillern" (170). The exploitative dimension of this endeavor is subsequently divulged: "So the State people didn't know that the children were their only source of income." Her willingness to make her living on the backs—figuratively if not literally—of other black people validates the summation that "despite all the evidence to the contrary, Mrs. Hedges and Lutie have more in common than either can admit" (Holladay 51). While Lutie's premeditated objectification of these children may not be as overtly heinous as Mrs. Hedges running a bordello out of her apartment or the systematic corralling of blacks into sepulchral tenement dwellings, it nevertheless hearkens back to African Americans' state-sponsored enslavement, as the warehousing of black bodies provided economic windfalls for the slavocracy. While it is inarguable that blacks may be "made monstrous by the white hegemony" (Lloyd-Smith 121) and that Petry is simply adhering to a female gothic discursive strategy that excoriates patriarchy, Lutie's willful commodifying—her own seizing—of black bodies is still a deplorable scheme that stems from some predatory part of her nature, or, in Fiedler's terms, her own "darker impulses": here she consciously becomes part of the "State's" objectifying apparatus by taking economic advantage of those least capable of advocating on their own behalf, African American children. The cumulative effect of such behaviors, in which Lutie more resembles the novel's constellation of villainous men and women—Boots, Jones, Hedges, Junto—than the innocent black damsel in distress, demonstrates Petry's effective variation on the standard but racially monocentric female gothic, which is ostensibly a corrective of the "patriarchal paradigm" where "the woman is motherless, that she is defective, and that she has for her God the male, not the absolute" (Fleenor 7); unstated but implied here is that "woman" and whiteness are conflated in this paradigm.

Another discursive dimension of gothic literature generally and female gothic specifically are the attempts to occlude the feminine legacy and the potential power of women's homosocial relationships. Several critics have looked at the gothic from this gyno-centered perspective: Hogle and his colleagues note the form's emphasis on the "repression of primordial feminine origins" (215); concentrating on the "mother-daughter plot," Becker claims that her analysis deigns to "make a case *for* the mother-figures, as gothic texture foregrounds the mother's demise as a horrific sign of cultural containment and her potential as a liberating force of female desire" (47–48); and while they were specifically commenting on women's ghost stories, Carpenter and Kolmar's point about mother-daughter conflicts in gothic being "much more ambiguous" (19) is nevertheless germane in my discussion of internecine familial, same-gender relationships in *The Street*. Recalling African American women authors such as Jacobs and Hurston, whose writings reinscribe the mother-daughter scenario with the grandmother acting in the mother's stead, Petry employs this discursive formation in depicting a comparably fraught same-gender relationship between Lutie and her deceased grandmother, "Granny." A veritable absence-presence, the chimera of Granny "haunts" Lutie's waking consciousness, though Lutie assiduously tries to repress or discount Granny's belief system when it conflicts with her own money-centric goals.

Lutie's near-slavish devotion to whites' values, which she perversely holds while also routinely abhorring and denigrating white people collectively, engenders her repression or containment of her central feminine/mother figure.[7] Though "Granny" is only mentioned sporadically, her personal principles invade Lutie's consciousness without warning: "Someone had told Granny once that the butchers in Harlem used embalming fluid on the beef they sold in order to give it a nice fresh color. Lutie didn't believe it, but like a lot of the things she didn't believe, it cropped up suddenly out of nowhere to leave her wondering and staring at the brilliant scarlet color of the meat" (61). In this taut description, Petry weaves a ghastly image—the semantic conjoining of the chemical process by which dead bodies are preserved and the horrid hastening of blacks' sociophysical death through their protracted, deliberate poisoning by (presumably) white grocers. Granny, a spectrally indomitable presence that can't be shuttered, had also given her granddaughter irrefutable warnings about the sentience of *evil*, the raison d'être of gothic literary discourse. Lutie contemplates that she would have assessed Jones thusly: "Granny would have said, 'Nothin' but evil, child. Some folks so full of it you can feel it comin' at you—oozin' right out of their skins'" (20). However, especially telling is Lutie's incredulity about and discounting of Granny's ancestral, folk wisdom, which contrasts sharply with the modernity represented in the Chandlers' meretricious and arid values. A few pages later, encumbered with familial and economic woes, she again recalls Granny's homespun insight vis-à-vis Pop's willful obtuseness:

> And Pop didn't believe in discussing problems—"Just goin' out of your way to look for trouble," was his answer to anything that looked like a serious question. Granny could have told her what to do if she had

> lived. She had never forgotten some of the things Granny had told her and the things she had told Pop. Mostly she had been right. She used to sit in her rocking chair. Wrinkled. Wise. Rocking back and forth, talking in the rhythm of the rocker. (76)

The tension between Lutie's financial fetishism and Granny's folk epistemology, magnified by Granny's absence, dramatizes a mother-daughter predicament prevalent in the female gothic, a point Diane Roberts addresses in assessing classic gothicists such as Poe, Charles Brockden Brown, and Mrs. Radcliffe. These writers, Roberts writes, "hurl their young heroes and heroines into a hostile world where the mother lives only as a memory of virtue and nurture. Much menace derives from the protagonists' lack of maternal protection and moral guidance; the gothic world suppresses actual mothers and tries to destroy potential mothers" (43). Though this discursive situation is not as pronounced in *The Street*, Lutie's inability and/or unwillingness to recoup and apply the folk wisdom of her female ancestor bespeaks Lutie's privileging of Anglocentric values. Instead, her chosen role model/spiritual mentor is, unsurprisingly, a great white American forefather, Ben Franklin, to whom she frequently compares her quest for economic fulfillment.[8] Her monomaniacal crusade for money in her northern dystopia displaces ancestral folk wit, a decidedly black, alternative epistemological base reflected in Granny's wise counsel.

With insightful voices like Granny's a faint memory, the predominantly female residents of Lutie's Harlem tenement may appear to be the archetypal agency-less gothic female subjects. However, this conclusion would belie women like Mrs. Hedges and Min, who attempt to intervene upon their respective oppressions. Ostensibly, the "haunted" residence, like the splintered Usher mansion, externalizes the emotional/physical travails of its occupants, a point Roberts posits in her discussion of the gothic underpinnings of *Uncle Tom's Cabin:* "As the haunted house is both a space where women are violated and abused and a representation of the woman's body itself, the haunted house becomes both the emblem of the slave woman's damaged body and a site of resistance to slavery" (49–50). Correspondingly, the tenement exemplifies the physical and psychological incursions the women suffer but also comes to stand as a bulwark against multiple assaults.

Junto

In considering how patriarchal power and untrammeled desire undergird most of the characters' actions and destinies, the sole white protagonist, Junto, emerges as the architect—*master*?—of most of the characters' fates. He clearly instantiates what Hannah Arendt classically delineated as the "banality of evil"; his largesse and seeming equanimity mask his insidious, "dark" desires underneath a patina of (white) benevolence. His innate diabolicalness is highlighted by both Boots and Mrs. Hedges' misguided interpretation of his racial ideology; she goes as far as to exorcise his whiteness: "I put up with you because you don't ever stop to think whether folks are white or black and you don't really care. That sort of takes you out of the white folks class" (251). But, of course, the indiscernible and unhindered power he wields throughout the Harlem ghetto—materialized in his commercial colonization of Harlem's licit and illicit business enterprises (the Junto Bar and Grill, Mrs. Hedges' brothel, the apartment building itself)—hearkens back to the so-called golden age of 1920s' black Harlem, when white-owned clubs and cabarets barred blacks as patrons while admitting them as performers.

In more appositely symbolic terms, Harlem functions for the covertly racist Junto as a reincarnated plantation, even as he appears to empower blacks in his economic-sexual ventures. For instance, he enlists both Mrs. Hedges and Boots as minions in his plot to cajole Lutie into sleeping with him. Mrs. Hedges sternly warns Jones that Lutie is "marked down" for Junto, a phrase that twins the marketing of black flesh and the simultaneous devaluation of that flesh. Comparably, Boots will stanch his own appetite for Lutie once Junto warns him to "keep your hands off her" (262) and indicates that he both "made" Boots and can thereby also "break him" (264) by relieving him of his relatively cushy gig as pianist/bandleader at the Junto Bar and Grill; this language as well conjures images of both economic dispossession and the sexual policing of black desire as well as slave masters' wide latitude in "breaking in" their chattel by any means necessary. In a gesture that is both self-policing and self-neutering, Boots acquiesces, promising Junto that "that babe will be as safe with me as though she was in her mother's arms" (274). Though his actions may not approximate the sadistic sexual threats posed by lecherous masters such as Dr. Flint and "Captain" Aaron Anthony, who subjected black women to gruesome sexual and psychological violence, Junto's compromising and exploitation of blacks as vestibular to his monomaniacal sexual longings buttress my claim that the novel employs the discourse of enslavement, thereby girding its gothic substructure. That Mrs. Hedges and Boots so acquiescently agree to facilitate Junto's jaundiced sexual machinations situates them in the role of "sexual overseers" who work unscrupulously and unquestioningly on behalf of the neo-slave master Junto.

In addition to his sexual voraciousness, Junto's economic voraciousness dovetails with what Hogle identified as the gothic's engagement of class tensions: "the connection of both that [haunted, antiquated] setting and [hidden primal] crime to the class climbing and property-seeking drives in the major characters" (215). With Mrs. Hedges' unwavering assistance (she played an indispensable role in his rise from junkman to entrepreneur; it is she who suggested he start investing in Harlem's tenements), Junto is propelled up from slavery—he goes from being economically *niggerized* to having access to all of the rights and privileges that have historically accrued to men of his own race. Though his contemptible deeds signify a gothic reversal, with *whiteness* now reinstalled as the spectral, contaminating presence, Petry further underscores this point through descriptions of both his physical appearance and the enterprises over which he presides.

As evidenced by the marks that a fire grafted onto Mrs. Hedges' body, Petry often amplifies her characters' menacing and predatory qualities through physical markings. Not limited to the scarified Mrs. Hedges, Petry images most of the novel's major characters as physically disfigured; consider, for instance, the "long, ugly scar" that adorns Boots's face, which he sardonically calls a "souvenir" (another term connotative of lynching/sexual castration) left by a girlfriend who knifed him in self-defense. But while these deformities may appear consonant with historically pervasive conceptions of blackness as aesthetically less appealing than whiteness, Petry deconstructs notions surrounding the black body's grotesqueness by foregrounding Junto's own physical defects.

In a canny counter-theorizing of race and beauty vis-à-vis Thomas Jefferson's classic aesthetic devaluing and animalizing of blacks, Morrison's neo-fictive slave novel *Beloved* abrogates the notion of whites' aesthetic/intellectual superiority and the attendant fiction of blacks' physical repugnance and intellectual inadequacies:

> Whitepeople believed that whatever the manners, under every dark skin was a jungle. Swift unnavigable waters, swinging screaming baboons, sleeping snakes, red gums ready for their sweet white blood. . . . The more coloredpeople spent their strength trying to convince them how gentle they were, how clever and loving, how human, the more they used themselves up to persuade whites of something Negroes believed could not be questioned, the deeper and more tangled the jungle grew inside. But it wasn't the jungle blacks brought with them to this place from the other (livable) place. It was the jungle whitefolks planted in them. And it grew. It spread. In, through and after life, it spread, until it invaded the whites who had made it. Touched them every one. Changed and altered them. Made them bloody, silly, worse than even they wanted to be, so scared were they of the jungle they had made. The screaming baboon lived under their own white skin; the red gums were their own. (198–99)

In language that is concurrently vampirish, ethnographic, poetic, and corrective, Morrison cannily deconstructs blackness in the white imaginary, transubstantiating it into a fantasy displacement construed to camouflage their own monstrous behaviors and desires—the inapprehensible horror of whites' native psychoracial bestiality. Prefiguring Morrison's consummate de- and re-construction of whiteness, Petry inscribes Junto's own physical loathsomeness as emblematic of his sexual degeneracy, as those blacks within his racial-economic orbit frequently liken him to something hideously malformed: "He was squat. His shoulders were too big for his body. His neck was set on them like a turtle's neck. His skin was as gray in color as his eyes. *And he was white*" (245–46; emphasis added); at another juncture, Boots reflects that "Junto's squat-bodied figure was all gray—gray suit, gray hair, gray skin, so that he melted into the room" (275). While his "gray" pigment may symbolize his miscegenational designs as well as his racial dimorphism (see Mrs. Hedges' removal of him from the exclusively "white" category), Petry sketches him as cadaverous and gnome-like, almost alien. Indeed, while he may conceive of Harlem as a "jungle" ripe for his sexual/economic gorging, it is he who is the "red-gummed" baboon-vampire whose own heart is incorrigibly dark.[9]

Correlatively, Petry patterns Junto after more conventionally gothic nineteenth-century figures such as Dr. Frankenstein and the male half of the Usher dyad. When Boots rails against being drafted to fight for an American citizenry which, "no matter how scared they are of Germans," are "still more scared of me" (258), he exhorts Junto to "fix this thing." Engineering a plan that spares Boots the humiliation of enlisting in a Jim Crow army, Junto at first appears magnanimous in agreeing to render Boots unfit to serve, though of course he has a vested economic interest in his superbly talented pianist. Junto dispatches him to a doctor "who performed a slight, delicate, dangerous operation on his ear. 'You'll be all right in a month or so,' said the doctor. 'In the meantime mail this letter to your draft board.' The letter stated that Boots Smith was ill and unable to report for a physical examination. And, of course, when he was finally examined, he was rejected" (261). While Junto's doctor is no Josef Mengele, Junto's demoniac takes on a more sinister turn here: Albeit at Boots's request, Junto's ability to alter the black body for his own ends conjures images of racial maiming endured by blacks in slavery as well as medical "experiments" such as the calamitous Tuskegee "bad blood" episode that commenced in the 1930s.[10] Conjunctively, Lutie imagines Junto's bar in similarly palliative terms—the bar being an embodiment of Junto's faux "healing" powers with respect to black bodies; she contemplates how the bar mitigates "the haunting silences of rented rooms and little apartments" by providing her an oasis when she's "caged in that apartment" after interminably dreary workdays (147). Presiding over physical alterations while also providing a faux shelter, Junto becomes a synthesis of Shelley's fiendish physician and a plantation master who permits a modicum of enjoyment for those whom he otherwise victimizes through sexual and economic subjugation.

Junto's co-opting and circumscribing of African Americans, bodies which he like his slaveholding paternal forbears finds contradictorily sexually repellent, sexually boundless, and carnally irresistible, reach their zenith in the novel's climax. At this point, Boots lures Lutie to his own apartment by promising to help her financially. Pimping for his neo-master, whom he's stashed in his bedroom for an unsuspecting Lutie, Boots pawns him off to her as "a good guy" to which she screams, "Get him out of here! Get him out of here! Get him out of here quick!" (422–23). In her verbal resistance and claiming of her own sexual subjectivity, Lutie contemplates, "Junto has a brick in his hand. Just one brick. The final one needed to complete the wall that had been building up around her for years, and when that one last brick was shoved in place, she would be completely walled in" (423). Lutie's summation, couched in terms of sexual subjugation and live interment, again recalls Poe's immortal tale of sexual degeneracy, consanguineous violation, and misogyny. As Poe's narrator observes that "sympathies of a scarcely intelligible nature had always existed between" Roderick and his prematurely buried twin, Madeline (34), with its implication of sibling incest and the violation of one of America's unpardonable taboos, Junto's miscegenational inclination represents a similarly transgressive act. Petry's prose here radiates with sexually insinuative language—"brick" euphonically and scatologically suggesting male genitalia; "shoved in place" more than hinting at forced penetration; the "wall" around Lutie suggestive of her own genitalia which Junto would like to "wall in," Dr. Flint style, for his exclusive pleasure. Boots too metamorphoses into a witting Roderick in a sense, facilitating the violation of his African American (soul) "sister" (significantly, Boots will try to rape Lutie once the Junto-Lutie liaison he's engineered goes awry). Petry deftly connects Junto to a tradition of literary monsters, primeval scourges whose inherent evil may take a variety of visages but cannot be extirpated.

William "Supe" Jones

In appraising Junto's colonized Harlem as a neo-plantation, I concur with several gothic feminist critics. Though not speaking of Petry specifically, they consistently argue that women writers have exploited the form to protest patriarchal excess and prerogative. Still, hers is a much more complicated racial/gender calculus than the simple equation of whiteness and maleness with the profane and blackness and femaleness with the sacred. On the one hand, in light of Allan Lloyd-Smith's assertion that Bigger Thomas is the re-figuration of Frankenstein's creature "made monstrous by the white hegemony" (121), it is not a stretch to read characters such as Junto as the apogee of the ineradicable and irremediable white male hegemony. On the other hand, if doubling is one of gothic's more identifiable conventions, then to concentrate on Junto's demonism without looking at those who might be his counterparts simplifies Petry's complex rendering of white, black, male, female—*human*—behavior. Given that Junto is the vaporous white presence behind several blacks' chronic misery, then it is necessary to explore how Petry employs doubling not only to expose the corrosive aspects of patriarchal excess but also to depict how blacks—enacted in the parasitic actions of both Mrs. Hedges and Boots Smith—can inculcate and replicate its most debased dimensions, behaviors that can't be overlooked or rationalized simply because they themselves have been victimized by it. As it does so prominently in gothic literary discourse, space functions tropologically; here it evinces black men's misguided imitating of behaviors that ultimately diminish the humanity which they fervently blame whites for denying.

If Junto is the often undetectable presence wielding unheralded power throughout his *spoil*(ed) Harlem, then William "Supe" Jones is his sepia doppelganger. Superficially, he emerges as the novel's most recognizably "gothic" figure, evidenced by live-in companion Min's brandishing of a cross to repel his borderline evil behavior: "When she spoke to him, he no longer looked at her for fear he would see, not her, but the great golden cross she had hung over the bed" (232); and in a volatile confrontation, Min "made the sign of the cross over her body," as the stunned Jones "backed away from her" (358–59). Clearly, Petry interpolates overtly gothic iconography by summoning the legacy of the tradition's most ghoulish antagonist; without a doubt, she concocts an ebony Dracula who lurks as "the satanic figure responsible for the upkeep in this hell of a place to live" (Harris-Lopez 72). Given Jones's deranged presence in an equally deranged black dystopia, we witness a subversion of the prevalent "madwoman in the attic" trope, with Jones as a sort of "mad brother in the basement." Germane here are Diane Roberts's insightful comments on the gothic undercurrents of *Uncle Tom's Cabin:* "While Legree's plantation is a gothic realm where women are abused, it is also represented in 'genital' language, identifying it with the female body. In the gothic castle, the dungeons or cellars signify female genitalia, the 'dark places,' the recesses of the body" (48). Correlatively, the Harlem tenement becomes an organic edifice, a space of female containment and multiple incursions. Petry echoes Stowe in portraying Jones's basement as the hood-inflected version of the "dungeon" and thereby a potential site of female violation—most notably when, "trembling with his desire," Jones "dragged her [Lutie] toward the cellar, and the dark hall was filled with the stench of the dog and the weight of his great body landing on her back"; ultimately, his omnipresent foil, Mrs. Hedges, thwarts his attempted rape (236). However, Petry simultaneously uses Jones's lair to symbolize his sexual mania and neurosis, disorders which have an array of sources, with white patriarchal aspirations as a possible symptom but not the sole root. Like the live burial that Lutie laments in the novel's final passages, copious images of male containment pervade Jones's entire life, rendering him a victim-cum-villain.

Ostensibly, Petry imagines William Jones as a wannabe slumlord-kingpin (a more ghettoized version of *The Narrows*' Bill Hod) who is reduced to collecting rents for invisible "white agents" and serving as the gatekeeper for the squalid slums which, in the words of a white policeman, aren't "fit for pigs to live in, let alone people" (386). As Junto's counterpart, Jones exists as a blackguard whose precipitous psychosexual degeneration is so severe and depraved that his very humanness is cast into doubt. The text is replete with diagnoses from the women with whom he shares common physical if not emotional space, all assessing him as having devolved into something more hoofed than Homo sapiens: Lutie grouses that as he conducts her tour of the apartment, Jones is "snuffing on my trail, slathering, slobbering after me like some dark hound of hell seeking me out, tonguing along in back of me" (25); one of his young girlfriends refers to him as an "old goat," as she reviles "stay[ing] in this stinkin' apartment with you slobberin' over me" (87); after having lived within his menacing midst for a while, Lutie vows to find a new residence with "no half-human creatures like the Super" (222); and his current girlfriend, Min, bemoans the fact that "living with him was like being shut up with an animal—a sick, crazy animal" (354). Satyr-like and repellent, on the surface he appears to conform to prototypical gothic monsters, which Ellen Moers characterizes as "creatures who scare because they look different, wrong, non-human"; moreover, she concludes, a device in Victorian gothic literature was to create monsters by "the crossing of species, animal with human" with the result being "animaloid humans" (101–2). Clearly, Petry delineates Jones's benighted character by mongrelizing him. However, she tempers this profile by, again, using the trope of space to embody internal human frailties—in this instance as a metaphor for psychosexual pain, deprivation, and alienation.

Furnishing the reader a comprehensive if disconcerting psychic profile, Petry encapsulates the arc of Jones's life, one spent relegated to the most dreary, mundane work environments that severed him from human contact and made him "deadly" lonely: "It was a loneliness born of years of living in basements and sleeping on mattresses in boiler rooms. The first jobs he had had been on ships and he stayed on them until sometimes it seemed to him he had been buried alive in the hold" (85). Jones's is an interstitial existence, an afflicted life spent enclosed "in the basements and hallways of vast, empty buildings that were filled with shadows, and the only sound that came to his ears was that made by some occasional passer-by whose footsteps echoed and re-echoed in his eardrums" (86). Petry concludes this brief but morose mini-history with a roadmap outlining how Jones ends up in his first-floor tenement flat and the basement over which he presides, a crypt-like space where he performs many of his mind-numbing tasks as building superintendent:

> He had been on 116th Street for five years. He knew the cellars and the basements in this street better than he knew the outside of streets just a few blocks away. He had fired furnaces and cleaned stairways and put washers in faucets and grown gaunter and lonelier as the years crept past him. He had gone from a mattress by a furnace to basement rooms until finally here in this house he had three rooms to himself—rent free. (86)

This virtual volunteer slavery again recalls the entombment of the Middle Passage; what Jones perceives as his economic liberation precludes human growth and emotionally healthy relationships with his fellow blacks. In his Dantean subterranean hell, he metamorphoses into what Min describes as resembling "Satan—black and evil" (114); similarly, Mrs. Hedges pronounces, "You done lived in basements so long you ain't human no more. You got mould growin' on you" (237). An extreme example of the pathological effects of chronic interment, Jones deteriorates into a wicked, very visible (unlike Junto) essence who rules a dark netherworld devoid of community and, most deleteriously, love. His figurative live burial—racial, economic, spatial—eventuates in his psychosocial death and becomes the external manifestation of a mind shattered by protracted isolation. Thus, Petry provides an etiology of Jones's mental degeneration, which results in a welter of different neuroses; especially revelatory are the psychosexual perturbations exhibited when he visits Bub during Lutie's absence and displays instances of cannibalistic desire.

One of the novel's most disquieting episodes occurs when Jones visits Bub on the pretense of keeping him company during Lutie's absence, though Jones's ultimate goal is to fulfill his maniacal desire to "see her bedroom" (101).[11] A conniving father manqué (think, too, of Lutie's faux/forefather, Franklin), he fosters a false filial camaraderie by playing cards with Bub while seemingly indulging the boy's frantic rehashing of the plots of two movies he'd recently seen (appropriately about gangsters and financial double-crossing). Fixating on a tube of lipstick left on the table, Jones anthropomorphizes it, transforming it into a sexual synecdoche for the absent object of his corrosive longings. In depraved, near-ritualistic behavior that escalates, he begins by "staring at the lipstick"; afterward, he "pulled the top off and looked at the red stick inside" (105). Ultimately, the conflation of object and human reaches its peak: "He wanted to put it against his lips. That's the way her mouth would smell and it would feel like this stuff, only warm. Holding it in his hand he got the smell from it very clearly. . . . He raised the lipstick toward his mouth and the boy suddenly reached out and took it out of his hand, putting it in his pants pocket."

In Heather Hicks's apt description, this scene implicates Jones as a "compulsive scopophiliac" (25). As red has traditionally symbolized the feminine/vaginal, his insatiable desires have slipped into psychosexual deviation, marked in this bizarre commingling of hyper-olfactory sensitivity and quasi-transvestitism.[12] This sexually macabre encroachment climaxes with him entering (penetrating) her closet—a vaginal-like space, the intrusion of which recalls the female gothic trope in which home emblematizes the besieged and violated woman's body—where he seizes upon one of her blouses and "crushed it violently between his hands squeezing the soft thin material tighter and tighter until it was a small ball in his hands except the part where the metal hanger was near the top" (108). In effect, he enacts a symbolic rape, betokening the novel's climax in which Lutie imagines being buried by Junto's sexually and audibly insinuative "brick." Jones's cosmetic and vestment fetishisms, culminating in his mangling of Lutie's clothing, encapsulate not simply his psychosexual turpitude but also the intractably materialist/capitalist culture that impels women to self-objectify—most explicitly reflected by colossal clothing and cosmetic industries that promulgate the calumny that women's raison d'être is their desirability by men.[13]

Petry's daring foray into the subject of sexual psychopathology at a time when most contemporaneous African American authors were foregrounding interracial conflicts continues as she limns the devastating impact of Jones's severe isolation and the neuroses that it has bred. Sketching what amounts to a desire to "eat the Other," Petry integrates gastronomical images of consumption, where Jones seeks to devour Lutie as a sort of sexual road-kill.[14] His monomaniacal pursuit, described as his "being eaten up by some horrible obsession" (57), is most vividly rendered as his imagination runs amok. He contemplates presenting Lutie with a pair of stockings and caressing her "soft brown skin" as he helps her to put them on: "He would lean nearer and nearer, as the stocking reached the rounded part of her leg where the fatness of the curve came, until he was pressing his mouth hot and close against that curve. Closer and closer so that he could nibble at it with his mouth, nibble the curve of her leg, and her skin would be sweet from soap and cool against the hotness of his mouth" (98). Juxtaposed with earlier images of Jones "eating her up with his eyes" (25), this eerie craving captures the depth of his sexual debasement; recalling Milton's Satan, Jones's mind becomes a virtual hell unto itself. While this passage clearly invokes classical mythology, specifically the Sirens who wooed men with their melodious songs only to devour them in an early iteration of the "monstrous-feminine" (Creed 2), Jones's imaginings invert this classically gothic portrayal of the gyno-monster, as his gustatory impulses bear out his sexual pathology, which has its genesis in his prolonged periods of sequestration.

Moreover, as Peggy Sanday points out, "Cannibalism is never just about eating but is primarily a medium for nongustatory messages—messages having to do with the maintenance, regeneration, and, in some cases, the foundation of the cultural order" (3). In effect, Jones's appetitive yearnings are more about the restoration of a precarious patriarchal "order" that women like Mrs. Hedges, Lutie, and even Min upend as they—with varying degrees of success—shape their own destinies. With Lutie ardently spurning his sexual advances, and Mrs. Hedges constantly taunting him that there "ain't no point in lickin' your chops, dearie" (90) and her subsequent thwarting of his attempted rape, he is repeatedly foiled in trying to exercise his presumed phallocentric privilege. As rape is a crime about domination as much as it is about sex, Jones's carnivorous phantasms become compensatory mental strategies, given his inability to enact orthodox masculine praxes; in other words, the taint of blackness is a drag rope that hamstrings his presumed pedestalized place in the patricentric and patri-normative American culture. Forever frustrated by implacable racial and patriarchal hegemonies that permit once-impoverished white men such as Junto to own tenements, juke joints, and brothels—in effect, to colonize Harlem—William Jones incarnates the black man who can only mimic true manhood, his severely neutered power dwarfed in comparison to that wielded by unseen Anglocentric forces.

Ultimately, Petry's oppositional black gothic both appropriates and re-stages traditional narrative situations and strategies that are most closely associated with the genre. Clearly, Junto and Jones's mutual hypersexualization of and demented fantasies about women evince both men's misogyny, bearing witness to the "male disgust with woman's sexuality, the male hatred and fear of woman's awful procreative power and her 'otherness,' which lies at the root of the Female Gothic" (Stein 124). On the one hand, although they are racially and genealogically different, both become nonsanguineous "brothers" who envision women's bodies as well as the spaces women inhabit as territory to be seized, owned, and violated. On the other hand, Petry's insistence on complicating ostensible villains like Jones, linking the origins of his psychosexual dementia to the physical and racial encasement experienced by his enslaved ancestors, defies easy categorization of her novel as "Female Gothic"—she haunts b(l)ack, with a difference. And finally, though the "task of the classic Gothic heroine is to escape from the castle that has become her prison, to preside over its demystification, a process that usually requires its violent destruction, and to claim the fortune and lineage that the villain has sought to make his own" (Ellis 263), Petry integrates *and* undermines such formulae in the novel's denouement: Lutie's own psychic infrastructure crumbles and leads her to abandon Bub and her squalid home life. As well, Lutie's concluding act signifies on both social and literary convention with respect to women's essentialized "mothering" role and the notion that only men can flee such circumscribing gendered expectations. However, her train ride to Chicago is no underground railroad; at best it amounts to a transitory freedom, since she will presumably be pursued for murdering Boots. Meanwhile, the patriarchal structure over which Junto presides and for which Jones serves as literal and figurative custodian remains unvanquished.

While the "black man" may be what Fiedler decreed the "proper subject" of the Anglo-American literary gothic imagination, the demons that haunt Petry's characters and their reactions to them trouble shopworn binaries of white-evil versus black-good and pure-female versus predatory-male; it is as much the individual choices her protagonists make and their own moral vacuity that engender their emotional implosions. Like her first and most acclaimed novel, Petry's short fiction further demonstrates her hybridized, Africanized gothic, where she expands her discursive repertoire to include the ghost story and dark comedy to exhume the *madness* underlying race, gender, gender identity, sexual orientation, and class in America.

5

HAUNTING/HAUNTED B(L)ACK

Tormented and Tormenting Souls in "The Bones of Louella Brown" and "The Witness"

> And the entire bottom of the land is hemmed in by the town cemetery. Had to be half-witted—who'd want to own land near a graveyard, especially a darky who is known to be scared pantless of haints and such? They pocketed Nedeed's money and had a good laugh: first full moon on All Hallows would send them spirits walking and him running to beg them to buy the property back.
>
> —Gloria Naylor, *Linden Hills*

As evidenced in the previous, companionate chapter, *The Street*'s dingy tenement setting conjures up the inapprehensible dread of the slave ship and plantation—though the sites and experiences are not, of course, coterminous. Given Petry's long-standing valuation of alternative cosmographies and the unabating horror associated with and experienced by the black body, the gothic "eruptions" that reverberate throughout the novel are not anomalous; on the contrary, there are a surfeit of them throughout her novels and short stories. One such tale, evocatively entitled "The Bones of Louella Brown," is a sobering comedy of errors in which the bones of the eponymous black laundress and those of a white Boston Brahmin, the "Countess of Castro," are intermingled and rendered indistinguishable, with both becoming fodder for racialized "scientific" inquiry. The story unfurls as a literal and discursive "dark comedy," as Petry explodes the absurdity of posthumous segregational cemetery practices as well as "liberal" New England's odious class biases.

Petry continues her serial deconstruction of a dystopic northern milieu in another tale. Darker and gravely unfunny, "The Witness" dramatizes the misadventure of Charles Woodruff, as tormented and emotionally splenetic a character as the morbidly idiosyncratic, hysterical Roderick Usher. Telling are Woodruff's gloom-laden ruminations after he and a young white girl, Nellie, have been kidnapped by a group of white adolescent misfits who subsequently rape her while a hapless Woodruff is forced to stand facing a wall, a prostrate and bound "witness" prevented from coming to the girl's aid: "He could see shadows on the wall. Sometimes they moved, sometimes they were still, and then the shadows moved again and then there would be laughter. Silence after that and then thuds, thumps, silence again" (225). From the funereal cemetery setting to the onomatopoeia-like descriptions that recall Poe's euphonically rich descriptions of horror, this event becomes a micro-text of a tale that is awash in racial, sexual, and psychic terror.

Indeed, Diane Roberts's designation of "the gothic prison of the South" (43) to describe African Americans' historic-geographic "Egyptland" accurately captures Petry's quasi-southern North, evidenced in one of her earliest short stories, "The Necessary Knocking on the Door" (1947). She fashions the Berkshires, a Massachusetts mountain idyll and the location of "the Annual Conference on Christianity in the Modern World," as a haunted milieu for protagonist Alice Knight, the event's lone black attendee: "There was no sound anywhere—either in this [her] room or, as far as she could determine, in any other part of the building. . . . Thus she became aware of the moonlight—pale, cold light that filtered through the small-paned windows, making grotesque patterns on the floor, the walls, the ceiling" (243). With Knight functioning as a female version of "Witness"'s Woodruff (both are English teachers from southern environs —in Knight's case, Washington, D.C.) in this southern-esque setting, Petry embroiders a mosaic of northern terror. The mausoleum-like atmosphere of Knight's room connotes that the North, too, can foment dread in the psychically dis-eased black subject.

Reflecting what she considers her own ambivalent place as a black woman in the putatively "liberal" New England, Petry recasts her native soil as a northerly annex of its southern counterpart—anywhere south of Canada becomes synonymous with *the* South and can thereby traumatize isolated blacks by inducing miasmatic racial-psychic fear. Cumulatively, the tableaux of the menacing images that pervade "The Bones of Louella Brown" and "The Witness" highlight what the epigraph from Gloria Naylor encapsulates: African Americans' existence in America has been beset by racially frightful experiences that affect—and infect—every facet of their lives.

"A Monst'us Bad Dream, A Nach'ul Nightmare": Dupes and Spooks in "The Bones of Louella Brown"

As he is an expert on gothic literature, David Punter's delineation of the form's distinguishing features and objectives holds immense currency: "an emphasis on portraying the terrifying, a common insistence on archaic settings, a prominent use of the supernatural, the presence of highly stereotyped characters and the attempt to deploy and perfect techniques of literary suspense." He adds as well that gothic is "the fiction of the haunted castle, of heroines preyed on by unspeakable terrors, of the blackly lowering villain, of ghosts, vampires, monsters and werewolves" (1). As I have argued earlier on, *The Street* contains several of these elements, though Petry troubles such swimmingly formulaic gothic waters with heroines who are villainous and predators who are simultaneously prey. With respect to Punter's gothic parameters, the *most* gothic of black literary texts is *Beloved*, Morrison's Pulitzer-Prize-winning epic of infanticide; through the titular child-ghost's haunting of the mother who slays her rather than relinquish her to the monstrously *peculiar* institution, Morrison unsheathes the specter of American slavery and its irrepressible legacy of physical and psychic horror. In my repositioning of Petry as literary foremother of so many contemporary women writers, I would install her 1947 short story "The Bones of Louella Brown" as a precursive text that employs the most transparent of gothic formulae, the visitation of the (un)dead's spirit, for both comic and weighty purposes. Relatively obscure and ignored in the dual realms of American gothic literature and black feminist criticism, this story exemplifies a mastery and manipulation of the form that prefigures Morrison's more feted (albeit somewhat over-analyzed) masterpiece.

The story's gothic components emblematize the paradigms that Eve Sedgwick and Jerrold Hogle outlined (see the previous chapter). To recapitulate briefly, Sedgwick pinpoints elements such as "the priesthood and monastic institutions," "subterranean spaces," "doubles," "unnatural echoes or silences," "the poisonous effects of guilt and shame; nocturnal landscapes and dreams; apparitions from the past" (*Coherence* 9–10); Hogle emphasizes "the haunting of an antiquated, *falsely* antiquated space by the monstrous specter(s) of a hidden primal crime which can be discovered only by probing through layers of memory, documentation, or buried physical evidence" and also the "repression of primordial feminine origins . . . to shore up a patriarchal hierarchy whose counterfeit grounding is increasingly exposed" (215). An outline of "Louella Brown"'s pivotal moments illumines how its gothic substructure transforms it into a morality tale of transgression, transformation, and redemption. While antiblack phobias haunt Petry's familiar New England terrain, trespasses relating to gender, class, and the landscape itself abound as well.

From its opening paragraph, Petry clearly outfits the story in the vestments of the gothic. Old Peabody and Young Whiffle, two elderly white morticians, relate a newspaper item regarding the exhumation of the Bedfords, "the most distinguished family in Massachusetts" (163): they are to be moved from the family plot at Yew Tree Cemetery and reburied in a private chapel, Bedford Abbey. Thus, the story's exposition conforms to the discourse's concerns with religious edifices and the sub-rosa world of dis- and re-interment. After undertaking this project, Old Peabody uses it as an opportunity to right what he sees as a long-standing racial-historical injustice: at the behest of his father—who was acting upon his wife's insistence—the family's laundress/maid had been buried in the all-white cemetery; the mass exhumation will permit the undertakers to banish her to "one of the less well-known burying places on the outskirts of the city" (165).[1] Magnifying this racial-social breach is the following revelation: "Louella's grave had been at the very tip edge of the cemetery in 1902, in a very undesirable place"; however, "due to the enlargement of the cemetery, over the years, she now lay in one of the choicest spots—in the exact center" (166).

Soon thereafter, Petry introduces the prototypic conceit of haunting: in the first of what will become numerous visitations, Old Peabody "suddenly saw Louella Brown with an amazing sharpness. It was just as though she had entered the room." Hired by Whiffle and Peabody to perform research on the bodies, Harvard medical student Stuart Reynolds enthusiastically embraces the project, which will also facilitate his "private study of bone structure in the Caucasian female as against the bone structure in the female of the darker race, and Louella Brown was an unexpected research plum" (166–67). But to the old men's dismay, Reynolds inadvertently mixes up Louella's bones with those of Elizabeth Bedford, "the Countess of Castro," who was "the nearest approach to royalty" in the family. Thus, the deceased women become posthumous twins, their twinning the story's cataclysmic event. The indeterminable bone structures of the black and white women generate a media circus, as the press hyperbolizes the mix-up to exploit both its class and racial implications. More pressing for the geriatric undertakers, however, is how to explain that their presumably segregated cemetery was in fact integrated, an unpardonable trespass that will mortify the liberty-loving New Englander as deeply as it would any peculiar-institution-sanctioning southerner.

Compounding this race/class/gender crisis are Peabody's increasing nightly "visitations" by Louella's ghost. Subsequently, the men's conflicting solutions regarding how they should publicly atone for the "sin" of interracial burial touch off a "violent quarrel" between them, triggering the dissolution of their business partnership. The collapse of their patriarchal "empire" and the frequent and unsettling hauntings by Louella kindle a personal conversion, as a racially enlightened Peabody consequently convinces the intractable Governor Bedford to rebury both women in the familial abbey with a gravestone that acknowledges not just their indistinguishableness but their common humanity.

Thus, Petry fashions the story in prototypically gothic terms: a milieu awash in death; buried family "sins" and the subsequent return of both the buried white countess and the "repressed" black woman, whose disinterred aura wreaks havoc on patriarchal, familial, and financial enterprises; the "unnaturalness" and senselessness of postmortem racism and classism. Certainly, the trajectory of her dark concerns harkens back to the late nineteenth century—think of the gothic ingredients of Charles Chesnutt's stories such as "Mars Jeems's Nightmare," where the conjure woman Aunt Peggy subjects the sadistic titular slave owner to a "Monst'us Bad Dream, A Nach'ul Nightmare" by transforming him into a flesh-and-bones nigger, his—and Chesnutt's white readers'—worst "nightmare"; Aunt Peggy subsequently restores the now racially enlightened Jeems's whiteness, as he is reborn as the most benevolent of masters. Chesnutt utilizes the trope of bodily invasion and transformation not to expose African Americans as irrepressible dark Others who bedevil the white American psyche, but to elucidate for a white reading audience how they themselves might feel if subjected to the very real horrors of slavery. As Justin Edwards incisively explains, Chesnutt employs "the gothic discourse of fluidly transformative identities to question the racial essentialism that marks blackness and whiteness as strictly autonomous. The gothic import, directed toward white supremacy, speaks of the horrors of slavery through the rejection of whiteness as an exemption from bondage" (90).

With respect specifically to "Louella Brown," its intertextual connections to "Mars Jeems's Nightmare" render Chesnutt's tale an unlikely but quite plausible intertext. Recall the previous chapter, where Petry's comments bespoke her respect for the cosmic and otherworldly—her abiding belief in conjure and respect for black folk and vernacular culture. Envisioning herself as a pen-wielding conjure woman, Petry becomes something of a *gyno-trickster*, for she too will employ not racial reassignment but bodily haunting and the ultimate white nightmare—blackness—to contest venomous but staunchly held American "values" such as congenital racialism, segregation, class stratification, and sexual chauvinism. In an instance of what Henry Louis Gates would deem "a joyous proclamation of antecedent and descendant texts" (xxvii), Petry, though not necessarily deliberately, performs a Chesnuttian manipulation to comparably limn the underside of the American ethos, specifically beliefs regarding the absurdity of inviolably racist burial codes and the presumed biological purity and superiority of white blood.[2] Petry does not foreground racial fluidity but instead blurs spatiotemporal boundaries separating life and death in constructing "Louella Brown"'s narrative architecture.

The death-in-life return of Louella Brown similarly permits Petry to address such incendiary issues in an ostensibly innocuous and even comic fashion. Such a narrative situation coheres with the notion that gothic writing "concerns itself with boundaries and their instabilities, whether between the quick/the dead, eros/thanatos, pain/pleasure, 'real'/'unreal,' 'natural'/'supernatural,' material/transcendent, man/machine, human/vampire or 'masculine'/'feminine'" (Horner and Zlosnik 1). The antithesis of gothic monsters such as the *enfant terrible* Beloved or Poe's disarmingly normal madmen, the Louella Brown who "visits" Old Peabody is "a small, brown woman with merry eyes" who "laughed and laughed" (177)—a comic sprite who nevertheless takes residence in the old undertaker's subconscious. However, the story's outwardly humorous agon belies its harrowing content: the insidious and entrenched nature of racism that carries over into the afterlife, and the fallacious but "scientifically" sanctioned belief in the black body's inherent physiological difference and primitiveness.

Horner and Zlosnik in *Gothic and the Comic Turn* elucidate what can be considered the story's thematic and rhetorical methodology: "Indeed, as Philip Stevic suggests that the heightened, distorted and sometimes comic quality of Gothic texts arises from their likeness to dream narratives so that whilst the story might seem ridiculous, even amusing, the 'coexistence of mythic seriousness, psychic authority and laughter' within the Gothic text reflects the disturbing authenticity of insight gained through an unconscious process" (8–9). True enough, while donning the (dis)guise of "Sambo" and even invoking memories of mammy, Louella is nevertheless the moral touchstone who will animate a reevaluation of long-standing racial attitudes and malignant cultural practices. Therefore, the "amusing" and "absurd" elements of the story function as comic subterfuge, which in fact amplifies the "terror" of the collective American soul—a terror not encased within the darkened Other, but in the dominant culture's morally jaundiced attitudes that result in the wholesale abjectification of the black body.[3]

The initial event that stokes the story's seriocomic machinery is Old Peabody's somber admission of his inadvertent role in the social crisis that Louella's dead presence nevertheless bestirs:

> "She used to be our laundress," he said. "My mother was very fond of Louella, and insisted that she be buried in Yew Tree Cemetery." His father had consented—grudgingly, yes, but his father should never

> have agreed to it. It had taken the careful discriminatory practices of generations of Peabodys, undertakers like himself, to make Yew Tree Cemetery what it was today—the final home of Boston's wealthiest and most aristocratic families. (166)

Petry employs both racial and gothic symbology, as topology becomes the material indicator of chronically pernicious views regarding both class and race. Just as the dark tarn outside the Usher mansion becomes a vortex emblematizing incest, mental illness, and live burial (not to mention the mansion's literal fissure, which bespeaks broken bloodlines and violated taboos), Petry's landscape is a tangled briar patch of meanings. Geographic space has, in fact, functioned as the master signifier of seemingly impermeable racial boundaries, evinced by a cursory glance at our divided racial/spatial historical lexicon: "free" North versus "slave" South, with the Mason-Dixon line instantiating the juridical oppression of blacks in one region and their (relative) freedom in another; the "other side of the tracks" as the physical divider for where blacks were and were not permitted to be; the "Black Belt," the dilapidated outlying areas of southern towns to which blacks were relegated; "sundown towns," places where dusk provided a celestial semaphore signaling blacks to disappear or die trying; even the now quaintly nostalgic "chittlin' circuit," less-than-glamorous venues to which black performers were relegated for decades—all of these geographical "fissures" particularize proscribed territory that concomitantly reflects the gothic's emphasis on the concentricity of social, racial, and psychic spaces.[4] Moreover, the seeming absurdity of the story's watershed event, the dis- and re-interment of the odious black body, nevertheless has historical precedence.

Posthumous segregation was, at least until the 1970s, as certain as death and taxes. Writing about this ignoble practice, literary/cultural critic Karla Holloway addresses startling but historically accurate protocols surrounding the rancid racializing of southern burial—racial protocols that interface with the segregationist codes of Petry's fictitious northern cemetery: "White violence, including the vicious practice of lynching, was complicit in too many black deaths, and whites were often as disrespectful to black bodies in death as they were in life" (*Passed On*

16). And though one might be inclined to conjecture whether Petry may have fallaciously ascribed this comprehensibly "southern" practice to her more "liberal" native New Englanders, Angelika Krüger-Kahloula in "On the Wrong Side of the Fence: Racial Segregation in American Cemeteries" observes how even "biracial" northern cemeteries that "mixed" black and white corpses nonetheless followed "confederate" burial procedures:

> Following the hierarchical worldview, the graves of blacks in biracial cemeteries were "carefully relegated to the obscure corners of the ground, along with those of paupers and criminals." Projected onto the flat surface of the burial ground, this model of society assigned people of inferior social standing and outsiders the margins of the cemetery, as they had occupied the margins of the community. In Boston, grave diggers petitioned the town in 1744 to provide a place for burying "stranger [sic] and negroes." In Worcester, Massachusetts, blacks were buried in the far left corner of the Burial Ground on Mechanic Street, behind the strangers' section.[5] (133–34)

Hence, Petry's representation of racial positioning in burial clearly has its historical antecedents; in fact, Krüger-Kahloula exposes how blacks occupy a lower place on the burial totem pole than even "strangers," a bracing indication of the intransigence of northernized Jim Crow policies. Factually or fictionally, there has existed a de facto politics of racial interment that informs and sanctions the actions of Petry's white morticians. Compounding the irony of the story's northern setting is the name of Louella's white employers: New Bedford was in fact the place to which "fugitive slave" Frederick Douglass fled and settled with wife Anna Murray, though he would subsequently lament blacks' tribulations on this less-than-hospitable northern soil. Indeed, there is nothing new about either the indignities the runaway chattel faced or the reprehensible actions of real and imagined undertakers and their venomous racial views, which are magnified in the story's other pivotal event.

Petry deconstructs the notion of racial difference, using satire to sharpen her withering critique of whites' seemingly ineradicable insistence on blackness as synonymous with contamination and subhuman-ness. While the discovery of the black corpse's proximity to the elite Bedfords sets off a minor crisis that is easily rectifiable, another "proximity," related here by the third-person narrator, will subsequently have a catastrophic personal and professional impact. After informing the reader of the Countess of Castro's royal pedigree, the narrative reveals the following: "Though neither Old Peabody nor Young Whiffle knew it, the countess and Louella Brown had resembled each other in many ways. They both had thick glossy black hair. Neither woman had any children. They had both died in 1902, when in their early seventies, and been buried in Yew Tree Cemetery within two weeks of each other" (167). While these "anthropological" resemblances among Homo sapiens might not ordinarily be cause for alarm, they take on an acute import because of medical student Stuart Reynolds's aforementioned "private study." Petry here most clearly invokes the vernacular of nineteenth-century "race science," specifically what has come to be known as the "American School of Ethnology."

The most "expert"—and notorious—treatise on the subject was authored by George Robins Gliddon, a British lecturer and self-styled expert on Egyptology, and Josiah Clark Nott, an Alabama physician. Literary critic/theorist Scott Trafton describes their seminal work thusly: "*Types of Mankind* is infamous today for being the representative text of the American School and thus for many the best example of racist science the Western tradition has to offer. It was a watershed event in the history of American culture; it was the signature text of the American School, and Nott and Gliddon were its self-appointed messiahs" (46). Among a bevy of physiologically dubious "findings," Nott and Gliddon conclude, "The Negro races possess about nine cubic inches less of brain than the Teuton" (qtd. in Trafton 48). In retrospect, the raison d'être of their work is indubitable: the nation's febrile fears of miscegenation, the outgrowth of the "amalgamation hysteria" that swept through post–Civil War white America.

Whether Petry had these two nominal "scientist"/supremacists in mind when she concocted Reynolds or Old Peabody–Young Whiffle is unknown; what is clear, however, is that "The Bones of Louella Brown" unreservedly dismantles the core claim of Anglo-American eugenics—a doctrine which may have reached its pinnacle in the nineteenth century but has nevertheless retained its currency in the twentieth century (and beyond) with the publication of scientifically legitimated works such as *The Bell Curve*.[6] The heretofore sanctioned epidermalization of difference is explicitly abrogated once the inept Reynolds mixes up the bones and has to probe beneath the skin: He astonishingly realizes "there was no way of telling the countess from Louella" (168). Though he momentarily allays his panic by returning to a prototypical marker of difference—"But the hair! How stupid of me. I can tell them apart by the hair. The colored woman's will be—"—he is further flummoxed upon realizing that "both women had the same type of hair" (168). Upon measuring the women's skeletons, he finally pronounces it "sensational" that "they were the same height, had the same bone structure" (168). Petry emphatically intervenes upon and vitiates the unscientific science of racial difference, which inarguably had its adherents when she published the story in the 1940s; she contests and supplants the myth of racial heterogeneity through her portrayal of the racially indistinguishable countess and laundress—the gothically benighted black body and its putative antipode, the pristine and genetically advanced white body, are, in fact, doubles.

Further, drawing into her critical orbit capitalist patriarchy's penchant for sensationalizing and capitalizing upon difference, Petry continues her long-standing critique of the press's fanning the flames of racial difference, as the newspaper headline sensationally exclaims, "Who will be buried under the marble floor of Bedford Abbey on the twenty-first of June—the white countess or the black laundress?" (170). In the wake of the ignominious public ogling of Saartjie Baartman (Hottentot Venus) in the early 1800s, the parading of Louella Brown and Elizabeth Bedford (at one point heralded for being "as famous as movie stars," 171) exhibits how women's bodies—pigmentation and century notwithstanding—become fodder for unscrupulous patriarchal enterprises (faux-scientific or journalistic) that simply mirror and amplify—but not create—society's entrenched anxieties about racial difference.

Unpacking the slave narrative as a quintessentially gothic medium, Katherine Henry observes that "the anxiety registered in the slave's appearance as the citizen's Gothic Other, then, is the anxiety not of difference but of sameness" (34). Indeed, refiguring arguably the most dominant trope in American/African American literary traditions, the fear of miscegenation, Petry revises this discursive formation with the *anxiety of homogeneity*—the unbearable sameness of genes and, more terrifyingly, races.[7] The sheer horror of the heretofore incontrovertible certitude of racial heterogeneity is evidenced in the old men's apoplectic responses—Young Whiffle more so than Old Peabody—to the public exposure of the mixed-bone fiasco. Witness the former's frantic response to "this dreadful mix-up" (170): "Young Whiffle was breathing hard. 'The house [their undertaking business],' he said, 'the honor of this house, years of working, of building a reputation, all destroyed. We're ruined, ruined—' he choked on the word" (170). Aside from the power of blackness to snuff out these patriarchs' long-standing corporation, significant here is the highly insinuative use of the word *ruin*, which has traditionally connoted women's sexual "promiscuity" and attendant "impurity." Petry's invocation of the term here subverts the antiblack and antiwoman connotations that it usually carries. Instead of women's sexuality being responsible for white men's "ruination"—think here of Faulkner's masterpiece *Absalom, Absalom!* as Thomas Sutpen's dalliance with an enslaved woman he owns produces the inveterately contaminated black body (daughter Clytie, one of two children he sires with black women); in Sutpen's mind, the black woman and *her* offspring despoil the *ueber*-patriarch's grand design—it is the black woman's decidedly nonsexual death-in-life presence that effectuates his economic downfall.

Conjunctively, this bizarrely tripartite necrophobia-Negrophilia-Negrophobia unleashes in Young Whiffle a *racial panic*, a strain of the amalgamation hysteria that cannot be stemmed.[8] Right in the midst of another haunting by the uncontainable Louella, whom he "very clearly" envisions, Old Peabody gamely attempts to bring a bit of sobriety to the rapidly unraveling situation: "She might have been Irish. . . . And a Catholic. That would have been equally as bad" (171). However, he still insists on blackness as the ultimate malignity: "'Nonsense,' said Young Whiffle pettishly. 'A black washer-woman is infinitely worse than anything you've mentioned. People are saying it's some kind of trick, that we're proving there's no difference between the races. Oh, we're ruined—

ruined—ruined—' Young Whiffle moaned" (172). Indeed, Petry betokens what Morrison writes of in *Beloved* as Anglo-America's ineradicable terror: *Blackness*, specifically black people, become synonymous with untrammeled savagery and the quintessential threat to a simon-pure white American civilization ("swift unnavigable waters, swinging screaming baboons, sleeping snakes, red gums ready for their sweet white blood" [198]). The stratified ethnic deck that Peabody ticks off—one that exposes the contextually accurate New Englander's anti-Irish and anti-Catholic prejudices—is not so much contested by Young Whiffle as it is reshuffled.

That Petry uses two old white men to utter and argue the totemics of race and ethnicity not only serves the rhetorical purpose of exposing how northerners harbor the same perverted "amalgamation" hysteria that drives white southerners into spasmodic fits (and brutality), but it also dramatizes how difference serves a cohering function, codifying what whiteness is by delineating what it isn't. In what she calls a "Lacanian analysis of race," Kalpana Seshadri-Crooks trenchantly articulates this point: "By Whiteness, I refer to the master signifier (without a signified) that establishes a structure of relations, a signifying chain that through a process of inclusions and exclusions constitutes a pattern for organizing human difference. This chain provides subjects with certain symbolic positions such as 'black,' 'white,' 'Asian,' etc., in relation to the master signifier" (3–4). With the unpacking and routinizing of the "master signifier" comes not only anxiety but what amounts to a physiological distemper; specifically, the return of the repressed black feminine animates not only financial distress, but it begets something akin to racial mania, a type of mind-body convulsion—the transmutation/alchemizing of *dis-ease* into *disease*. Note how the reaction to the headline reporting the bone-excavation blunder destabilizes the story's most prominent patriarchal emblems, the elderly undertakers and the octogenarian Governor Bedford, Elizabeth's kinsman who set the calamitous wheels in motion with his exclusivist re-interment project: Young Whiffle "breathing hard" (170); "both suffered slight heart attacks when they saw the next morning's edition of the *Boston Record*" (175); Bedford "very nearly had apoplexy" upon seeing the headline. Clearly, illness functions metaphorically here, as the atrophying of the men's staunchly held racial taxonomies induces an internal spasmodic response—a response which externalizes the American body's seemingly incurably cancerous racial ethos. Indeed, the posthumous elision of racial hierarchies through a veritable homo-gendered, hetero-racial "coupling" augers doom in Petry's "enlightened" New England just as much as any southern patriarch/master's sexually profligate behavior would in the racially benighted Confederacy. Just as Sutpen seals his fate by committing the South's unpardonable transgression, miscegenation, Young Whiffle too is "niggerized" in Petry's droll but unsparing portraiture: like Huck Finn, he hightails it to the white man's north, relocating "all the way to California, and chang[ing] his name to Smith, in the hope that no man would ever discover he had once been a member of that *blackguardly* firm of Whiffle and Peabody, Incorporated" (178–79; emphasis added).

Moreover, we see Petry at her lexically mirthful and subversive best, as she plays on the word "blackguard" for which *Merriam-Webster* provides this dual definition: "the kitchen servants of a household" and "a person who uses foul or abusive language." Wielding her semantically sharpened ink scalpel, Petry coyly appropriates and subverts these meanings: In Louella she conjures an omnipowerful maid-cum-haint whose earthly domain may have been limited to the kitchen or laundry room; but in her reincarnated form, Louella need not employ sass or invective—rhetorical stratagems black women often employed as means of resistance (consider how both Harriet Jacobs/Linda Brent and her grandmother "talk b(l)ack" to the libidinous and predatory Dr. Flint).[9] Instead, lodging herself indelibly in Old Peabody's dreams as "a small, brown woman with merry eyes" who "put her hands on her hips, threw her head back and laughed and laughed" (177), Louella reemerges as both the deceptively comic maid and simultaneous fear-promoting "spook" who in fact uses silence as a weapon to *spook* and disrupt the citadel of patriarchal racism and, subsequently, to occasion Old Peabody's racial redemption. And comparable to her eponymous gyno-trickster persona, Petry turns the discursive tables in two key ways: by ostensibly protesting the perniciously absurd burial protocols in the putatively free Bay State that practices southern principles; and, concurrently, by appropriating and *Africanizing* the comic gothic form, deploying it as an antidote to the univocal "Wright school of social protest," the orthodox masculinist discourse that dominated black literary expression in the 1940s.

One narratologically vexing question that this gravely comic ghost story raises is Petry's choice of someone as seemingly benign as a maid to interrogate the North's odious "southern" practices and its more indefensible insistence on blackness and whiteness as inassimilable. Less physically daunting than a Frankenstein or even her literary contemporary Bigger Thomas, the woman described as "small," "brown," "merry" and "laughing" might seem an odd choice of a "haint" to disrupt hierarchies of race and class. But given the legitimacy of Allan Lloyd-Smith's claim that "one of the great strengths of the Gothic is its ability to articulate the voice of the other" (8), the black female domestic may in fact be the ultimate "other" who occupies the lowest rung on the race-class-gender pecking order. Though Petry does not provide a profile of a living Louella, the character's status as a laundress/domestic would make her susceptible not only to the drudgeries of mundane household chores but also possibly the sexual abuses of her "madam's" licentious husbands. Again, I return to the hermeneutically salient notion of gothic space—physical, social, psychic—to address possible rationales for Petry's choices.

Almost de rigueur in gothic literary studies is Freud's 1899 study *The Uncanny*, in which the father of modern psychology takes up literary if not specifically gothic concerns. Citing Daniel Sanders's work on German etymology, *Worterbuch der Deutschen Sprache*, Freud quotes the following (translated) definitions of *Heimlich:* "belonging to the house, not strange, familiar, tame, dear and intimate, homely, etc."; "intimate, cozily homely; arousing a pleasant feeling of quiet contentment, etc., of comfortable repose and secure protection, like the enclosed, comfortable house" (126–27). Freud then quotes definitions of *Unheimlich:* "concealed, kept hidden, so that others do not get to know of it or about it and it is hidden from them" (129); "arousing uneasy, fearful horror" (131). "Uncanny is what one calls everything that was meant to remain secret and hidden and has come into the open" (132). Freud goes on to delineate these words' connectivity: "For us the most interesting fact to emerge from this long excerpt is that among the various shades of meaning that are recorded for the word *heimlich* there is one in which it merges with its formal antonym, *unheimlich*, so that what is called *heimlich* becomes *unheimlich*" (132). Complementarity, not antithesis, informs the psychiatrist's lexical theorizing of concepts.

In effect, Freud argues the close semantic proximity between the canny and uncanny, which takes on especially salient racial implications historically as well as in Petry's narrative configuration. The *canny* notion of the "tamed" black with whom whites are "comfortable" might explain the mammy's enduring presence in white households as evidence of America's cultural *Negrophilia*, where blacks were permitted close physical proximity to whites as long as they occupied clearly delineated "nonthreatening" positions (e.g., "the house nigger"). Concomitantly, however, the archetypal mammy's portrayal in the popular and literary imagination has rendered her persistently *uncanny*, as her "withheld" personal life amounts to a type of "concealing" of her core self. Revealingly, the attendant definition of the uncanny as "weird, arousing gruesome fear" also relates to America's chronic *Negrophobia*. Hence, "The Bones of Louella Brown" astutely conjoins these concepts to show the potential of the "familiar" and presumably "domesticated" to terrify the American psyche and to effect the collapse of its familial and financial institutions. A far cry from the wildly popular mammy figures of the day—think of the simpering Prissy and the tyrannical Mammy of *Gone with the Wind* fame, both figures upholding the white supremacist imperatives of the southern plantation through obsequious fealty to their masters and mistresses—Louella functions as both "anti-mammy" and indestructible feminine. Harking back to the redoubtable Lady Madeline Usher, whose self-excavation engenders the genetic and literal fall of the patriarchal Usher line/manor, Louella haunts Old Peabody's unconscious in triggering the dissolution of what Young Whiffle deemed the men's venerable burial "house" (i.e., "the honor of this house, years of working, of building a reputation, all destroyed" [170] and "the ancient and exclusive firm of Whiffle and Peabody, Incorporated, went out of business" [178]), a cankerous business institution that has promulgated toxic racial-sexual-class biases.

Deploying what Sharon Holland calls the "subjectivity of death," which "allows marginalized peoples to speak about the unspoken" (4–5),

Petry ironically withholds Louella's actual, corporeal self: since it is the figment of the white male unconscious, the author makes the Chesnutt-like maneuver of recuperating and empowering the abjectified black subject (individually and collectively) without assaulting white sensibilities with a "militant" and potentially off-putting black protagonist. Because Louella resides exclusively in the realm of the numinous, the narrative becomes potentially more frightening: existing as the possible figment of whites' repressed racial guilt, Louella functions as a cautionary presence-absence, a harbinger for the ensuing and ineradicable black occupation of the white psyche that will wreak havoc if racial transgressions aren't addressed and rectified. As with the racially converted Mars Jeems, Petry's oppositional gothic insists that it is *whites* who can be rehabilitated: Old Peabody undergoes a racial exorcism and conversion, becoming an evangelistic agent for social change. Insisting that the obdurate Governor Bedford "put the names of both those women on the marble slab in Bedford Abbey" (179), and admonishing him that "it is always best to be at peace with this world and any other world that follows it, when one dies," the racially "reborn" and enlightened Old Peabody is cleansed and made new, demonstrating that whites of any age are capable of purging an entrenched racist ethos (and Bedford follows Peabody's directive). In "The Bones of Louella Brown," the consummate gyno-trickster Petry cunningly crafts a synchronously antiracist, feminist, anticlassist, and even ecclesiastical gothic morality tale, where fear and loathing give way to enlightenment and redemption.

A Good Black Man Is Hard to Find: Gynophobia, Anglophilia, and Homoeroticism in "The Witness"

While no tangible evidence suggests that Petry read the most gothic of southern women writers, Flannery O'Connor, "The Witness" nonetheless demonstrates Petry's similar tropologizing of space. Whereas O'Connor uses gruesome random violence as a touchstone for the South's religious/spiritual torpor and its inbred fear and demonization of a litany of Others—blacks, women, homosexuals, the physically disabled—Petry traverses southern thematic terrain in a frighteningly similar northern landscape.

While Charles Woodruff, a milquetoast African American English teacher recently transplanted from Virginia, is the stark antithesis of the belligerent drifter/serial murderer "the Misfit" from O'Connor's grim short story, Woodruff is nevertheless a gothic antihero in the sense that he is also psychically alienated, physically displaced, and beset by multiple terrors. Unlike the illuminative denouement of "The Bones of Louella Brown," the culmination of "The Witness" is endarkenment, withdrawal, and flight.

The baroque plot unfurls as a series of nocturnal horrors that commence at the "Congregational church in Wheeling, New York" (213), where Woodruff will assist white Dr. Shipley in a rehabilitation class comprised of seven "delinquent" white adolescent boys (214). The action then shifts to a cemetery shed, which provides a fitting backdrop for these same boys' gang rape of a young white woman and their subsequent physical-psychic assault on Woodruff. The story concludes on a sunlight-drenched morning with the emotionally battered Woodruff fleeing for fear that the boys will frame him for their savage crime. With its juridical, religious, and moral implications inhered in the title, "The Witness" traces Woodruff's long day's journey into the nocturnally irrepressible horrors of physical and psychological violence that are motivated by race, gender, and class; his own nagging self-loathing; sexual disequilibrium; and his ultimately aborted attempt to forge a new identity in—yet again—a counterfeit northern promise land.

A cursory character sketch of Woodruff reveals a psychically destabilized man who summons comparisons to Poe's most notoriously "normal" madmen. Resembling the frantic, hypersensitive narrator of "The Tell-Tale Heart," who maniacally proclaims his sanity though stricken by a disease that has "sharpened" his senses and made his hearing "acute" (138), and the emotionally teetering narrator of "The Black Cat," whose grisly and unmotivated axing of his wife engenders a festering guilt and consequent psychosis, the nonhomicidal Woodruff nevertheless epitomizes the emotionally unbalanced male gothic subject. His interior monologue consists of a welter of thoughts by turns comic, manic, and disquieting. Debating with himself in front of the church amidst a "blowing snow" that is "stinging his face" (212), Woodruff imagines his dead wife, Addie, upbraiding him for what she would consider his unfettered spending on a dark gray cashmere coat; this internal argument even leads him to "[speak] to her aloud," followed by hasty self-chastisement: "He stopped abruptly, thinking he must look like a lunatic, standing in the snow, stamping his feet and talking to himself" (213). He immediately imagines the all-white town's response to this rather incongruous sight, a black man talking to himself in front of a white church amidst a blanket of ivory: "If he kept it up long enough, someone would call the state police and a bulletin about him would go clattering out over the teletype: 'Attention all cruisers, attention all cruisers, a black man, repeat, a black man is standing in front of the Congregational church in Wheeling, New York; description follows, thinnish, tallish black man, clipped moustache, expensive (extravagantly expensive, outrageously expensive, unjustifiably expensive) overcoat'" (213). Upon hearing the boys' ramshackle car backfire, Woodruff "jumped and then winced because he heard a sound like a gunshot" (216). Cumulatively, the expository details are consonant with Sedgwick's comments about the nineteenth-century novel *Private Memoirs and Confessions of a Justified Sinner:* "Reasons for considering it Gothic are that . . . it is lurid, that it is 'psychological' (i.e., literalizes and externalizes, for instance as murder or demonic temptation, conflicts that are usually seen as internal), that its action seems to be motivated by religious absolutes, and, most importantly, that it richly thematizes male paranoia" (*Between Men* 97). Though innocuous on the surface, Woodruff's hearing of voices, the subsequent internal dialogue, and the imagined surveillance bespeak a peevishness if not outright neurosis. Indeed, this personality capsule suggests a protagonist at once Poevian and Prufrockian: psychically menaced—and perhaps emasculated—by his dead wife's ghost, he simultaneously imagines himself through the delimiting lens of the white judicial apparatus. The confluence of various "paranoias"—spaced, gendered, classed, raced—produces a character who is as much bedeviled from within as he is from without.

At the core of his internal demons is the death of "dark-skinned, intense, beautiful" Addie (213). Ostensibly, Woodruff's stated purpose for relocating to rustic Wheeling and teaching high school English there is the void left by her death, which occasioned his fervent desire "to escape his old environment" (214). But the character profile that Woodruff provides of his recently deceased wife belies the pensive, still-mourning visage he presents; in fact, her presence looms as an ominous one that corresponds to the gothic trope of the repressed feminine. Like Louella Brown, Addie is not corporeally present; instead, she is filtered through and animated by her husband's consciousness, and his memories of her are almost uniformly unflattering. Imagining her response to his purchase of the $500.00 cashmere coat, Woodruff intuits that "she would have argued with him fiercely, nostrils flaring, thin arched eyebrows lifted" (212); in effect, he mentally projects her as the "monstrous-feminine"—a far cry from the "beautiful" spouse whose passing he claims to lament. Correspondingly, when he returns home after Nellie's rape and a physical assault that results in the loss of his glasses, he retrieves an old pair and recollects another less-than-endearing memory: because of their outdated style, "Addie had made him stop wearing them. She said they gave him the look of another era, made it easy for his students to caricature him—the tall, slender figure, slightly stooped, the steel-rimmed glasses. She said that his dark, gentle eyes looked as though they were trapped behind those little glasses" (228). Such memories render Woodruff powerless and passive vis-à-vis the austere Addie ("Daddy"?), resulting in a lingering resentment; indeed, a tableau of a conflicted relationship comes into sharper focus, where the roles of wife-mother become enmeshed in his less-than-fond remembrance of his purportedly beloved spouse. Woodruff appears infantilized, alternatively reprimanded and ridiculed as a fiscally irresponsible, geeky man-child. Though I wouldn't extrapolate latent uxoricidal desires from these belittling episodes—he is clearly not bedecked in the dark hues in which Poe fashions his wife-killing madman—I believe his bitterly tinged memories of his deceased spouse raise questions about the gender-geography nexus, a recurring leitmotif in gothic literature.

Invariably Woodruff, like Malcolm Powther (*The Narrows*), John Forbes ("Has Anybody Seen Miss Dora Dean?") and William Jones ("In Darkness and Confusion"), is afflicted by a masculine anxiety that stems at least partially from geographic displacement. Though focused on the South's incomparably grim statistics regarding its state-sanctioned execution of scores of black males, Houston Baker provides a gloomy though accurate summation of the southern black male subject: "However, in our day-to-day United States life, we scarcely ever reflect that Texas, Louisiana, and Oklahoma—all southern territories of the actual present—are sites of mass black- and brown-body incarceration . . . and extermination" (94). While Baker's dismal assessment emanates from these states' warehousing and liquidating of black male bodies, his analysis of the South as dystopia is apropos when considering Woodruff's native Virginia as the cradle of the Confederacy, the *original* southern state. Given its malignant history, one way of explaining Woodruff's exodus from South to North is in fact the region's historical identity as the site of black male devaluation, a place that exacerbates his sense of sociopsychic if not actual imprisonment.

In effect, Woodruff might perceive the South as a geographic externalization of his attenuated racial-masculine positionality; conjunctively, black women, wittingly or not, become complicit in this narrative, on some level acting as surrogates for white male hegemony and the constrictions it imposes. Commenting on the topography-gender nexus, Diane Roberts cogently specifies how the South generally and Virginia especially are often metaphorically feminized and eroticized in Harriet Beecher Stowe's gothically inflected novels: "The very naming of the first Southern colonies after women demonstrates the colonisers' [sic] commitment to seeing the 'New World' as a feminine space to be 'taken': Virginia implies not only a compliment to Elizabeth I but an ideology: virgin land to be possessed, to be made fruitful" (28). Virginia becomes a veritable floating signifier, connoting a mélange of freighted meanings related to gender, race, and sexuality. Etymologically and historically, the Virginia/vagina from which Woodruff exiles himself emblematizes his dead wife, the indestructible and irreducible feminine who sternly infantilized if not feminized him. Unable to conquer his wife in life, and daunted by his memories of her as overbearing, he resembles the prototypical gothic *maiden* as he, too, must extricate himself from the gendered prison that the unconquerable feminine reifies both corporeally and geographically. Thus the sexually liminal—if not androgynous—Woodruff emigrates to the North in a desperately recuperative gesture, an attempt to escape the clutches of the foreboding feminine and restore the masculine prerogative which a castrating, "feminized" South so imperviously usurped.

Analogously, Woodruff's denuded status compounds his racial distemper: not only is he unable to wield power over women in Virginia/vagina, but his racially tarnished status means that, unlike the "colonisers" (Roberts's term) who preceded him, he cannot devalue others, since blackness is the apogee of Otherness. Wheeling, New York, in essence becomes his Canada, a potential male sanctuary where he can fulfill an elusive masculine prerogative. His position of authority as an English teacher at a white high school engenders a specialness—"His students liked him and told him so" (214)—a privileged position that could only be imagined in the racially and sexually fraught South. In fact, his repatriation into this "frozen Northern town," an all-white enclave, might be read as his own latent desire to remake himself in accordance with the very standards of white patriarchal masculinity that left him so emotionally bereft in the cradle of the Confederacy.

What might be deemed his latent Anglophilia first surfaces in the aforementioned purchase of the "dark gray cashmere coat, lined with nutria and adorned by a collar of black Persian lamb" (212); his longings for masculine bourgeois privilege are stoked by a sycophantic salesman's insistence that purchasing it will "make you feel like a prince." In Woodruff's mind, clothes might help "make *the man*," a chestnut that obliquely hints at his white patriarchal aspirations. Moreover, the service Dr. Shipley drafts him to perform—assisting in reforming seven "new young outlaws spawned by the white middle class" (216)—bestows a paradoxical sense of satisfaction. Recruited as Dr. Shipley's helpmeet in the boys' rehabilitation, Woodruff is potentially accorded a quasi-white male status. Logically but misguidedly, he delights in this racially topsy-turvy situation, where indeed he can claim race and class superiority. Unashamedly, Woodruff revels in the fact that, ultimately, the boys are "the white man's problem. This cripplingly tight shoe was usually on the black man's foot. He found it rather pleasant to have the position reversed" (216); note again how Petry uses apparel as a metaphor for Woodruff's subjectivity. Put plainly, his smugness stems from having America's culturally and lexically encoded shorthands for African American maleness—thug, criminal, menace—uncharacteristically transferred onto white juveniles. He thus becomes something of a racial minstrel, at once basking in the regal status garnered through his extravagant purchases of a new car and coat (the salesman designating him a "prince" with the purchase of cashmere) and thereby masking the always deleterious blackness, while expressing his relief that the white boys over whom he assumes conditional authority are in fact niggerized. As Carol Henderson astutely explains, "In particular, Petry's focus on material 'enslavement' serves to underscore the bondage awaiting those who foolishly embrace the seductive lure of wealth at the expense of the integrity of their mortal souls in an effort to embrace America's promise of prosperity" (147). This "enslavement" ephemerally manumits him from his almost always devalued position on the low rung of the South's intractable racial ladder.

Because it connotes an unhealthy (and in some cases pathological) form of attraction, I have deliberately invoked the neologistic Anglophilia to convey Woodruff's gendered and racial anxieties, motivations, and aspirations. Implicit in his apotheosizing of whiteness is a seemingly incongruous fear that as he ascends on the racial ladder, he is simultaneously and nervously eclipsing the pigeonholing albeit familiar racial space he occupied in the South. For instance, when he tries to intervene upon the boys' kidnapping of Nellie by questioning their intentions, he immediately censures himself: "He spoke with the voice of authority, the male schoolteacher's voice and thought, Wait, slow down, cool it, you're a black man speaking with a white man's voice" (221). Coupled with his minstrel-like inclinations, this racial ventriloquism suggests Woodruff's dis-ease with a power that he presumably covets. His racial genuflecting, where he alternatively craves and eschews whiteness, further evinces itself in his sardonic, self-deprecating comments.

Prior to his encounter with the boys, we glimpse Woodruff's propensity for self-mockery when his thoughts encroach upon the third-person narrator's: "And the search [the Wheeling school system's quest to find "the one," a lone black teacher to "integrate" the school system] yielded that brand-new black widower, Charles Woodruff (nigger in the woodpile, he thought, and then, why that word, a word he despised and never used so why did it pop up like that)" (214). Albeit parenthetical, his interpolated self-appraisal mitigates his witting attempts to don the accoutrements of whiteness; indeed, in his own mind's eye, he is nothing more than an insect futilely attempting to "bite off" the trappings of white supremacy/success without making any discernible progress. Correlatively, he conjures a replica of this pest-like, Kafkaesque image of himself: standing outside the church awaiting Shipley and the white delinquents, "he envisioned himself as a black beetle in a fur-collared coat silhouetted against the snow trying to scuttle out of danger" (217).[10]

To be sure, Woodruff's self-diminution coheres with Julia Kristeva's theorization of the abject: "If it be true that the abject simultaneously beseeches and pulverizes the subject, one can understand that it is experienced at the peak of its strength when that subject, weary of fruitless attempts to identify with something on the outside, finds the impossible within; when it finds that the impossible constitutes its very *being*, that it *is* none other than abject" (5). Woodruff's self-conceptions, steeped in the language of the parasitic, bestial, and apparitional, hypostatize the archetype of Kristeva's wretched subject who ultimately locates self as the locus of Otherness and even nonhumanness. In effect, by cloaking himself in the vestments of white bourgeois culture while simultaneously self-minimizing, he ultimately seems to destabilize the very racial, gender, and class identities he hoped to reconstruct and reinvent by fleeing a South which was so burdensome. In effect, his self-belittlement amounts to an internalizing imprisonment that is consonant with the physical-juridical apparatuses Baker posited as the South's official means for containing black male subjects. Additionally, Woodruff's external Anglophilia masks a complementarily malignant Negrophobia.

If Woodruff's internalized racialism is traceable to a southern past that has historically occluded black male subjectivity, then the white male adolescents who terrorize both him and Nellie might at first appear to be stock demons in the black literary imaginary. On the one hand, the story's historical-temporal context is noteworthy: "In the midst of an era [late sixties/early seventies] when American women and minorities are demanding equal rights, the town's most intellectually promising white boys exhibit an appalling hatred of others, especially blacks and women" (Holladay 109). However, in discursive terms, Petry's portrayal of them marks a subverting of prototypical gothic convention that conflates blackness and evil. Their very presence evokes a palpable dread in Woodruff that probably conjures images of the venomous Ku Klux Klan and other white men committed to terrorizing blacks ad infinitum; the boys' attire—"the click-clack sound of their heavy boots" and their "great quilted dark jackets that had been designed for European ski slopes" (217)—evokes images of the twentieth century's most iniquitously xenophobic and genocidal killers, the Nazis. As well, these sociopathic seven boys incarnate the specter of white death that Woodruff presumes he's escaped. At the outset of the Sunday night class in which Woodruff and Dr. Shipley will endeavor to reform them, Woodruff offers this bracing description: "They sat silent, motionless, their shoulders hunched as though against some chill they found in the air of that small book-lined room. Their eyelids were like shutters drawn over their eyes. Their long hair covered their foreheads, obscuring their eyebrows, reaching to the collars of their jackets" (214–15). Moreover, as the meeting progresses, Woodruff's fears are not allayed; if anything, prolonged exposure to them magnifies his sense that they are in fact Satan's white emissaries:

> Woodruff glanced at the boys and then directed his gaze away from them, thinking, if a bit of gilt braid and a touch of velvet were added to their clothing, they could pass for the seven dark bastard sons of some old and evil twelfth-century king. Of course they weren't all dark. Three of them were blond, two had brown hair, one had red hair, only one had black hair. All of them were white. But there was about them an aura of something so evil, so dark, so suggestive of the far reaches of the night, of the black horror of nightmares, that he shivered deep inside himself whenever he saw them. Though he thought of them as being black, this was not the blackness of human flesh, warm, soft to the touch, it was the blackness and the coldness of the hole from which D. H. Lawrence's snake emerged. (218)

Reminiscent of the death-in-life whiteness that Mr. Norton represented to Invisible Man, these boys, too, exemplify whiteness in all of its hideousness; the fiendishness they exude approximates that of Dr. Frankenstein's spawn or some other gothic monstrosity.

A subsequent defense of cannibalism on the part of "Rambler," the group's ringleader—"Well, if the cats who go for this human flesh bit don't think it's a sin and if they eat it because they haven't any other food, it isn't a sin for them, is it?" (218)—firmly establishes them as typically insolent adolescents but, more ominously, as representative of *Anglo-America's* own unacknowledged, festering darkness.[11] In fact, Dr. Shipley's preliminary description of them sounds not only sanguine but prototypically American. They are "about sixteen. Very bright. Still in high school. . . . As a matter of fact, if they weren't so bright, they'd be in reform school" (215). To be sure, the boys, like the ineffectual Dr. Shipley, occupy a Currier and Ives pastoral, snow-nestled suburban North that approximates the mythological place that "middle America" holds in our collective conscience: "It [middle America] is a space defined by financial status, social stability, family structure, sexuality, and still, perhaps, race. It is a space located antithetically to that of the criminally unspeakable" (Tithecott 53). Their discordant ghoulishness and cherubic Americanness prefigure the similarly placid (white) all-American personas of Eric Harris and Dylan Klebold, the homegrown juvenile terrorists whose 1999 massacre at Columbine (Colorado) High was explicably, inimitably American. Petry keenly turns the tables here, recalling Justin Edwards's perspicuous comment about Chesnutt's narrative jujitsu in "Mars' Jeems's Nightmare," where the author's inversion of white and black "simply calls attention to the fragility of the gothic's true colors by situating whiteness—as we have seen with Poe's Tsalalians—as the inspiration of fear and a more appropriate shade of the gothic" (Edwards 90). The feral menace that Anglo-American culture has historically and perpetually projected onto its darker Br/Others is merely a refraction of its native depravity; like Kristeva's abject, it is ultimately the white self that is the enemy within—the monstrously unspeakable that's interminably assigned to blackness.

Thus, in considering this representation of whiteness as wretched and benighted, Petry can be said to have embroidered a richly woven reverse, oppositional gothic that connects both white women and black men as objects of unspeakable violence. The hypergothic catalytic narrative events speak for themselves: the boys' abduction of Nellie, their simultaneous theft of Woodruff's luxury car and seizing of him as their ersatz "witness," the gang rape of Nellie, and the physical and psychological violence inflicted upon Woodruff. All of the events transpire, appropriately enough, in the most conventional and moribund of gothic settings: the kidnappings originate at a church, and the ensuing crimes occur in a cemetery. And reminiscent of Poe, Petry interlards these scenes with stock images of live burial, as we ourselves witness the aura of immobility, entombment, and suffocation that besieges Woodruff: "They kept moving in, closing in on him. Even on this cold, windy night, he could smell them and he loathed the smell" (221). "They took his coat off and put it around him backward without putting his arms in the sleeves and then buttoned it up. The expensive coat was just like a strait jacket—it pinioned his arms to his sides" (222–23). Petry brings the transience of Woodruff's manufactured Anglicized status—garnered through the superficial trappings of commodities as well as his geographic relocation—into focus in what amounts to both a physical assault and a type of psychic *male* rape. The narrative presents the leveling of his highly polished facade in terms of immobility and asphyxiation:

> He [one of the boys] pulled a black wool cap down on Woodruff's head, over his eyes, over his nose.
>
> He couldn't see anything. He couldn't breathe through his nose. He had to breathe through his mouth or suffocate. The freezing cold air actually hurt the inside of his mouth. The overcoat immobilized him and the steady pressure of the fur collar against his windpipe was beginning to interfere with his normal rate of breathing. . . . He frowned, thinking what a simple and easily executed method of rendering a person helpless—just an overcoat and a knit cap. (223–24)

In effect, the trappings of bourgeois privilege, the pricey gewgaws he assumed would exorcise his blackness, eventuate his socioracial death if not his actual one. Petry spotlights the glaring irony of Woodruff's physical and psychoracial encasement as well, the black wool cap symbolizing the ineradicable prison of color which he cannot vanquish, and the simultaneity of his constricted windpipe and gaping wordlessness indicative of his racial emasculation and voicelessness. The horror of horrors, then, becomes whiteness—and Woodruff's elevation of it—in all of its multifarious forms.

Making Woodruff an unwitting accomplice by forcing him to touch the naked Nellie, the boys frame and frighten him into silence. Echoing the kidnapping and assassination of Link Williams by members of the white industrial elite, the teenage miscreants orchestrate what amounts to a northern version of a psychic lynching, since the fear of miscegenation remains the ultimate taboo, so taboo, in fact, that Woodruff experiences a blinding and debilitating epiphany: "They were bright enough to know that he would quickly realize how neatly they had *boxed him in* and thus would keep quiet. If he dared enter a complaint against them they would accuse him of raping the girl, would say they found him in the cemetery with her. Whose story would be believed?" (230; emphasis added). The boys' derisive nicknaming of Woodruff as "ho-daddy," a malediction they fling at him throughout the course of Nellie's rape, is the ultimate insult, since Woodruff is the antithesis of the sexually predatory black male menace who haunts the American cultural imaginary. Consequently, the boys deftly exploit the unassailable image of the stereotypical black brute (compare Rodney King, Willie Horton) to enslave and de-voice a man who cultivates the image of the "safe Negro," one whose fealty to whites trumps any racial consciousness. Though this harrowing Walpurgisnacht ends in standard Petrian fashion, with the physically and emotionally shattered Woodruff fleeing for the relative solitude of Virginia (think here of other characters for whom flight becomes a last resort—*The Street*'s Lutie Johnson, "Miss Muriel's" Bemish), this subtle but riveting depiction of Woodruff's *sexual* (aside from racial and gender) anxiety pushes the story in a differently gothic direction in a departure that might be considered radical for a black woman writer in 1971, when "The Witness" appeared in *Redbook* magazine.

H. L. Malchow has made the following observation regarding conventional gothic writing: "The typical late-nineteenth-century gothic story revolves around the problem of confused, vulnerable, or secret identities, fear of exposure, evil masquerading as respectability, or respectability built upon a hidden corruption" (127). Clearly, "The Witness" is a descendant of such nineteenth-century texts: Woodruff's emotional instability and attendant racial confusion, the marauding white boys' patina of respectability concealing their perfidy most obviously reifying the traits Malchow identifies. Moreover, the issue of Woodruff's "secret identity" and "fear of exposure" lends another layer of complexity to Petry's work and offers daring thematic vistas for the still largely unrecognized and underexamined black gothic literary tradition: the specter of sexual difference.

One of the more fascinating occurrences vis-à-vis the politics of black literary canonicity is how texts which foreground same-gender sexual desire are usually relegated to the back of the critical and popular bus—or are summarily barred from the bus altogether. The paucity of attention paid to works such as Bruce Nugent's "Smoke, Lilies, and Jade," Langston Hughes's homoerotic poems—not to mention Baldwin's *Giovanni's Room* and *Just Above My Head*, which remain undertaught and understudied—reflect a major lacuna in African American literary scholarship. Only with the emergence of so-called "Queer Theory" have such texts begun to receive the critical attention they merit; Nella Larsen's *Passing* perhaps more than any other text has been the beneficiary of this concerted interest in intra-gender desire, reflected by the heightened critical attention the novel has garnered in the past ten to fifteen years. I would contend that perhaps Petry, like Larsen before her, slyly interweaves into the narrative same-gender desire on frequencies not initially perceptive to readers and critics not attuned to such resonances in African American literature.

Woodruff's gynophobia—I'm distinguishing *fear* here from outright misogyny—and compensatory Anglophilia may camouflage the quintessential "abomination" in much of the black community: homosexuality. Intentional or not, the story's gothic overlay serves a vestibular function, enabling a foray into the "other" tabooed territory—"amalgamation hysteria" being the first, as evidenced by Woodruff's fear of sexual blackmail. I'm not suggesting that this is necessarily "new" thematic territory vis-à-vis white Euro-American gothic literary discourse; as Eve Sedgwick has argued, "A less obvious point [regarding gothic's burgeoning interest in its heyday] has to do with the reputation for 'decadence': the Gothic was the first novelistic form in England to have close, relatively visible links to male homosexuality, at a time when styles of homosexuality, and even its visibility and distinctness, were markers of division and tension between classes as much as between genders" (*Between Men* 91). But for an African American woman writer, especially during the maelstrom of the Civil Rights/Black Power movements which dared homosexuality to speak its name (e.g., March on Washington organizer Bayard Rustin's unceremonious expulsion from positions of relative power in the movement, a concession made by Martin Luther King, Jr., in response to cross-dressing FBI director J. Edgar Hoover's threat not only to expose Rustin but to spread the lie that Rustin and the incorrigibly heterosexual King were lovers), the gothic provided something of a cover, given its abiding connections to what Sedgwick calls "the decadent." In the aforementioned examples that focused on his relationship with his deceased wife, Woodruff emerged less as a partner/helpmeet and more of a naughty little boy—hence, the adumbration of his potential sexual otherness. Thus, his escape from the South/Virginia-Vagina/White Power might speak to his need to flee the confines of heteronormativity which his role as husband, albeit a widower, would impose. Perhaps the North's allure is manifold: Woodruff can extricate himself from the South's racially constrictive mores; he can escape the South's compulsory heterosexuality that proscribes sexual fluidity; and, conjunctively, he is free to pursue those unsanctioned sexual desires on a "new frontier" where he is not bound by the black community's parochial sexual strictures. Not just his racial Canada, the North now becomes his sexually libertine Paris as well.

To be sure, the manicured and self-indulgent Woodruff, bedecked in an "elegant overcoat" (232) of cashmere and fur while loathing the boys' smell—"cigarettes, clothes washed in detergents and not rinsed enough and dried in automatic driers" (221)—epitomizes a mimetic, sepia New World decadence. Though no Wildean aesthete, he nevertheless embodies yet another Petrian dandy who troubles gender boundaries through his very dress if not by his overt sexual behavior. And as evinced throughout her canon, Petry here names with a purpose: She signals the gaping discrepancy between society's gender mores and Woodruff's self-fashioning through nomenclature, as his very surname—Wood-rough—connotes a bucolic, frontier masculinity that his chic dress and manicured mien clearly undercut. With further regard to names, "Nellie" also stands out: though clearly denoting a female character in the story, the name has traditionally been synonymous with "sissy" as a derogatory term for an effeminate man presumed to be homosexual. While Woodruff's dandified male persona would on the surface seem to counterpoise the socially orthodox masculinity displayed in the teens' rowdy hyper-aggressiveness and even more reprehensible sexual aggression, the hypermasculinity they radiate gives rise—metaphorically and perhaps even literally—to forbidden feelings that the "nellie" Woodruff possibly suppressed on his native southern soil.

While Woodruff appears affronted by their unbridled, antisocial behavior, Petry describes his encounters with the young hooligans as more than mildly homoerotic. Once the class is dismissed, Woodruff

> left almost immediately after the boys, carrying in his mind's eye a picture of all those straight, narrow backs with the pants so tight they were like elastic bandages on their thighs, and the oversized bulky jackets and the long, frowsy hair. He thought they looked like paper dolls, cut all at once, exactly alike with a few swift slashes of scissors wielded by a skilled hand. Addie could do that—take paper and fold it and go snip, snip, snip with the scissors and she'd have a string of paper dolls. (219–20)

This plangent passage becomes a micro-text of Woodruff's multivalent anxieties—anxieties teeming with paradoxical and even contradictory suggestions about place, race, sexuality, gender. On the one hand, the adolescents' very whiteness, as the thing Woodruff both longs for and disparages, makes his blackness even more stark and emotionally discomfiting, a dynamic well articulated by Kalpana Seshadri-Crooks: "Psychoanalytically, we can perceive the object cause of racial anxiety as racial visibility, the so-called pre-discursive marks on the body (hair, skin, bone) which serve as the desiderata of race" (8). Thus marked by difference, Woodruff psychically aligns himself with that which is racially normativized and esteemed. Further, as with the previous example, his homoerotic impulses are subsumed within the realm of the heteronormative—thus, his emphasis on the boys' feminizing "long, frowsy hair." Perhaps in the most bizarre of conflations, we witness the reemergence of Woodruff's gyno- and geophobia as, again, the specter of the mother/wife Addie turns up (think of the indestructible, death-defying home wrecker played by Glenn Close in the 1980s gothic-tinged thriller *Fatal Attraction*) as the *castrating* monstrous-feminine. In this weird psychoracial, psychosexual coagulation, he and the boys become coterminous victims—he of a racist and homophobic culture, they of a homogenizing one that conspires, in Dr. Shipley's words, "to turn them into God-fearing responsible young citizens" (215). The concomitant victims of an autocratic white hegemonic system that co-opts black women, Woodruff and the boys are niggerized and feminized, "snipped" "paper dolls" whose agency and distinctiveness are eclipsed by the scourges of white patriarchs and the physically deceased but posthumously invincible black woman.

Try as he might, Woodruff cannot expunge the boys' indelible image within his racially and sexually haunted psyche. For instance, in the example quoted earlier, where Woodruff conceived of them as Satan's earthly ambassadors, note the sensuousness of the language: "Though he thought of them as being black, this was not the blackness of human flesh, warm, soft to the touch, it was the blackness and the coldness of the hole from which D. H. Lawrence's snake emerged" (218). This passage oozes with imagery of the love that dare not speak its name: the sensual way Woodruff images the *blackness* they are not—which of course suggests some proximity as its opposite as well as our culture's inexorable equation of *blackness* with licentious and unsanctioned sexuality—alongside the sexually insinuative hole/snake symbols, which intimate both anality and phallicism. Even during their initial meeting, where he observes that their "collective stare" was "so hostile," there is also this: "Their legs, stretched out straight in front of them, were encased in pants that fit as tightly as the leotards of a ballet dancer" (215); hence, their accompanying gaze, to which he "felt himself stiffen and sweat broke out on his forehead," is again more than moderately sexually pregnant. Indeed, given his conceptualization of their clothing and demeanor as masculine *and* feminine, one wonders if Woodruff is tormented by the prospective violence they represent, or if he is plagued by his ungovernable sexual arousal despite his being conditioned to repress such same-gender attraction. Ironically enough, he uses the phrase "crime against nature" (214) to describe what he initially viewed as Dr. Shipley's attempts to transform the boys into working-class automatons; unconsciously, he may have also been parroting society's condemnatory mantra against his possibly buried homoerotic longings.

In effect, Woodruff's encounters with and violations by the "young animals" (227), the white boys whom he ostensibly loathes, reflect the commingling of multiply proscribed or distressing desires: homoerotic—and, perhaps, ephebiphilic—miscegenistic, Anglophilic, and androcentric. The homoerotic iterations in "The Witness" surface in examples such as the aforementioned Lawrence allusion, one of a handful of purple passages that conflate same-sex desire, fear, and even death in Woodruff's afflicted un/conscious. Repulsed after the class ends, he frets that " I feel as though I had spent the entire evening lying prone under the unrelieved weight of all their bodies" (216)—this another instance of Woodruff's irrepressible concern with suffocation manifesting itself in a fantasy at once erotic and necrophilic (Faulkner's murderous necrophiliac Emily Grierson comes to mind here). After the boys seize him and Nellie in preparation for the trip to the cemetery at which they'll rape her and implicate him by making him touch her thighs, Woodruff "was forced into the back seat, two boys on each side of him. They were sitting half on him and half on each other" (223); once in motion, the jarring car ride launches "all of them on top of each other" (224). In a sort of Freudian knot, these passages cumulatively mark the wedding of the sex and death drives: while the North might provide the sexually distressed Woodruff a homosocial utopia—note the absence of women in his social milieu—it also threatens the deeply ascetic mask he has donned to conceal the faintest of same-sex urges which threaten to irrupt at any moment.

"The Witness" may indeed be Petry's most gothically effusive tale, as the tendrils of Woodruff's multiple fears and anxieties represent festering classism, masculine inadequacy, (same) sex repression, and, ultimately, self-loathing. Thinking that he will replace a racially, sexually, and masculinely plagued life with a sybaritic one in which his race can be subsumed by whiteness and conspicuous consumption, Woodruff embodies what Louis Gross identifies as gothic's distinction from what he calls "traditional narratives": "While the classical quest ends in the regeneration of a decaying world and the integration of the hero into society, the Gothic quest ends in the shattering of the protagonist's image of his/her social/sexual roles and a legacy of, at best, numbing unease or, at worst, emotional paralysis and death. The Gothic may then be described as a demonic quest narrative" (1–2). Incontrovertibly, Charles Woodruff is no Huck Finn or Bigger Thomas or Milkman Dead: His circular journey, replete with dehumanizing and objectifying experiences, doesn't engender a newly realized, empowering subject position. Fearfully retreating from the now uninhabitable "tomb" of the North and hightailing it back to the "womb" of "Ole Virginny"—a space he heretofore found monstrously feminine and racially intransigent—Woodruff ends his quest with a heightened feeling that his mongrelized statuses as racially and sexually different are irreconcilable.[12] Petry concludes the story on a note of derision and psychological death, as the timorous, mis-monikered Woodruff frantically drives while his car radio serenades him with a randy blues ditty sung by a "husky-voiced woman": "I'm gonna turn on the big beat/I'm gonna turn up the high heat/For my ho-daddy, ho daddy,/For my ho-daddy, ho-daddy" (234). Just as physical distance couldn't erase memories of the censorious Addie, the song's mention of "ho-daddy" intimates that the boys' physical/psychic assault (recall that they mocked/marked him with this sobriquet during the kidnapping) will impinge upon his thoughts no matter how far he roams. Far from the pimp who wields economic-phallocentric prerogative or the virile lothario who drives women to sexual ecstasy, the muted, not-so-"husky" Woodruff incarnates the deracinated black subject whose geo-psychic, racial-sexual quest ends not in Douglass-like enlightenment and hope, but in emotional paralysis and metaphorical endarkenment if not somatic death.

Though not as calculatedly gothic as the New England of her male literary forebear Hawthorne, Petry's northeastern terrain is as palsied as its façade is deceptively pastoral. Perhaps Charles Woodruff's ultimate impressions prior to his return southward—"The moonlight was so bright that he could see wisps of tall grass in the meadow—yellow against the snow" (230)—provide the most fitting tableau of Petry's fictivized North, be it Harlem or Wheeling: that it is a pestilential Eden, a cancerous nonrefuge whose various -isms are as sickening as the stench from any southern strange fruit. Petry's composite portraiture is of a desacralized North, not simply the site of ineradicable racial oppression but of multiple transgressions—blacks terrorize whites; blacks terrorize blacks; and whites terrorize blacks and women and less-than-manly men, such wrongdoings usually occurring with impunity. That Petry so often uses weather, specifically snow, metaphorically to convey the discrepancy between the pristine landscape and its jaundiced denizens sets the stage for *Country Place*, where a raging whirlwind provides the backdrop for white lives so deceptively and dizzyingly out of control.

6

"ENTOMBED WHILE STILL ALIVE"

Images of Domestic Terror and Monstrousness in Country Place

> I shouted his [Mr. Norton's] name above the roar of the men, and got no answer. He was out again. I shook him, gently, then roughly, but still no flicker of his wrinkled lids. Then some of the milling men pushed me up against him and suddenly a mass of whiteness was looming two inches from my eyes; it was only his face but I felt a shudder of nameless horror. I had never been so close to a white person before. In a panic I struggled to get away. With his eyes closed he seemed more threatening than with them open. He was like a formless white death, suddenly appeared before me, a death which had been there all the time and which had now revealed itself in the madness of the Golden Day.
>
> —Ralph Ellison, *Invisible Man*

> How terrible it will be for you teachers of religious law and you Pharisees. Hypocrites! You are like white-washed tombs—beautiful on the outside but filled on the inside with dead people's bones and all sorts of impurity.
>
> —Matthew 23:27

Given the critical and popular acclaim—not to mention the profits it reaped for Houghton Mifflin as the first million-selling novel by an African American woman—that accompanied *The Street*'s publication, the academic and reading publics might have indulged Ann Petry had she chosen to repeat the book's surface naturalistic and protest formulae. To be sure, playwrights have reaped astronomical profits by writing plays that follow a proven formula; think of the slew of lucrative Broadway musicals by Rodgers, Hammerstein, and Hart, who would have been Petry's contemporaries. Why, indeed, should novelists be any more reticent about parlaying a winning blueprint into commercial success? Ostensibly, Petry's decision to train her scalpel-like critical eye on an overwhelmingly *nonblack*, bucolic Connecticut milieu would seem an odd choice, a 180-degree turn away from the gritty "urban realism" that became a discursive shibboleth for and staple of 1940s' African American texts that foregrounded white perfidy, black pain, and racial disaffection. As Bigger Thomas's northeastern counterparts, the racially traumatized denizens of Petry's hardboiled Harlem ghetto occupied quarters as emotionally and economically devitalizing; in effect, the novel's depiction of Lutie Johnson's unrelenting exploitation by whites and the black men and women they co-opted resonated as the black woman's racial/sexual/economic plights writ large. Concomitantly, this narrative scenario dovetailed all too well with the "data" on the so-called "Negro Problem," the sociocultural appellation holding sway in the 1940s that identified blacks as a sort of quadratic riddle to be solved with mathematic precision through objectifying sociological metrics that obfuscated what might more aptly have been deemed *whites' problem* with blacks. The compelling question for me as a literary critic interested in the raced *and* gendered politics of literary expression becomes not only why Petry chose to abandon the de rigueur racial literary framework but also the stakes involved in a black woman calculatedly choosing to dissect what for the black writer was softly spoken if not entirely unspeakable: whites' problems with other whites. Because of its relative obscurity not only within the microscopic world of Petry scholarship but in the macroscopic one of canonical African American literature, I will begin my discussion of *Country Place* by commingling commentary on its reception and its emplotment.

Reflecting the intermingled lives of *The Street*'s characters, the novel is organized around what Hilary Holladay calls a "concentric logic" (31). As in her first novel, Petry interlaces stories within a fairly compact narratological schematization, as she dexterously braids a narrative with multiple strands. *Country Place* opens with an anonymous narrator laconically ruminating on Lennox, Connecticut, the titular "country place" in which all of the action occurs. Lennox, a not-so-thinly veiled double for Petry's native Old Saybrook, is, as promised on the dust cover of the 1950 Signet edition, a place rife with "hidden sores and pollution"; indisputably, the novel's surface plot is a lurid web of adultery, greed, and emotional ennui. Critics have keyed in on this, articulating it in various ways: the venerable Robert Bone adduces "the novel probes beneath the quiet surface of a country town to the inquisitiveness, bigotry, and malice which are typical of its inner life" (181); and two relatively early critics in 1974 (early given the scant attention accorded the novel in the sixty-odd years since its 1947 publication) reach comparable conclusions: Roger Rosenblatt observes that the novel "is concerned with the narrowness and maliciousness of small town life" (138), while eminent Howard University African American literature scholar Arthur Davis concludes that it "deals with the class lines between aristocrats and nobodies, the antiforeign, anti-Roman Catholic prejudices, and the sexual looseness and the ugliness and viciousness found behind the innocent-appearing life" of the town (194). These conclusions cohere with the narrator's (Doc's)—and I would add Petry's—explicit intention to expose the "vein of violence running under the surface quiet" (*Country Place* 7).

Primarily though not exclusively through the eyes of Doc, whose narrative vision is more tinted and tendentious than he imagines, we're introduced to the central players: "Over the years I have acquired an intimate, detailed knowledge of all of them: Johnnie Roane and his wife, Glory; Mr. and Mrs. Roane, who were Johnnie's mother and father; Mrs. Gramby and her son, Mearns; Ed Barrell; The Weasel; Neola; the Portegee [Portulacca]; Daniel Rosenberg; and, of course, Lil, who was Mearns Gramby's wife" (7).

From what he perceives as his reportorial, objective perch, the first character Doc foregrounds, the Weasel, drives the "town taxi" with a pulse on the collective townspeople's frailties and the sexual calisthenics in which many engage. More than that, the Weasel figuratively "drives" the action by exposing or threatening to unsheathe such dalliances. Early on, as told to Doc by the Weasel (thereby undermining the former's presumed narrative omniscience), we get our first glimpse of twenty-four-year-old Johnnie, a less-than-heroic World War II veteran whom the Weasel picks up from the train station. Johnnie returns to his idyllic hometown, feeling rather disillusioned about the war given the emotional and physical toll such militaristic violence takes on its combatants. Though his mother and father welcome him with the requisite adulation and deference, Glory eschews his sexual advances. He reflects on her rebuffs and his response to them as follows: "This is what rape is like—to hold a woman close to you, and force your body on hers, ignoring her protests" (25). In fact, his sexual homecoming and its attendant violence results in Johnnie leaving "the clear imprint of his hands" on her throat. Recalling Lorraine Hansberry's trailblazing exploration of black women and the issue of abortion/ sexual reproduction in *A Raisin in the Sun*, Petry addresses marital rape at a time when few if any African American authors dared broach the subject for fear of being salacious or sensational.

The remaining plot lines and their various intersections come together through the Weasel and the omniscient narrator more so than the presumptuous Doc. Just as Glory is portrayed as vacuous and opportunistic, her mother's actions suggest that the fruit hasn't fallen far from the proverbial tree. The covetous Lil marries (Peter) Mearns Gramby, the hypochondriacal son of town matriarch Bertha Gramby, in order to improve her social standing. The ill-matched couple resides in the Gramby mansion, on which Lil sets her sights along with the collateral fortune. Lil's voraciousness along with Mrs. Gramby's equally corrosive resentment of her working-class status (prior to marrying Mearns, Lil was the town's seamstress) and her marrying Mearns for money make the women fast enemies. Though "Lil" is an abbreviation for Lillian and not Lilith, she is nevertheless a devilish wife (most of the characters describe her in demonic terms, e.g., a "witch" with a "white ghost-ridden face" [118]). Lil attempts to hasten her access to the Gramby fortune by leaving a box of chocolates near her diabetic mother-in-law, who has an equally voracious appetite for food generally and chocolate especially. Though Lil thinks her plot indestructible—she does this on a day when Mrs. Gramby's black maid, Neola, and the Portuguese gardener, Portulacca, are not working—Lil's death-by-chocolate scheme is foiled, her maliciousness exposed if not immediately punished.

The town's moral turpitude is rounded out by revelations of Glory's affair with "good old" Ed Barrell, an inveterate albeit rather feeble womanizer who had a brief fling with Lil and is currently carrying on one with Glory (upon Ed's death, one townsperson rhapsodizes on how Ed "would give you the shirt off his back," to which another retorts, "Maybe. But at the same time he'd take the shirt off your wife's back and all her other clothes, too" [184]). The conniving Weasel exposes Lil and Ed's tryst to the Grambys, while Johnnie stumbles upon a barely clad Glory at Ed's cottage following a violent nor'easter. The novel reaches a somewhat deus-ex-machina-like climax: the obese Mrs. Gramby tumbles down the steps of the town hall, managing to topple along with her Ed ("the man who has broken my son's heart" [182]) as both hurtle to their deaths. Her Jewish lawyer, David Rosenberg, then presides over the reading of the will: Mrs. Gramby predictably dispossesses Lil; leaves several other characters varying amounts of money (including several thousand dollars to Johnnie to help him embark upon his dream of becoming a painter in New York, safely away from the parasitic "country place," and $500.00 to "Mr. Weasel" for "his careful driving and for the chivalrous assistance he had so cheerfully offered to an old woman"); wills her diamond ring to "Mr. George [Doc] Fraser," her "devoted admirer"; and in an act that so inflames Lil that she unleashes a torrent of anti-Semitic, antiblack, and anti-immigrant expletives, Mrs. Gramby bequeaths both money and the Gramby mansion to "Cook," Neola, and Portulacca, the latter two planning to marry upon the finalization of Neola's divorce (186).

Given its rather overwrought dramatic schema, *Country Place*—replete with bed-hopping, skullduggery, and villainous characters who get their comeuppance—might seem like a bizarre (non) sequel to the muckraking, sociologically correct *Street* (which was obviously informed by Petry's stint as a reporter in Harlem). As the above summary suggests, the novel's exposition seems as tawdry as any dime-store romance, a genre which was especially popular during the 1940s. In light of W. Lawrence Hogue's assertion that *The Street*, along with works by Wright, Chester Himes, William Attaway, and Willard Motley, was judged as "fine" because it upheld the critically correct discourse of naturalism (29), one might wonder what compelled Petry not merely to de-center the prevailing narrative of white racism/black victimization but to veer into an entirely different direction altogether. Certainly, Petry is not the first African American writer to abandon racial antagonism as the crucible for all her literary creations—Paul Lawrence Dunbar, Zora Neale Hurston, Wright, and James Baldwin have all contributed to the ill-named "raceless" literature category.[1]

A profitable way to consider Petry's decision to follow an unabashedly *raced* novel with a *raceless* one might be to contemplate the second novel of her more acclaimed contemporary and the writer to whom she was usually compared, Wright. One of the trio of authors on the Mount Rushmore of 1940s/1950s black writers, Wright followed up his lavishly praised first novel with one that drew a comparable disparagement. *The Outsider* (1953) departed appreciably from the wildly popular, critically acclaimed "document" of black protest, Wright's fictive magnum opus that dramatized in excruciating detail nefarious whites and the blacks whom they torment without reprisal. Of course this skeletal encapsulation is reductive; *Native Son* (1940) is rightly considered a staple in the African American/American canons for its rigorously complex portraiture of race, and it was vital in the formation of a black postmodernist aesthetic. But the critical castigation accorded Wright's second novel revealed a certain prescribed and circumscribed racial-literary politics that confined black writers to a literary ghetto which mandated that they showcase if not resolve the ill-labeled "Negro problem." As the late Claudia Tate has written of Wright's existential tour de force, critics who expected "Native Son II" were less than receptive: "Rather than locating interpretive models more suited to *The Outsider*'s polemics than social realism, Wright's critics have generally lamented the absence of the familiar racial plot in this novel and the corresponding presence of tedious philosophical discourse and extravagant violence" (88). As a result, Wright's sepia existential tragedy was roundly panned; to most critics, Wright's immersion in French culture and its heady philosophical exegeses were inconsonant with the American "race problem," the black writer's compulsory topic from which he/she was encouraged not to stray.

Given the gendered politics of black publishing, Petry's publication of *Country Place* might have been thought to be even more of a gamble. However, unlike her male counterpart's second book, it didn't garner the opprobrium of critics: While sales fell far short of the handsomely praised *The Street*, its reception was far warmer than that of *The Outsider*. The reviewer for the *New Yorker* gushed that "on the whole the author kept up to the form she displayed in *The Street*," while the *Atlantic Monthly* commentator remarked that Petry's "writing in this second novel shows much of the improvement one was led to anticipate on reading her first"; and in an especially fulsome claim, the *Saturday Review of Literature* concluded that "out of materials very like those of *Country Place*, you get a

Madame Bovary" (all qtd. in Hughes 240–41). One might extrapolate from the vastly different critical appraisals that there was a certain patronizing and tacit gender essentializing at work: *the* anointed black writer de jour—Wright—being expected to engage in more lofty, "serious" excursions into the bowels of interracial conflict or black intraracial despair and dysfunction; women authors—in this instance, Petry—indulged in their forays into stereotypically, frivolously "feminine" concerns regarding the discomforts of the domestic sphere, regardless of their protagonists' racial identities. But I would hypothesize that the misnomer "raceless" novel does a disservice to the subversive components of *Country Place* in terms of race. Just as James Baldwin's also raceless second novel, *Giovanni's Room*, waged a frontal assault on what Baldwin considered white Americans' enslavement to delimiting notions of masculinity and calamitously constrictive definitions of love by casting a gay white male as a sexual "nigger"—a surrogate receptacle for all that heterosexual Americans find repulsive and unclean—*Country Place* enabled the black writer to focus her artistic lens almost singularly on those who are denominated as *raceless*—the always normative, always unmarked, always aproblematical: whites.[2]

At its most dissonant, *Country Place*'s foregrounding of whites' problems becomes an intervention upon and antidote to the misdiagnosed "Negro problem" that has its genesis in the "race science" quackery of the nineteenth century (see *Types of Mankind* and *The Negro: His Ethnological Status*) and in her own time was perpetuated by writers/academics such as Gunnar Myrdal (*An American Dilemma: The Negro Problem and Modern Democracy*, 1944). I concur with Emily Bernard's assessment of one of Petry's primary reasons for placing whites under her fictive microscope: Bernard contends that in *Country Place* Petry "represents white characters in order to destabilize conventional assumptions about whiteness and universality." In flipping the spectatorial script, Petry presages bell hooks' unpacking of the asymmetrical white-black critical gaze, where blacks are routinely viewed through an often astigmatic white gaze; hooks concludes that many whites "are shocked that black people think critically about whiteness because racist thinking perpetuates the fantasy that the Other who is subjugated, who is subhuman, lacks the ability to comprehend, to understand, to see the working of the powerful" (hooks, "Representing Whiteness" 168). Even in *The Street*, which at the very least portrayed whites and blacks as equally monstrous in their ravenous devouring of Lutie Johnson, Petry makes a point of niggerizing even the most prototypically all-American of (white) families, the Chandlers: Observing the vitriol they freely heap upon each other, Lutie ruminates that "it was nice to know that white people had loud common fights just like colored people" (46). Petry expands her disassembling of whiteness in her second novel, interrogating what one critic calls the "White family values" that were and still continue to be held up as evidence of an infallible, mythic postwar white America.[3]

To be sure, writing in the so-called raceless vein becomes emancipatory, allowing the black writer to transcend the limiting but prescriptive and sanctioned discourse of protest through which the literary establishment countenances their exposure of whites' systemic and chronic disenfranchising of blacks.[4] Petry's donning of the "raceless" fiction mask thus allows her to camouflage what might not have been tolerated by whites in nonliterary venues: a black person forsaking the "Negro problem" and turning her critical eye exclusively to whiteness and what the novel's dust jacket calls the "polluted" lives of the predominantly white Lennox denizens. This particular form of contamination heretofore has most readily been associated with the Bigger Thomases of the literary world. As John Charles rightly notes, Petry's "emphasis on the psychological dynamics of white family life avoids the re-inscription of black suffering that the traditional 'protest' narrative typically requires" (113). While one of the novel's contemporaneous critics lamented in 1948 that by refusing to stay in her aesthetically consigned place of black writer as combination muckraker/spokesperson for the everlastingly downtrodden black masses—"Mrs. Petry has been diverted from a subject which she could treat with special understanding to one about which she can be merely repetitive" (Butcher 113)—*Country Place* displays Petry in subversive mode, her demythologizing and dissection of whiteness unremitting. From the novel's narrative architectonics, in which Petry cloaks her lacerating critique through the guise of a seemingly nondescript white male narrator, Petry's deft ability to, as Morrison would say much later, "say without saying," puts her on par with the dean of literary tricksters Charles Chesnutt, a pioneering master of discursive (dis)guises that facilitated his piercing assault against slavery within the outer packaging of the nostalgic "plantation" tradition. And if Faulkner's injunction that a writer should concentrate on her "own little postage stamp" has any merit, then Petry's not-so-imaginary Lennox, Connecticut—not necessarily the Harlem on which she reported for the *Amsterdam News* but in which she did not actually reside until adulthood—is the locus for her subject matter; indeed, it is the generative landscape that engenders the white lifescapes she crafts so ingeniously in *Country Place.*

In my repositioning of Petry generally and recuperation of *Country Place* specifically, I think it necessary to situate her not only within a neglected New England black literary tradition—think of the prodigious and prolific authors hailing from or associated with this region: Phillis Wheatley, Harriet Wilson, Pauline Hopkins, W. E. B. DuBois, George Schuyler, Marita Bonner, and Dorothy West—but also in a geotextual one that included Anglo-American inscribers of what Lawrence Buell calls "New England Strangeness" (353). He argues that this designation applies to Nathaniel Hawthorne's fiction; in addition to Hawthorne's phantasmagoric narratives, we might also think of the calcified, Bergman-esque world that Robert Frost conceives in poems about psychically chilled New Englanders atrophying in equally chilly environs ("Mending Wall," "Home Burial"), and the domestic tragedies of Eugene O'Neill, who chronicles this idiosyncratic "New England Strangeness" in dramas shot through with incest, abject isolation, drug/alcohol addiction, and familial implosion (*Mourning Becomes Elektra, The Iceman Cometh, Long Day's Journey Into Night,* et al.).

Writing in the same year that Morrison published *Playing in the Dark: Whiteness and the Literary Imagination* (1988), critic Joseph Bodziock echoes Morrison's thesis regarding canonical white writers' equation of blackness—specifically, black people—with the always lurking primal and barbarous; he contends that "Blackness entered the literature of Hawthorne and Poe, as well as a multitude of other white American writers, as a common metaphor for sin, corruption, dirtiness, and moral depravity" (34). In effect, Petry makes a midcentury intercession upon this pervasive fictive episteme. Her Anglocentric New England, a land once inhabited by self-styled "Puritans" with the blood of countless Native Americans on their hands, is peopled with descendants whose "corrupt" and "depraved" behaviors don't quite rise to the level of the genocidal violence inflicted by their ancestors. Still, what stands out in *Country Place* is Petry's adroit "Othering" of that which is routinely treated as normative and indistinctive. The sepia shadows that permeate her Lennox, Connecticut, are cast by white New Englanders whose personal and moral turpitudes were so often downplayed by Petry's white literary forebears (if not necessarily by her twentieth-century counterparts), who instead installed the culturally familiar dark-skinned Other as the metonym for the "sin" and "corruption" which Bodziock specifies.

Petry arrays *Country Place* in gothic adornments, beginning with what she claims as the novel's genesis: "I wrote *Country Place* because I happened to have been in a small town in Connecticut during a hurricane—I decided to write about that violent, devastating storm and its effects on the town and the people who lived there" (O'Brien 161). The force with which the storm lacerates the defenseless Lennox evokes fear and contemplation in several of the characters, as Doc surmises that "the beat of the rain against the windows, the ever-increasing force of the wind, had set all of us to a reluctant examination of our lives" (105). The external storm sets off within the characters exacting reflections on the emotional violence they have meted out and undergone, and it also forces them to reconcile their experiences within the larger cosmological forces of good and evil. The entire novel, especially those chapters in which the storm serves as symbolic backdrop, is steeped in gothic leitmotifs, language, and symbology. After he runs over a black cat, which is "flattened in the road, smashed into flat, black fur and dark red blood" as he ferries the newly arrived Johnnie from the train station, the Weasel concludes that "this was an omen of evil" (18); while waiting for her mother in the Gramby mansion, Glory reckons that only "a horrible old woman like Mrs. Gramby would want to own three striped tiger cats and name all of them Leon [meaning *lion* in several Romance languages]" (45). Through these feline references, Petry invokes both white and black iconic gothic works: Poe's titular black cat, which is equated with the protagonist's gynophobia and eventual wife-killing; the cat that the guileful six-year-old Dick Wright "lynches" in a psychoverbal battle royal where he literalizes words his father meant figuratively; and the white cat which frightens Bigger as he smothers Mary Dalton within range of her blind but acutely aware mother.[5]

Petry's dramatization of the storm itself and the disequilibrium it rouses in the characters is steeped in gothic trappings: Doc wonders if it "had not brought with it some ancient spirit of evil, long suppressed" (107). The storm's fury is felt especially at the Gramby mansion, where it "beat at the windows like an evil spirit, bent on entering the house, bent on violence" (112). Inside, Mrs. Gramby "turned away from the sight of Lillian's white ghost-ridden face. . . . 'Two hundred years ago I would have said you were a witch and that you had bewitched my son'" (118); and the matriarch then surmises, "I will be entombed here with her" (119). The mansion's morgue-like aura is further iterated by Lil, who decries how "Mrs. Gramby's hostile servants—her insolent cook, her silent gardener, her indifferent maid—had all helped seal her inside that one room [her and Mearns's bedroom]" (121). This feeling envelops Lil even when she's in another macabre milieu, Miss Susie Brandford's boardinghouse; subbing for Mrs. Gramby as "the fourth and necessary person" during a rather mirthless game of bridge with "two old ladies and a [aptly named] Mr. Wormsley," Lil silently broods that she feels as if "she had been entombed while still alive" (166–67). In a way reminiscent of Poe's mournful poem "The Bells," Petry describes the sounds from the nearby Congregational Church which further ensconce the house and its inhabitants in dread: "The church bells were still ringing—ominous, slow; as though they were tolling the death of the town" (123). Though speaking more generally about American gothic vis-à-vis its German antecedent, Allan Lloyd Smith captures the uniqueness of our homegrown literature of fear and fright: "The house, not the castle, becomes the site of trauma; its terror deriving from the familiar inmates instead of some external threat, and its terror therefore what Poe called a terror of the soul, and not of Germany" (75). And just as Poe uses the miasmic tarn and the structurally splintering Usher mansion to exteriorize the family's decomposition, Petry's ferocious landscape becomes the external correlative for a family that is as doomed as Poe's cadaverous twins.

Apropos of its antipastoral, storm-ravaged setting, the occupants of the mausoleum-like Gramby mansion are beset with maladies that approximate those of the "first families" of twentieth-century American gothic literature, Poe's Ushers and Faulkner's Griersons. Like those of the Grambys' literary predecessors, their once august name has suffered a precipitous decline in stature, and the continuation of that fading name is in severe jeopardy. As well, the Grambys cannot forestall their genealogical extinction: "The name would disappear, lost down the reaches of time. No heirs, no issue, the line ended" (61–62). Though Petry spares us the most gruesome scourges that bedevil Poe's and Faulkner's families—live burial, poisoning, necrophilia—the Grambys inculcate the worst traits of an atrophying New England Brahmin class. Inhabiting the "largest house in Lennox," Mearns and Mrs. Gramby are "the town's wealthiest citizens"; Mrs. Gramby especially incarnates a petty, resentful bourgeoisie, given her disdain for those not so well-positioned: She exclaims, "I am not charitable" (63) while bemoaning the rise of people of Lil and Glory's ilk. Moreover, Mrs. Gramby is preoccupied with her late husband to the point of obsession, his spectral presence permeating the mansion and memorialized in a "horribly alive-looking portrait" that "hung over the mantel" (45). Finally, her overprotection of their only child, Mearns, has contributed to his hypochondria and neurosis: he is little more than a "middle-aged man who was addicted to vitamin pills and mouthwashes" (62). In fact, her very name, Bertha, invites comparisons to one of gothic literature's most prominent female characters, the original "madwoman in the attic," the imprisoned Bertha Mason of *Jane Eyre;* this intertextual connection is even more stark when we learn that Mrs. Gramby occasionally "walked through the house at night, even going up to the attic, just to look at the rooms, cool, high-ceilinged, subtly changed because they were faintly lit by the moon or the street lamps" (111). But unlike her infallible, victimized fictive predecessor, Mrs. Gramby both articulates and embodies Petry's maxim that "we're all mixtures of good and evil" (154); as depicted in *Country Place,* Mrs. Gramby's behavior resembles the "monstrous feminine" that permeates past and present gothic literature.

Our first glimpse of Mrs. Gramby, occurring as the Weasel drives Johnnie from the train station, establishes her leviathan presence and grim bearing: "A bulky, slow-moving figure, clad in a long black cape, paused in front of the church"; the Weasel then pronounces the town's less charitable appraisal: "Folks been betting she'll hit the ninety-year mark. . . . But I dunno. Her waterworks are pretty well shot to hell and her false teeth slip and she can't get none that will stay in her mouth" (17). Glory adds to this snarky assessment when she sees the Weasel's car "bend" under Mrs. Gramby's girth: "I bet she's all of two hundred pounds, short like she is and wide. They ought to put her on a diet. Momma says she eats like a pig" (46). Like the monomaniacal narrator of "The Tell-Tale Heart," who hatches a scheme to murder his elderly, wealthy host and lay claim to his gold, the diabolical but inept Lil tries to kill her mother-in-law by exploiting her food fetish, leaving a box of forbidden chocolate nearby on the servants' day off and removing her insulin from its drawer. Albeit it is a harebrained scheme, Mrs. Gramby nevertheless succumbs: "Selecting a chocolate, she ate it quickly; then another, and another, without pausing to wonder who had put the box on the table" (153). While her gluttony does induce the diabetic coma Lil has sought, Mrs. Gramby's life is saved by her indispensable black maid, Neola. Glory furthers this hulking image of Mrs. Gramby, comparing her to a "monstrous bird, flapping its big black wings as it walks awkwardly along the ground" (46). In addition to the foreboding, morose shadow Mrs. Gramby casts, her ponderous, near-predatory image comes to symbolize the notion of gothic excess, evinced not only by her rapacious appetite for food, but also by a near-fetishistic materialism.

During the ravaging storm, Mrs. Gramby seeks comfort by adorning herself in "a string of pearls from a worn velvet case" and a "diamond ring which she forced over the swollen knuckles of her little finger" (112).[6] Such palliatives—chocolate and the "worn," now ill-fitting gewgaws of a passing and increasingly impotent life—emblematize a psychological devolution, an unraveling self-conception that Anna Sonser speaks to in her study *A Passion for Consumption: The Gothic Novel in America:* "The loss of historical and social particularity exacts a price and, therefore, the byproducts of commodification are two-fold. Subjectivity is unstable, transient, fluid, and always contingent on commodity signs and, as such, encourages deviation from social constraints and the responsibilities of morality, ethics, conscience, and other forms of social affiliation" (2). As Mrs. Gramby's behavior makes increasingly clear, her subjectivity is "unstable" as the aging matriarch of a once-proud but now deteriorating family. To be sure, her "deviation from social constraints" and wavering moral compass are exposed not only in her hostile encounters with the crass, avaricious Lil; more forebodingly, her rapacious consumption of luxury items and food augers an even more daunting relationship between her and those men closest to her, be they deceased or living.

Petry's depiction of the Grambys' less-than-beneficent universe—and more specifically, the increasingly insular and ominous world Mrs. Gramby inhabits—vivifies what Lawrence Buell has deemed "provincial gothic," which he argues "takes impetus from the awareness of social change but is grounded in the premise that institutions and values resist change. This insight, in turn, supplies the ideological foundation for provincial gothic's assimilation of the standard theme of entrapment (typically imaged by symbolic houses that function as extensions of familial and cultural restraint) and for the standard plot elements of ordeal by immurement, suffering, resistance, and escape" (358–59). Johnnie Roane reinforces her waning stature, deeming her a "half-forgotten landmark" (17); and though she is not confined to her home, her mansion is a virtual prison given that she cannot leave without assistance because of both her age and her physical enormity. Further "resisting the change" of which Buell writes, Mrs. Gramby frequently bemoans feeling "useless" and "defeated" (113). Thus, burdened by her near-nonagenarian status and cultural diminution, Mrs. Gramby clutches at a patriarchal authority through an obsession with and invocation of her late husband (see: Glory recoiling from his "horribly alive-looking portrait" in the living room). Prefiguring Lena Younger's frequent appropriation of her late husband Big Walter's voice to consolidate her authority in *A Raisin in the Sun*, Mrs. Gramby attempts to refurbish her tattered subjectivity through a sort of imagined transvestitism: in order to retain her fleeting ability to control those under her roof, she recuperates and reenacts a patriarchal masculinity that she assumes will restore a fleeting subject position.

Analogous to Mrs. Hedges' masculine re-fashioning as a compensating mechanism for her sexual devaluation, Mrs. Gramby's androcentric desires are multifold. At one level, she feels a similar worthlessness vis-à-vis Lil's ornamental attractiveness and vanity, marked by the latter's slimness: when Mrs. Gramby invites Lil to share some cakes during the storm, Lil retorts, "'I never eat sweets.'. . . She [Lil] meant to enlarge on this remark, pointing up her words with meaning glances at Mrs. Gramby's feather-pillow waistline" (114). Further, Lil remarks upon Mrs. Gramby's stark grotesqueness in terms of the latter's vanishing femininity: "She has now reached the stage where she is completely sexless—that heavy gray mustache over her mouth, that mountain of flesh inside that loose black gown, could belong to a man just as well as to a woman" (122). On the one hand, these remarks could be attributed to the homo-gendered competition that a patriarchal society foments—thus, such "catty" comments might seem deplorable but understandable in a society that pits women against women. But more saliently, they bespeak the cultural ethos that women are valuable only inasmuch as they are attractive to men, an appeal that recedes as they age and become hormonally more "masculine." We witness Mrs. Gramby lamenting her lost allure when she recalls her late husband's comment that "my knees were so perfect they should have been immortalized in marble" (178); even this endearment objectifies and historicizes her as an *object d'art.* While her feminine anxiety/masculine envy rears itself in odd ways—upon seeing lawyer Rosenberg, the object of the town's sneering anti-Semitism, she ruminates, "But if I were given the chance I would change places with him—now, at this moment" (65)—it is clear that she astutely grasps the gender/ethno-religious hierarchy: being a male subjected to the community's xenophobia is still preferable to being an aging woman of any race or class.

Thus, Mrs. Gramby's grasping for the accoutrements of masculinity—control, implacability, ownership—is directly proportional to her expanding size, increasing age, and concomitant "sexlessness." In effect, she finds it far easier to remake herself into the dead patriarch than into the floozyish daughter-in-law who had "the temerity to marry" her son (151). While I am wary of symbol-mongering, I find it nevertheless insinuative when, upon exiting the Weasel's cab during a rainstorm, Mrs. Gramby "unfurled the late Mr. Gramby's oversize umbrella" (66), a phallically implicative act that hints at a desire for masculine if not phallocentric dominance. She is both haunted by the loss of an adoring husband who conferred on her femaleness and by her impending mortality; consequently, her home comes to emblematize her own psychic tomb and her attempts to sequester and dominate others as well, evidenced by the iron fist Mrs. Gramby brandishes in ruling over Lil within her domestic fiefdom. Thus, without compunction, she "had pushed Lillian into a corner and kept her there" (152), while declaring that "I never cared where she went or what she did; how she spent her days; so long as she understood her place in my house" (153). A plutocratic, patriarchal past, with its impenetrable class barriers, is giving way to a more class-fluid, female-dominated present that gives rise to money-grubbing vulgarians like Lil and her daughter (think of *The Waste Land*'s crude "Mrs. Porter and her daughter" desecrating the hallowed Christian foot-washing ritual by bathing their feet in "soda water"). As John Charles trenchantly concludes, "The Gramby house—a resonant symbol of traditional patriarchal authority, is in a sorry state; it is dominated by women with 'excessive desires' and there's not a (white) man in sight capable of bringing them in line" (115).

The gothic situation that Petry designs here recalls what James Twitchell observed in *Dreadful Pleasures:* "The early gothic usually tells the story of a single and specific family run amok: 'father' has become monstrous to 'daughter.' It seems to make little difference if the father role is shunted to uncle, priest, duke, landlord, or devil, as long as his relationship with the young female is one of paternal dominance" (qtd. in Louis Gross 53). The Gramby homeplace, the site of "paternal dominance," replicates this schema in the form of matri/patri-hegemony and subjugation. With Lil positioned as a low-rent "damsel in distress," Mrs. Gramby functions alternately as duke, landlord, and even devil; Lil actually calls her an "old devil" (116), thereby implying a sort of perverse kinship between them, since Mrs. Gramby similarly imagines Lil a sinister presence (recall too Lil as Mrs. Gramby's bridge-playing surrogate in chap. 23). As well, the home is alchemized into a quasi-plantation—like enslaved blacks, Lil must "know her place"—and a site for white female enslavement, as Mrs. Gramby's classism, internalized sexism, and physical disfigurement intermesh and bring into sharp focus her monstrous presence in Petry's postlapsarian, "strange" New England.

Though Mrs. Gramby doesn't evoke comparisons to Morrison's mother-succubus figures—no filicidal Sethe Suggs or Eva Peace here—Petry nevertheless paints her relationship with her sole heir as infected by debilitating excess. If cleaving to notions of patriarchy transmogrifies Mrs. Gramby, then her relationship with son Mearns marks her consolidation of patriarchal authority and maternal domination to the point of pathology, not only in terms of Mearns' identity formation, but also as it relates to his sexual subjectivity. While the "sins of the father" has persisted as a dominant trope in American and other literatures, Petry insists that fulsome displays of (s)mother love can be just as paralyzing and calamitous.

In her androgynous role of domineering patriarch-matriarch, Bertha Gramby has suffocated her son to the point of rendering him emotionally stunted and neurotic. One senses that Mearns has experienced a lifetime of petty demands—for instance, she commands him to "put on your glasses" because the sight of him fumbling with them "sickened her" (110; recall the previous chapter's discussion of Woodruff being similarly chided by wife Addie over his glasses). At another moment, reminiscent of Caroline Compson's counterfeit mother-martyrdom in *The Sound and the Fury*, Mrs. Gramby's identity is subsumed by the suffering mother role: She sententiously opines that she stands and contemplates the "sorrow" of Mearns being cuckolded, "though standing is painful, making my knees, my thighs ache unbearably" (152). Such a surfeit of mother love has in all likelihood created a puerile, dependent adult son beset by physiological neuroses and gender anxiety. Doc informs us that "he's been a walking medicine cabinet ever since he was born—eye drops for his eyes, cough drops for his throat, those expensive ones from the Liverpool Throat Hospital; and a gargle and a mouthwash, specially made up for him. He takes vitamin pills and sedatives, even mild laxatives" (97). Mearns is little more than a middle-aged man-child, a hypochondriac whose chemical and medicinal dependencies are traceable to both an insular life and one short-circuited by overpowering mother-love. In fact his very stilted name, P. Mearns Gramby, evokes images of another enfeebled sybarite, J. Alfred Prufrock, whose behavior from the very outset of Eliot's second most famous poem is compared to that of an "etherized patient" and whose sexual depredation has rendered him an impotent shell of a man.

As well, in the image of "prude-frock," one can even detect more than a hint of the feminine in Mearns's multiple addictions, considering that "sedatives" and "laxatives" have often been associated with women entertainers as diverse as Judy Garland, Marilyn Monroe, Dinah Washington, and Phyllis Hyman. His marrying of Lil in his late forties, from this psycho-pharmacological standpoint, becomes a desperate attempt to shore up a destabilized masculine identity. When Mrs. Gramby grouses that "at forty-seven he had married Lillian—a hard, shallow woman with an acquisitive, seeking mouth, a woman who dyed her hair and starved herself in order to stay slender" (61), the tri-headed Oedipal family portrait comes into full relief. Lillian becomes both incarnation and antithesis of his domineering mother: monstrously feminine in her masculinized appetite for power and status symbols while sexually tempting in a meretricious kind of way, the opposite of his estrogen-deficient mother. Mrs. Gramby herself hints at this unhealthy triangulation, admitting that "she had stood guard over him, believing that she could keep him safe because she was stronger than he" (61). Mearns becomes the devitalized damsel who cannot flee the monstrous mother's castle-dungeon, even after he marries.

Quite rightly, Louis Gross asserts that "incestuous relationships in American Gothic fiction are primarily about brother-sister pairings; they rarely involve children (though *The Turn of the Screw*'s ambiguity may involve hints of childhood incest) or parents and children (Alfred Hitchcock's *Psycho* [1960] is an important exception here)" (54). I would amend his observation a bit, given that Faulkner also hints at father-daughter incest in "A Rose for Emily" with the obdurate patriarch Grierson cloistering daughter Emily and violently repelling would-be suitors. Still, when one thinks of incest in Anglo-American literature in the twentieth century, *The Sound and the Fury*'s Compson children and Sutpen's black and white offspring in *Absalom, Absalom!* immediately come to mind; it would take until the early 1950s for black writers to broach the subject, which wasn't then addressed for almost two subsequent decades. Ralph Ellison, Toni Morrison, Alice Walker, James Baldwin, and, more recently, novelist-poet Sapphire would eventually explore proscribed intrafamilial sexual conduct in works from 1952 to the present. Thus, in raising the specter of mother-son incest, we see Petry charting new ground for the black writer in appropriating this gothic discursive formation, hinting throughout *Country Place* that postlapsarian New England, like its degenerating southern counterpart, is awash in sexual immorality bordering on the taboo and corroded.

While Mrs. Gramby's behavior might ostensibly be considered emblematic of the overbearing mother-succubus, it takes on an Oedipal tinge in the context of her own widowhood and her obsession with and surveillance of Mearns and Lil's sex life. Of course, it is not uncommon for mothers to become fixated on sons in the event of the father's death or dissolution of their marriages—for the sons to, in effect, fill the void left by the father's absence by becoming their mother's companion and de facto surrogate husband. We get more than a trace of this when Mrs. Gramby enviously sizes up the newlyweds sauntering up her walkway: "When I saw Lillian, leaning on his arm as they walked up the path to the front door; saw her brushing against him, kissing him, patting his cheek while she talked baby talk to him, I could not bear it. The sight of those cold eyes under that beflowered hat, the sound of her shrew's voice carefully pitched to tenderness, nauseated me" (152). This snapshot is clearly Oedipally inflected, as Lil now supplants Mrs. Gramby as mother—Lil infantilizes him just as she herself did—while also filling a role that by "natural" law of propinquity is off limits to her, that of lover.

More malevolently, Mrs. Gramby's mammoth presence is rendered sexually and spatially as well. For starters, the mansion's appellation—the "pink house," as Doc informs us on the second page—intimates an image of the female body as foreboding and colossal if not necessarily vaginally consuming (perhaps an anti-Sirenic image?). And further conjuring images of Bertha Mason, the *ur*-madwoman in the attic, Lil complains to Mearns as they lie in bed, "Your mother's in the attic. . . . What's she doing up there this time of night?" (116). Powerless to halt the behavior of a mother-in-law whom she understandably calls "that old devil," Lil legitimately complains, "She is the boss here, she is the one Mearns turns to for advice, she is the one that Mearns gives his money to—not me. If she could she'd sleep in the same bed with him and put me in the servants' quarters" (116; consider Mrs. Gramby's insistence that Lil "know her place"). These pregnant remarks make plain the simultaneity of variously dysfunctional family dynamics—Mrs. Bertha Gramby as de facto mother-wife who supplants Mrs. Lil Gramby; Mrs. Gramby as sexual interloper/incestuous mother; Mrs. Gramby as malevolent patriarch who relegates Lil to a subordinate slave-wife position.

The commingling of the patricentric/incestuous undercurrents so long associated with gothic come into full view when, again, Mrs. Gramby herself acknowledges the perverseness of her spatial/sexual surveillance and dominance of Mearns-Lil while providing insight into why her detested daughter-in-law sought solace in Ed Barrell's bed: "If she were someone else's daughter-in-law, I would say that I could almost see how she came to intimacy with that bowlegged man. For she must have been desperately disillusioned, too, what with the bedroom door kept open at night, the cats stalking in and out, the cats sleeping on her bed; no money of her own, no place of her own in another woman's house" (153). The last line especially speaks volumes, as Mrs. Gramby, in essence, has transformed herself into the "other woman" who impedes upon Lil's presumed wifely position. This description of a bedroom alchemized into a Poevian chamber of sexual horrors approximates the tomb in which Roderick Usher buried his living sister, only to have the self-exhumed, bloody-robed Lady Madeline fall "heavily inward upon the person of her brother, and in her violent and now final death-agonies, bore him to the floor a corpse, and a victim to the terrors he had anticipated" (40). Petry too provides the contours of the gothic incest narrative, dramatizing the form's unresolved, quasi-Oedipal mother-son plot, with Lil positioned as the mediator/trespasser in this consanguineous erotic triangle. Having set forth the "cats sleeping on" Lil's bed—these feline creatures functioning as Mrs. Gramby's feminized minions—Mrs. Gramby vitiates the conjugal union, as the "stalking" animals become extensions of her own (s)mother-monster eye; they freely encroach upon a space she herself desires to occupy but is prohibited from doing.[7] In this scene, she exhibits her parasitic proclivities, what at one point being meddlesomeness now edging into psychosexual pathology. Though she superciliously laments that "the line between good and evil had been rubbed out" (63), she fails to recognize her own complicity in its effacement.

The novel's climax—Mrs. Gramby plummeting down the city hall steps and managing to shove Ed Barrell to his death as well—is in a sense hyperdramatic to the point of comic absurdity: "Her huge body entangled in the folds of the voluminous black cape. . . . Ed Barrell had one foot extended in front of him, reaching for the next step, when Mrs. Gramby pushed him" (182). But I think Avril Horner and Sue Zlosnik's *Gothic and the Comic Turn* offers a useful framework for interpreting a seemingly quasi-theatrical climax:[8] they pinpoint the "hybridity of most Gothic novels, which includes their juxtaposition of incongruous textual effects" (3). Affixing such a melodramatic ending to a novel that almost elegiacally records a town in the throes of multiple deaths—historical, personal, psychological—heightens the sense of passing and finality. The physically violent demise of two of its most omnivorous and monomaniacal citizens—Ed, who resembled Mrs. Gramby in that the town considered him "an institution" (184) as he guiltlessly bedded most of the town's married women, and Mrs. Gramby, whose stultifying relationship with her son amounted to a sort of sociopsychic filicide—might usher in new possibilities in this socially and psychically deformed New England hamlet. Again, I turn to Horner and Zlosnik: "If the Gothic text demonstrates the horror attaching to such a shifting and unstable world, it also, in its comic dimension, celebrates the possibilities thereby released" (9).

On the one hand, the deceased Mrs. Gramby now morphs into the body of her late husband, occupying the same position of posthumous patriarchal authority that once belonged to her living-dead spouse. Safely immured, she can now exert the power to facilitate or stymie the financial fates of those within her orbit, notably dispossessing the venal Lil and funding Johnnie Roane's flight to New York, where he can pursue a career as a painter, away from the contaminated, putrefying "country place." But with her bequeathing the Gramby home to "Cook, Portulacca, and Neola" (187), an upheaval of the racial-class stratum is perhaps on the horizon; those associated with servitude are now elevated.[9] Moreover, with the impending marriage of the Portuguese Portulacca and the African American Neola, perhaps Petry is reversing the racial pox that Faulkner suggested at the end of *Absalom, Absalom!* with the mentally deformed, mixed-race Jim Bond as Thomas Sutpen's sole heir, thereby signaling a catastrophic end of the megalomaniacal patriarch's quest for a racially "untainted" lineage because of Sutpen's own miscegenistic excesses. Unlike its biblical and southern predecessors, Petry's potentially restored New Eden/New England does not exclude blacks and other ethnicities/nationalities, nor does it sanction tiers of power and privilege based on accidents of birth.

In exploring the gothic resonances of *Country Place*, I was struck by Petry's highly connotative use of the name Glory, which reminded me of the title of the second section of Wright's *Black Boy* (1993), "The Horror and the Glory" (recall that this section was originally published separately as *American Hunger* in 1977). This second half of Wright's autobiography chronicles his post-Mississippi trials and tribulations in Chicago as a young adult and aspiring writer. The overt connection I observe here is that both authors, with equal fervor, deconstruct and demythologize a northern environ that is in some ways merely an inverted southern dystopia. But with her downplaying (if not total elision) of the well-worn tropes of the often-clichéd protest discourse, Petry's portrayal is not so much in conversation with Wright's as it is a pathbreaking attempt to cast a glaring light on post–World War II America. She peoples *Country Place* with an array of whites whose actions are governed by fear and loathing if not by the astringent antiblack ethos of their southern predecessors. Indeed, the dwellers of the quaint but spurious idyll face a phalanx of horrors—this portrayal in diametric opposition to our glorification of the "Greatest Generation," which presumably faced down evil in Europe in upholding our presumed superior values. The values supposedly inherent in "Old Glory" have been sullied not only by "cheap people" (79) like Lil and her ironically named daughter—alternately referred to as "Morning Glory and Angel Face and Glory Hallelujah" and "Lana Turner" (35, 56), the quintessence of whiteness and blondness and physical allure—but by the entire Anglo-dominated community: from the psychosexually contaminated relationship between the aristocratic but morally flaccid Mrs. Gramby and her neurotic son; to the inert, ineffectual Doc and his grimy co-narrator, the Weasel; to the self-deluding Johnnie, who clings to the belief that "he had never lost [Glory] anywhere except in his imagination" (95), even though he knows of her unfaithfulness and vacuity. But if WASPy Lennox has devolved into a palsied paradise, Petry simultaneously adumbrates a still-germinating American landscape that is more heterogeneous. Presaging our internecine debates regarding America's changing ethnic demographics, Petry in her intermingling of black and Portuguese in the novel's conclusion may have unwittingly anticipated a seismic shift in our racial-ethnic terrain, the ethno-demographic aftershocks continuing to pulsate well into the twenty-first century.

7

"A QUEER MIXTURE OF VIOLENCE AND LOVE AND HATE AND TERROR"

(Wannabe) Gangsta, Gothic, and Grotesquerie in "In Darkness and Confusion"

For me, one of the great moments of American culture actually occurred in August of 1955. Very few people want to talk about it. In 1955, of course, Emmett Till was murdered by fellow citizens, a victim of U.S. terrorism, the body thrown in the Yazoo River, the Tallahatchie Bridge, under the Tallahatchie Bridge [sic]. But his body was brought back to Chicago, and the first major civil rights demonstration took place, 125,000 fellow citizens walked by to take a look at Emmett Till. His mother left the coffin open so they could see. It was at Pilgrim Baptist Church, led by the Reverend Julius Caesar Austin. And he introduced Mamie Till Mobley, and she walked to the lectern. She looked over at her baby, whose head was five times the size of his normal head, and she looked in the eyes of America as well as the folk at south side Chicago. She said what? I don't have a minute to hate. I'm going to pursue justice for the rest of my life. That's a level of spiritual maturity and moral maturity that does not give up on the Socratic attempt to interrogate the mendacity and the hypocrisy of American life, but is rooted in something deep. It's rooted in an attempt to keep track of the humanity of the very people who have dehumanized you. Use *that* as a standard of responding to terrorism, in light of the last two and a half years. My God. How fascinating. Here's Moms Mobley speaking on her behalf and speaking for the best of tradition. Martin King's in the background. Fanny [sic] Lou Hamer's voice is there. A. Philip Randolph's voice is there. And many nameless and anonymous black leaders who knew they had to deal with a situation in which they were unsafe, unprotected, subject to random violence, and hated for who they were. That's what it meant it mean [sic] to be a nigger. Unsafe, unprotected, subject to unjustified violence, and hated. Now, after September 11th, all America feels unsafe, unprotected, subject to random violence. And hated. You say, hmm, now that the whole nation's been niggerized, let's see what the response is going to be.

—Cornel West speaking at the Lannan Foundation, 2003

Terror in our contemporary sociopolitical idiom has become an arabesque of fraught and contested meanings. Right-wing politicians speak alarmingly and gravely of the self-professed "war on terror," using the notion of a "pre"- and "post"-911 America as a cudgel to bludgeon opposing politicians and critics as nay-saying and yellow-bellied, insufficiently "American." Unsurprisingly, the term is inexorably raced, with Arabs and Muslims supplanting African Americans as the savage, rampaging Other. In this patriotically correct, Americentric narrative, the "towel-headed," not-as-dark peril now constitutes the sinister, genocidal new niggers who brandish airplanes and suicide bombs that wreak far more havoc than any single bestial and unruly black dick ever could. Never mind that terror is as American as Roger Clemens and the late Senator Helms—see Wilmington, North Carolina; Tulsa, Oklahoma; Fannie Lou Hamer; the "Four Little Girls"; James Byrd, Jr.; Arthur Warren; or Sean Bell.[1] As cultural critic/scholar Cornel West opined, post-911 white America for the first time experienced the ontological fear/dis-ease of being "niggerized," of having one's entire existence constantly besieged by feelings that any moment he/she could be individually or collectively "neutralized" (to revive a favorite euphemism of King-baiter and cross-dresser J. Edgar Hoover) for *being* while black. Our once impenetrable domestic "homeland" could no longer focus exclusively on the domestic but familiar brown enemy/Other; the very landscape—its monuments of power and its citizenry—was now in the crosshairs of a more brutal Arab/Muslim/Islam/Islamofascist menace; despite almost daily evidence to the contrary, distinctions are seldom if ever made, even in post–Timothy McVeigh America.

Early forefathers and foremothers, too, battled domestic Others, a conundrum given that the identities/markers "Native Americans" and "African Americans" semantically imply both Other and kin. Leonard Cassuto theorizes the concept of "grotesqueness"—the monstrously Manichean opposite of whiteness, order, civilization—in discussing the stratified identities upon which constructions of a prototypical Anglo-American self and nation are based: "For American Puritans, the Indians were grotesque. For nineteenth-century Americans, the objectified African slave and his descendents came to occupy a similar shifting space in the system of meaning and value. Neither the Indian nor the slave was seen consistently as a person in the Western worldview" (7). As I discussed in chapters 4 and 6 respectively, *The Street* and *Country Place* represented fictive countertexts where the "grotesque" gets refigured in many guises—white as well as black, female as well as male. As well, "In Darkness and Confusion" can be read both within and outside a female Anglo-American/African American gothic tradition, which figures notions of domesticity and terror in far different hues than Petry's white New England forebears.

As Elaine Showalter and scores of feminist critics have demonstrated, the distaff side of the literature-of-terror genealogy has inveighed against the scourges of patriarchal prerogative, with the domestic homespace as a veritable haunted house. Women's truncated social, economic, gendered, and even artistic possibilities are configured spatially—detention in mansions, basements, garrets as most indicative of their quartered lives. From the Brontës to Kate Chopin to Charlotte Perkins Gilman to Joyce Carol Oates, "home" has not been a protective bower of bliss but a dungeon-like enclosure that sentences women to the horrors of marriage, the cult of true (white) womanhood, motherhood, hysteria/madness, and countless other scourges. Though largely ignored in this tradition, black women writers too have fictivized the miseries of patriarchy and untrammeled phallocentrism in decidedly raced ways. Perhaps the most illustrative historical example is Dr. Flint's attempted imprisoning and making a concubine of "Linda Brent" in Harriet Jacobs's 1861 "black captivity narrative," *Incidents in the Life of a Slave Girl.* More contemporarily, Toni Morrison's harrowing *Beloved* depicts the nightmare of slavery in terms of enslaved women's corporeal and psychic mutilation; the white torture chamber, the "Sweet Home" plantation with its gruesomely ironic name, becomes the locus of racial-sexual terror. Even Petry's New England black literary foremother Harriet Wilson chronicled the horrors that could befall a "mulatress" born in reputedly *safe* northern terrain (Boston) in *Our Nig; or, Sketches from the Life of a Free Black, in a Two-Story*

White House, North. Showing that Slavery's Shadows Fall Even There (1859); this lexically labyrinthine subtitle foregrounds geospatiality as a trope for gendered and raced oppression. On this continuum, twentieth-century writers such as Nella Larsen in both *Quicksand* (1928) and *Passing* (1929) and Gloria Naylor in *Linden Hills* (1985) have also imaged black women as figuratively buried alive not only in the imprisoning domiciles to which they're confined, but by marriage, the institution snuffing out their own sexual subjectivity and creativity, with black men often patterning their own behaviors after (if not mimicking) those of their malevolent white patriarchal predecessors.

As she did so masterfully in adorning *The Street* in the vestments of "naturalism" all the while subverting its conventions, Petry's under-read short story "In Darkness and Confusion" similarly troubles the conventions of what might be called the Anglo- and African American feminist gothic traditions. While the story traverses concerns native to such traditions—marital alienation, emotional isolation and the spatial confinement that hypostatizes it, different forms of pain, and gender disequilibrium—Petry inverts the predominant discursive formation underlying works such as *Incidents*, *Our Nig*, and *Linden Hills:* the black *male*, more so than the black woman, is besieged and beset by an array of domestic terrors—marriage, the workplace, the South. Similar to West's re-racing of terror in the amnesiac American consciousness, Petry ingeniously expands notions of domestic terror as limited to the black woman's most harrowing nightmare. Ostensibly a tale of the visceral turmoil that engulfs the Jones household—which consists of wife and husband Pink and William, along with Annie May, Pink's niece whom they have reared—Petry's story wrenchingly dramatizes the family's racial-psychic implosion and the larger black community's malaise and disempowerment. Enlacing issues as diverse as architecture, geography, masculinity, and the homosocial, "In Darkness and Confusion" like *The Street* resists reductive categorizations: Here, too, the perpetrators of terror and its victims have no prescribed race or gender.

The story highlights Petry's penchant for dramatizing her characters' moral foibles through their physical extremes and grotesqueness, reminiscent of what she so cleverly did in *The Street* (the story was published in 1947, a year after the novel). Within the context of Mikhail Bakhtin's notion of the grotesque—"Exaggeration, hyperbolism, excessiveness" (303)—I think "In Darkness and Confusion" also employs corporeal extremes/polarities as effective objective correlatives. William Jones (perhaps a reincarnation of *The Street*'s William "Supe" Jones?) is haunted by a mélange of perceived deformities, fears, and phobias; foremost is the bodily puniness that evokes derision and self-deprecation. To be sure, if Bigger Thomas embodies the untamable, alpha black male brute lodged in the white American imaginary ("He looks like an ape," as one white observer in *Native Son* exclaimed), then the lightweight Jones is his antithesis. Indeed, in a culture that equates manhood with the ability to impose one's physical will, he is the brunt of verbal harassment and belittlement within and outside the home. When he tries to assert himself by threatening the insolent Annie May with a beating, she quickly retorts, "You and who else?" to which Pink "roared with laughter" (256). When he subsequently demands that his "niece-in-law" either stop "runnin' around the streets until four o'clock in the mornin'" or "get some other place to stay," she replies, "Oh, I don't know why Auntie Pink married a little runt like you for, anyhow. It wouldn't bother me a bit if I never saw you again" (271). Clearly, she's hit an emotional vein, as her cheekiness causes Jones to bemoan both the verbal barbs and his somatic deficiencies: "What'd she have to say that for, anyway, he asked himself. Five feet five wasn't so short for a man. He was taller than Pink, anyhow. Yet compared to Sam [their son], he supposed he was a runt, for Sam had just kept on growing until he was six feet tall" (272). Jones's lament exposes his own inculcation of socially sanctioned but deleterious protocols of masculinity in which 1) male subjectivity is measured by the ability to intimidate, if not tame, women and 2) an unyielding homo-gendered competition undergirds relationships between men based on the assumed superiority of those more physically imposing. In effect Jones is both the perpetuator of these atavistic gender indices—physically threatening his niece, competing with his own son—and their pitiable victim as well.

At the opposite extreme of the severely diminutive Jones, Pink embodies another dimension of Bakhtinian grotesquerie, as Petry consistently brings attention to her mammoth size. Petry first architecturally implies what we will eventually discern as not only their discrepant sizes but Pink's superior strength. While William putters in the kitchen in preparing himself an unsatisfying breakfast, he is audibly attuned to—assaulted by?—Pink's "moving around in the bedroom" and the "thud of her two hundred pounds landing in the rocker by the window" (253). He is then stunned by her actual appearance in the kitchen doorway:

> She was a short, enormously fat woman. The only garment she had on was a bright pink slip that magnified the size of her body. The skin on her arms and shoulders and chest was startlingly black against the pink material. In spite of the brisk brushing she had given her hair, it stood up stiffly over her head in short wiry lengths, as though she wore a turban of some rough dark gray material. (253–54)

If William Jones marks the author's reincarnation of *The Street*'s conniving custodian, then the description of Pink unequivocally hearkens back to the jet black, gargantuan Mrs. Hedges. The quoted description of Pink here seems almost dialectical. Though Pink does work as a maid for a white family, Petry interrupts and revises American society's historically demeaning relegation of large black women to subservient roles in upholding what literary critic Trudier Harris calls the "mammy myth," whites' self-ameliorating fiction that "black women who cared for their children really *loved* those children" and that "except through animalistic, debased interactions" black women could not "tempt those [white] men away from white women, their perceived 'rightful' partners" (*Saints* 7). Lingerie-clad and even voluptuous, Pink's body gainsays the abjectified and asexual "mammy," with Petry resituating her into economies of the erotic.

Contrapuntally, however, in terms of the story's foregrounding of what I've deemed Jones's multiple hauntings and anxieties—in the domestic and external realms—Petry's portrayal of Pink personifies Barbara Creed's conclusion regarding sociohistorical renderings of women as destructive forces: "All human societies have a conception of the *monstrous-feminine*, of what it is about woman that is shocking, terrifying, horrific, abject" (1; emphasis added). While I would stop short of comparing Pink to the ogre-women Creed examines in films from *Whatever Happened to*

Baby Jane? to *Basic Instinct*, I do think Petry uses her enormity and potential grotesquerie (note too her Medusa-esque hair complementing her colossal frame) to dramatize the possibility of the domestic sphere as a perilous environ for a black man. Contrarily, a more apposite comparison of Pink as tormentor—if not "terrifying" and "shocking"—might be African American women (imagined and real) such as Elvira in Gloria Naylor's *The Women of Brewster Place* (1982), who physically threatens her craven husband Ben for being insufficiently obsequious to Mr. Clyde, the white man on whose land they sharecrop but who is also sexually violating their crippled daughter, or the sexually-psychologically abusive mother-daughter tandem who torment the preadolescent eponymous figure in the biographical film *Antwone Fisher* (2002).

Again utilizing the trope of entombment that so vividly exteriorized the characters' physical deformities and emotional fears in *The Street*, Petry employs confinement in "Darkness" not merely to suggest blacks' truncated social space but specifically Jones's sense of claustrophobia and impotence within the homespace. He expresses "distaste with their apartment" because "the rooms weren't big enough for a man to move around in without bumping into something" (261). On the one hand, there is the black masculinity theorist Maurice Wallace's legitimate claim that the "masculinist fondness for the home, the shanty, the underground room, the crypt, and the closet, then—as opposed to the Oedipal dread of them as domesticating, even emasculating, constructions (inasmuch as our cultural logic of sex and space renders the inside place feminine)—speaks for a longing to abscond from the neurotically uncanny experience of social spectragraphia by a retreat away from the public sphere where the gaze tyrannizes into the remote interiority of that other construction of space: consciousness" (123). Indeed, home in its many manifestations can be a sanctuary, hidden from the surveillant, potentially hazardous public, hegemonic gaze ("social spectragraphia"). But, on the other hand, the types of spaces Wallace also specifies suggest something a bit more foreboding than refuge: the "crypt," "underground room," "closet"—considered collectively, they connote at the least a sense of forced sequestration and proscribed sexuality, claustrophobia, and immobility; and at worst they intimate the specter of slavery and accompanying feelings of dread and death. Home, then, becomes the site of gender upheaval and disorientation; far from being a black man's hiding place/refuge, home exacerbates and concretizes Jones's multiple malaises, gender disorientation being perhaps the most paramount.

Ostensibly, the story's opening positions Jones as an example of "moderated masculinity," Marlon Ross's term for black male characters who attempt to dismantle traditionally anachronistic but debilitating notions of masculinity that are rooted in brutality, dominance, phallocentricity: "William Jones took a sip of coffee and then put his cup down on the kitchen table. It didn't taste right and he was annoyed because he always looked forward to eating breakfast. He usually got out of bed as soon as he woke up and hurried into the kitchen" (252). While Jones's performance of these "domestic" duties signals a progressive, counter-masculine masculinity, it is problematized by a more comprehensive portraiture of his position in the marriage and household. Anxiously awaiting a letter from Sam (who's stationed in Georgia), Jones "decided that as soon as she [Pink] came into the kitchen he would go back to the bedroom, get dressed, and go to work" (253). He then takes cover, "clos[ing] the bedroom door behind him gently" (254). Gingerly moving between two traditionally female spaces, Jones takes on the mien of a long-suffering wife who furtively calculates his every move lest he disturb his tenuous sense of bliss by provoking his spouse.

Petry further dramatizes the authority/disempowerment/gender nexus through her emphasis on voice, where Jones's sense of impotence is counterpoised with women's verbal dominance and control. Both Pink's and Annie May's tendency toward domination is hinted at through harsh vocal intonation and verbal ridicule, not to mention the impending threat of physical intimidation. In addition to Annie May's piercing attacks on his physical stature, the tenor of Pink's voice transmits derision and violence: "'Good mornin', Mr. William Jones. Does the weather suit you this mornin'?' Her voice was *sharp*, like the crack of a *whip*" (262; emphasis added). Her patronizing tone underscores a coexistent puerilization alongside Jones's feminization—this in addition to the obvious analogizing of Pink's acute verbal jabs and slavery's metonymic emblem of pain and punishment. At another juncture, Pink scolds him for "talk[ing] so mean to Annie May" (275), again engaging him not as a lateral partner but admonishing him like adolescent who dissed a younger sibling.

In sharp contradistinction to his perpetual silence/silencing, Jones at least once appears to be on the cusp of voicedness, when he and Pink are in church. He inwardly decries being subjected yet again to a sermon in which a "buttery voice[d]" minister disregards chronic racial inequities while encouraging blacks to wait patiently for an afterlife where they will prosper on "streets of gold up in heaven" (273). Not lost on Jones is the crushing architectonic irony here, given his and Pink's not-so-heavenly upper rooms: "They'd lived on this top floor for years" and were habitually confined to it because "the top floors cost less" (257). Having reached his threshold for tolerating the minister's ineffectual analgesics, Jones is poised to proclaim his displeasure publicly: "One Sunday he'd actually gotten on his feet . . . the words were right on the tip of his tongue when Pink reached out and pinched his behind sharply. He yelped and sat down. Someone in back of him giggled" (273). Pink's corralling of Jones reifies what Trudier Harris brands an "ideology of domination," where physically imposing black mothers/mammy figures "inadvertently replicate the power dynamics of masters over enslaved persons, for they seldom allow anyone to challenge their authority" (*Saints* 11). Its slapstick and juvenile qualities notwithstanding, this public restraining with its quasi-violent underpinnings is degrading, exhibiting not only Pink's formidable power and Jones's childlike gesticulations but also the quelling of Jones's festering protest voice—not unlike the kitchen and bedroom where he takes cover and suppresses his own voice.

Finally, one of the most telltale remarks emblematizing Jones's gender anxiety and powerlessness occurs prior to the church censoring, when Pink reassures Annie May that her uncle's attempts to discipline her should be disregarded: "Don't you pay no attention, honey. He don't mean a word of it. I know menfolks. They's always tired and out of sorts by the time Saturdays come around" (272). Here we see a complete inversion and recasting of female "hysteria," as Pink's disavowals echo Janie's famous feminizing of Joe Starks, when she reduced her pompous husband to a menopausal woman: "When you pull down yo' britches, you look lak de change uh life" (Hurston 75). As with the publicly emasculated "Jody" (the name itself evoking both the puerile and the feminine), Jones's peevishness is ascribed to its being "that time of the week [month]"—"Saturdays" engendering a sort of menstrual crankiness to be indulged but, ultimately, disregarded.

Free of the imperious gazes of Pink and Annie May, Jones perhaps imagines a modicum of freedom outside of the kitchen, bedroom, and church—all of which become regulative, voice-abnegating enclosures. However, his outdoor Harlem environ is far from a halcyon, consoling homeland; on the contrary, the petrifying landscape corporealizes his internal demons:

> Even these [trees] were a source of danger, for at night shadowy, vague shapes emerged from the street's darkness, lurking near the trees, dodging behind them. He had never been accosted by any of these disembodied figures, but the very stealth of their movements revealed a dishonest intent that frightened him. So when he came home at night he walked an extra block or more in order to go through 125th Street and enter the street from Eighth Avenue. (260)

As if this journey through his native, obsidian Harlem-Hades weren't traumatic enough, Jones recalls walking the street alone in "broad" daylight, ruminating that "the bold-eyed women who lived in these houses would lounge in the open windows and call to each other back and forth across the street. Sometimes when he was on his way home to lunch they would call out to him as he went past, 'Come on in, Poppa!'" (260). The catalyst for Jones's horror is now, again, ascribed to the feminine, as these women's brazen invitations amount to verbal sexual assaults, not unlike the male jeers to which women are subjected when they happen upon construction sites or other disproportionately gendered spaces; like the women navigating androcentric work zones, he "would stare straight ahead and start walking faster." In light of the coterie of women who've thus far launched verbal attacks, the "bold-eyed women" are in effect *phallic women* who again expose Jones's chronic feelings of testosterone-deficiency.[2] Moreover, their derisive moniker, "Poppa," mocks not only his sexual inadequacy—think here of a pimp or some other sexually commanding male figure in the black vernacular tradition—but it also marks a commingling of his paternal shortcomings (see his impotent attempt to act as Annie May's "poppa" during a conference with her principal, who "buried [him] under a flow of words"—the principal described as "a large-bosomed white woman" [265]) and his sexual priggishness.

Jones heretofore being foiled in his attempts to rein in his wayward niece, it is not surprising that his efforts to fulfill both the patriarchal and matriarchal roles in Sam's life are less than successful. We witness what amounts to both a motherly impulse to shield his son from what he perceives as gargoyle-like, predatory figures and a self-serving desire to shore up his own feelings of devitalized masculinity vis-à-vis the physically strapping young Sam. Fulfilling a dual paternal/maternal instinct, Jones attempts to shepherd Sam through the sexual tribulations that mark adolescence:

> When Sam turned sixteen it seemed to him the street was unbearable. After lunch he and Sam went through this block together—Sam to school and he on his way back to the drugstore [where he works as a porter]. He'd seen Sam stare at the lounging women in the windows. His face was expressionless, but his eyes were curious.
>
> "I catch you goin' near one of them women and I'll beat you up and down the block," he'd said grimly.
>
> Sam didn't answer him. Instead he looked down at him with a strangely adult look, for even at sixteen Sam had been a good five inches taller than he. (260–61)

In typical Petryian fashion, this brief passage contains a cornucopia of interpretive possibilities. Perhaps consciously, perhaps not, she intertwines the epic and the gothic: this episode conjures images of Odysseus navigating his men through the Sirens' seductive but murderous melodies. As well, Petry evokes images of her New England literary forefather Hawthorne's classic 1835 tale "Young Goodman Brown," with Sam as the literal and metaphorical "brown" young man journeying through the sexually appealing, potentially consumptive feminine. Critically relevant here is the male character—and female author—figuring woman as menace if not grotesque. Commenting on the historicity of this representation, Margaret Miles trenchantly observes:

> Even with the most careful self-scrutiny and male surveillance, however, women harbored an irreducible element of monstrosity. For it was not only female behavior—loquaciousness, aggressiveness, stubbornness—that could at any moment reveal a woman's identity with Eve, but her body itself. Some women were seen as personifications of the grotesque; prostitutes, for example, epitomized the penetrable body, the body shaped by lust, the permeable body that produces juices and smells. The prostitute's body is opposite to the closed, self-contained, controlled male body, and the opposite of that of some virtuous women, especially of virgins, who were "gardens enclosed." (92)

Perceiving women thusly, Jones endeavors to "protect" his son from the "loquacious" and "aggressive," monstrous female corpora, which is clearly a modernized version of the historical notions of female grotesquerie that Miles lays out. However, such attempts are doomed to fail given women's "irreducible element of monstrosity" that resists attempts at "male surveillance."

Thus, the physically scrawny and emotionally wobbly Jones embodies a less-than-gangsta incarnation of black masculinity, given his diffidence as well as the multiple forces arrayed against him. To be sure, the inconsolable "trembling in his stomach" (267, 276) that brings about "a tautness and a tension in him that left him feeling as though his eardrums were strained wide open" (276) makes him more kith and kin to the physiologically plagued Roderick Usher than to Bigger Thomas. In effect, the effete and hypersensitive Jones becomes the apogee of a *gothicized* black masculinity, where the subject is assailed by ineradicable terrors from within and without; this state applies to an arc of Petrian males regardless of age—from eight-year-old Bub Johnson, left alone to battle the night terrors that envelop him during Lutie's absences, to the mid-sixtyish Charles "The Witness" Woodruff, so plagued with panic after the traumatic kidnapping/rape episode that he is stricken with "violent pains in his chest" (231) within the safe confines of his own home. And while the workplace has historically been an environment that conferred upon men status and a heightened sense of authority if not outright power, Petry again subverts this notion with respect to Jones's devaluation at his place of employment.

Accounts of southern black men forced to perform backbreaking jobs as sharecroppers, levee builders, and unpaid prison laborers are legion. While Harlem dweller Jones works as a porter, not necessarily a physically exacting job, he nevertheless experiences psychological emasculation vis-à-vis more masculinely sanctioned types of work. The humdrumness of his job is apparent enough—contemplating Sam being stationed in a virulently racist Georgia, Jones "would catch himself leaning on the broom or pausing in his mopping to wonder what had happened to him" (259). Completely oblivious to Jones's emotional anguish, the white storeowner rebukes him "sharply" (recall Pink's "sharp" voice) while bellowing, "Boy, what the hell's the matter with you? Can't you keep your mind on what you're doing?" (259–60). The owner's degradation, a more scalding *and* racialized form of Pink's verbal and physical mistreatment, renders an already physically tedious job now racially hostile as well. The internal malaise is externalized in terms of attire and the body in this poignant but doleful pictorial:

> When he hung up his soiled work coat in the broom closet at eight o'clock that night he felt as though he'd been sweeping floors, dusting fixtures, cleaning fountains and running errands since the beginning of time itself. He looked at himself in the cracked mirror that hung on the door of the closet. There was no question about it; he'd grown older-looking since Sam had gone into the army. His hair was turning a frizzled gray at the temples. His jawbones showed up sharper. There was a stoop in his shoulders. (265)

Beset by years of unsatisfying, physically monochromatic tasks, Jones glimpses a self virtually atrophying before his very eyes. Moreover, these decidedly unmasculine duties render him a sort of male mammy—the closet here a metaphor not so much for proscribed sexuality but attenuated masculinity. Cultural theorist bell hooks's historical perspective on African American men and work speaks to this issue: "Black men in America have rarely romanticized labor, largely because they have for the most part performed less desirable tasks. They knew that performing jobs society deemed menial with bosses and supervisors harassing and persecuting them was not fulfilling" (*Ain't I a Woman* 93–94). Domesticated at home and relegated to domestic drudgery outside of it, Jones becomes an interstitial subject, straddling several identities while a true, authentic one remains elusive.

While Jones's multiple distempers are concretized by the inhospitable and fear-inducing spaces he inhabits—the home, the drugstore, the church, Harlem itself—one might envision the barbershop as a potentially regenerating environ, given its near romanticizing in literature and film as one of the few habitats that promote black males' companionate bonds. Traditionally, it has functioned as an unmonitored venue where they can verbally enact an unfettered masculinity, holding forth on subjects from sports to war to women. For Jones, the barbershop might serve as a homo-gendered *third space*, an oasis and antidote to the verbal and psychic abuse so liberally dished out in insalubrious work and home environs. It is not surprising, then, when Jones relishes the opportunity to get a haircut, even though "he'd have to wait a long time before Al got around to him" (266); he goes on to imagine the impending camaraderie: "It would be good to listen to the talk that went on—the arguments that would get started and never really end." Upon his reaching this presumably male-dominated safe haven, "the instant he entered the barbershop he could feel himself begin to relax inside." In effect, the barbershop becomes a balm in Gilead, a sanctuary where persecuted and spiritually bereft black men can find respite—though it often proves only transitory.

The palpably male-centered aura of the barbershop emerges the moment Jones enters, as the polyphonous voices speak about race and sex undeterred. Sentiments such as "White folks got us by the balls—" and "Only thing to do, if you ask me, is shoot all them crackers and start out new—" are expressed without fear of retribution. To be sure, the barbershop becomes a site of ultramasculine performance, an arena where black men through the rituals of loud-talking, boasting, and signifying can experience the accoutrements of a socially orthodox masculinity too often denied in the outside world; in effect, it is a male womb. Though Jones's existence as a moderated version of "true manhood" still holds—"Some of the talk, he knew, would be violent, and he always avoided those discussions because he didn't like violence—even when it was only talk" (266)—the barbershop still becomes a theater in which he can don the persona of a more gangsta, and thereby socially sanctioned, masculinity. This is most evident when he inserts himself into a spirited debate about the war: "'Them Japs ain't got a chance—' he started. And he was feeling good. He'd come in at just the right time. He took a deep breath before he went on. Most every time he started talking about the Japs the others listened with deep respect. Because he knew more about them than the other customers. Pink worked for some navy people and she told him what they said" (266–67).

Cultural critic Mark Anthony Neal particularizes the conjoining of space, gender, and performance vis-à-vis this historically vital locale: "Black-owned barbershops are often less a space of personal disclosure and more so a space where black men continue to perform very rigid notions of black masculinity around acceptable topics of discussion such as politics, music, and of course sex" (77).[3] In effect, the barbershop becomes Jones's inviolable pulpit—no fear of Pink pinching him into submission or a white boss calling him out of his name. Seemingly, then, the barbershop "is a site where African American men, as do the men in the story, voice their opinions, rage, and fears about the war, economic realities facing both the individual and the community, and politics—all without facing reprisal from whites" (Raynor 108). However, Jones's performance becomes a compensatory and thus thorny endeavor: spewing jingoistic, Anglo-sanctioned epithets elevates him on both the racial and gender hierarchies. Jones offsets his boss's niggerizing him by a type of verbal jujitsu, as he dons the guise of faux white man who mends his frayed racial and gendered identities through the malevolent discourses of war, imperialism, and xenophobia. But as is always the case, Jones's epistemological superiority is mitigated by its twin sources—the seemingly irrepressible and omnipotent Pink, and the very whites who circumscribe his family's and race's entire existence. His performance of a sanctioned masculinist script is undermined by its *in*authenticity: Jones in effect remains the emotionally stunted man who parrots the diatribe of his more commanding superiors—and oppressors.

Jones's ersatz gangsta persona by way of nationalistic billingsgate vanishes against the material reality of America's entrenched georacial hierarchies. Just as quickly as Jones inflated his own sense of self through jingoistic slurs and militaristic chest-thumping, Scummy, Sam's army comrade in Georgia, confirms what Jones has suspected since he hadn't heard from his son: "He got shot by a white MP. Because he wouldn't go to the nigger end of the bus. He had a bullet put through his guts. He took the MP's gun away from him and shot the bastard in the shoulder" (268).[4] Sam's plight here upholds what J. Lee Greene observes about black soldiers' and civilians' "demand for greater participation in American democracy" after World War I: "Like a contagious disease, this demand infected large segments of the nation's black communities" (158–59). Predictably, Greene adds, "when petitions for better treatment were rebuffed, an angry black population responded with violence, and the white citizenry countered with violence." One can only conjecture Sam's reasons for entering the military in the first place—perhaps he was rejecting what he saw as his father's life of hand-to-mouth drudgery by entering an institution whose androcentric ethos would garner for him socially sanctioned masculinity through state-sponsored violence, a masculinity his broom-pushing father could only pay lip service to. Still, Sam's physical and spiritual maiming animates his father's racial-masculine rejuvenation, as Jones seeks refuge in another male-associated space.

Anticipating more famous (infamous?) bars—think of the bedlam Invisible Man experiences at the Golden Day or young Dick Wright's miseducation as a six-year-old taught to repeat obscenities by black drinkers in *Black Boy*—Petry uses the bar as a cataclysmic and resuscitative space in the formation of black male subjectivity. It is here that Jones witnesses firsthand the unhindered aggression of white hegemonic authority, the very kind that has left Sam physically injured and racially abjectified, thereby thrusting his father into unquenchable despondency. Here Jones encounters another soldier, whom he describes as "tall. Straight. Creases in his khaki pants" and who "looks likes Sam looked that one time he was home on furlough, he thought" (279). And like Sam, this unnamed soldier is again ambushed, this time while defending a "frowzy-looking [African American] girl" being harassed by a white policeman. After the soldier "grabbed the cop's arm and twisted the nightstick out of his hand" and discarded it, Jones witnesses an eerily alarming replay of Sam's wounding at the hands of the military police; from Jones's point of view we see what happens after the policeman fires at the soldier who'd gotten as far as the bar's doorway: "The soldier dropped. He folded up as neatly as the brown-paper bags Pink brought home from the store, emptied, and then carefully put in the kitchen cupboard" (280).[5] This rather unremarkable though bracing account is striking in that Jones mnemonically likens the black soldier to a "brown bag," with Pink analogically linked to indomitable supremacist police power that, not unlike its military counterpart, has license to extinguish the lives of black men with impunity. From his always-aggrieved perspective, Pink becomes an extension of white patriarchal hegemony (consider Mrs. Hedges fronting for Junto's heinous business ventures, which further buttresses the possibility of Pink as Mrs. Hedges reincarnated)—a position which foreshadows the climactic rioting he ignites. Ineluctably, the grotesquerie of black womanhood is aligned with the ferocity of white manhood, a marriage that black men must either brook or be willing to die in challenging.

What I read as Jones's epiphany occurs in the wake of the bar inhabitants' stunned horror at what has transpired: "He stood still, watching them. The anger that went through him was so great that he had to hold on to the bar to keep from falling. He felt as though he were going to bust wide open. It was like having seen Sam killed before his eyes" (281). Jones re-imagines Sam being shot in the soldier's veritably northern lynching, a re-creative doubling which has the effect of momentarily radicalizing the heretofore timorous Jones. Conflating the southern "justice" to which Sam was subjected and the equally debilitating northern unjustness of white-on-black violence, Jones exclaims, "Come on, what you waitin' for?" and leads the barricaded black bar patrons to another exit, where they witness an ambulance taking the presumably dead soldier to the hospital (the onlookers corroborate the soldier's murder: "'The soldier was dead when they put him in the ambulance.' 'Always tryin' to fool us'" [283]). Jones's newfound political fervor is marked by an attendant revived masculinity as well: "He got the feeling that he had lost his identity as a person with a free will of his own. It frightened him at first. Then he began to feel powerful" (282).

While quite clearly "the story makes it painfully clear that it is the state's recent attack on his son, in particular, and the long term destruction of his private life, more generally, that propels him into public action" (Charles 101), Jones's politicization and revitalization are evanescent; almost on cue, his feelings of omnipotence will be extinguished once Pink emerges from church. Two groups—the insurgent black bar patrons and the just-adjourned churchgoers—intersect on 125th Street, the epicenter of black Harlem. It takes little time for Pink to reestablish the power discrepancy that undergirds their marriage. First, she reasserts her authority through her laser-like gaze: "She was staring at him so hard he was suddenly horribly conscious of the smell of the beer that had spilled on his shirt" (286). This signals the restoration of the marriage's power disequilibrium, with Pink resuming the menacing mammy role to Jones's mischievous man-boy: "'What you doing out here in this mob? A Sunday evening and you drinking beer,' she said grimly" (286). Reconsigned, and resigned to his puerile status, Jones attempts to deflect her censorious comments while also providing an airtight excuse: not only does he blurt out that "this afternoon I saw a white cop kill a black soldier," but he subsequently discloses what he'd heretofore concealed but must now reveal lest the full weight of Pink's wrath engulf him: "I saw Scummy yesterday. . . . Sam shot the [white] MP. They gave him twenty years at hard labor" (286). Notwithstanding this momentary suspension of their roles—Pink temporarily in the supplicant position of parishioner, Jones as the race-man/rebel—both characters revert to the familiar, reinforcing the story's grounding in the absurd and grotesque as ways to dramatize psychic, spatial, gender, and racial destabilization.

While the 1943 riot in Harlem has been most famously fictivized as the climactic event occasioning Invisible Man's self-imposed subterranean exile, Petry dramatizes this seismic cultural moment for indeterminable ends. On the one hand, Pink's own feelings of melancholia and mourning regarding Sam's racial-social killing find their object in the white-owned businesses that line Harlem: With the shattering of stores' plate-glass windows, Jones thinks that "Pink had started this. He was proud of her, for she had shown herself to be a fit mate for a man of his type. He stayed as close to her as he could" (287). As Pink leads the looting of white businesses, Jones's feelings of agencyless-ness return: "The feeling of great power and strength left him" (288); and eventually, he is again relegated to the wifely status he occupies in the home: "Pink was striding through the crowd just ahead of him. He studied her to see if she, too, were feeling as he did. But the outrage that ran through her had made her younger. She was tireless. Most of the time she was leading the crowd. It was all he could do to keep up with her, and finally *he gave up the attempt—it made him too tired*" (289; emphasis added). Here the gender-spatial dynamics of their tomb-like Harlem flat are reenacted in the external realm, with Pink re-assuming the familiar position as indomitable disturber and destructor of a peace rooted in black hopelessness and white economic privilege. In a seeming reversal, Pink harnesses her "monstrous mammy" position not for domestic dictatorial ends, but to help bestow palpable, material agency to a long-suffering community. To be sure, she seems here to embody what Robin Lucy calls the text's inscription of "the revolutionary energy of black women, their capacity to analyze and resist the machinations of the war against the domestic front and reclaim the black home" (16).

Concomitantly, however, just as Sam's attempts to abrogate southern Jim Crow principles ultimately fail, so too do Jones's ephemeral feelings of supremacy give way to his own cravenness and Pink's ferocity. When Jones "snatched a suit from the window of a men's clothing store" (291), this becomes a dismal, last-ditch attempt to at least adorn himself in the outward trappings of masculinity; but while clothes may make the man for the white entrepreneurs who economically colonize Harlem, for Jones the suit will function as so much costume jewelry, giving the appearance of socially esteemed masculinity while camouflaging an unstable sense of self.

One might legitimately judge Pink's leading of a race-based economic insurrection as a corrective measure for decades of white businesses peddling rancid meat and exorbitantly priced items to black consumers redlined into squalid neighborhoods. In this scenario, the passing of Jones's rejuvenated gendered self might seem a small price to pay—it occurs for the greater racial good as the black community forges a counterforce against years of the epidermalization and juridicalization of oppression. I return to Bakhtin's theorizing of the grotesque body to unpack what might be considered Pink's "constructive monstrousness": "In grotesque realism, therefore, the bodily element is deeply positive. It is presented not in a private, egotistic form, severed from other spheres of life, but as something universal, representing all the people" (19). To be sure, one could argue that the story's climactic riot provides economic redress and heals racial breaches on multiple fronts. While the rioting may ostensibly seem "pathetic reactions to an institutionalized racism far beyond their [the rioters'] control" (Holladay 120), urban uprising may have an upside as well. At least temporarily, Pink in effect becomes the larger-than-life, almost Frankensteinian avenging archangel who marshals dormant ferocious energy that can potentially reinvigorate and restore a historically disconsolate people.

However, this potentially regenerative intervention takes on a harmful tenor when Pink and Jones encounter a group of young black men trying to demolish the gate outside of a liquor store. After handing her shrinking helpmeet the lamp, kettle, and coat she herself has pilfered:

> she walked over to the gate. "Git out the way," she said to the boys. Bracing herself in front of the gate, she started tugging at it. The gate resisted. She pulled at it with a sudden access of such furious strength that he was frightened. Watching her, he got the feeling that the resistance of the gate had transformed it in her mind. It was no longer a gate—it had become the world that had taken her son, and she was wreaking vengeance on it.
>
> The gate began to bend and sway under her assault. Then it was down. She stood there for a moment, staring at her hands—big drops of blood oozed slowly over the palms. Then she turned to the crowd that had stopped to watch.
>
> "*Come on, you niggers,*" she said. *Her eyes were little and evil and triumphant.* "Come on and drink up the white man's liquor." As she strode off up the street, the beflowered hat dangled precariously from the back of her head. (293–94; emphasis added)

This scene exhibits Petry's aptitude for melding the absurd, comic, and tragic. The visual image of the oversized Pink bedecked in the standard black churchwoman's hat wielding what Trudier Harris calls "suprahuman" strength (*Saints* 11) is ostensibly outlandish but also potentially empowering: again, Pink wreaks havoc on the citadels of white power—the business hegemony. Several nonblack entities have assembled conglomerates based on vices both legal (alcohol, cigarettes) and illegal (heroin, crack, marijuana), which too often are rooted in what Cornel West in *Race Matters* aptly terms "Nihilism in Black America" (9–32). Unlike the mammy who upholds the pillars of white supremacy, Pink is transmogrified into a "militant mammy" bent on demolishing the hallmarks of black economic enslavement.[6]

But just as the resourceful Mrs. Hedges both helped and hindered the black community—alternatively directing characters such as Min to folk remedies and saving Lutie from Supe Jones's clutches but also colluding with the invisible white patriarch Junto to oversee the pimping of economically disenfranchised black women—Pink's actions can be judged much more ambiguously and even problematically.[7] While seeming to help overturn a conscienceless white capitalist enterprise that narcotizes and anesthetizes beleaguered blacks, her subsequent directive for "you niggers" to "drink up the white man's liquor" recalls Jones's gesticulatory association of Pink with the white policemen who shamelessly murder the black soldier. In an act that would buttress the more malevolent "monstrous-feminine" prototype, she again colludes with a morally and economically rapacious white power structure that facilitates black self-debasement. While Pink's action might not be necessarily indicative of the domestic who "loses all sense of a black self and adopts the culture into which she moves" and thereby "concludes that white is indeed right and that it is correct to oppress Blacks" (Harris, *Mammies* 17), it is nonetheless racially contemptible; in essence she metamorphoses into a type of "monster-mammy." Incontestably, a chemically sedated community cannot engage in revolutionary acts to kindle its own liberation. Thus, the potentially racially emboldening act of sabotaging white business interests ultimately, if perhaps unwittingly, contributes to black men's chemical dependency and self-numbing. I admit my own uncertainty here, for

I contrarily think a case can be made for Pink's action as—perhaps—a revitalizing intervention: drunken young black men might at the least be spared the cruel fate of her only son, unjustly exiled to a southern military prison by an institution in which he was presumably "protecting" a country that classifies him as not fully a citizen. Indeed, "darkness and confusion" come into full view here: Behaviors that may appear to be violently revivifying and enlightening contradictorily induce black people's psychospiritual waywardness and potentially lead to physiological evisceration and death.

Just as the third law of thermodynamics maintains that systems ultimately become devitalized and inoperable, it is not surprising that Pink's frenetic energy subsequently burns out. Proving again futile in his spousal role, Jones cannot stem her inevitable demise: "Even as he put his arm around her she started going down. He tried to hold her up, but her great weight was too much for him. She went down slowly, inevitably, like a great ship capsizing. Until all of her huge body was crumpled on the sidewalk" (295). As with many of Petry's works, we are faced with a denouement that is as paradoxical as the culminating riot itself. It is conceivable that Pink's death will revitalize Jones, who exclaims the story's closing malediction—"the sons of bitches." Given the overwhelming trajectory of her orbit vis-à-vis Jones's perpetually eclipsed one, the conclusion may auger a reemergence of his often muffled, stifled blues voice. Perhaps Pink's passing emblematizes the Bakhtinian notion of how degradation "digs a bodily grave for a new birth; it has not only a destructive, negative aspect, but also a regenerating one" (21). Hence, maybe Pink's death is part of a cosmological cycle of life, death, and rebirth. While I might not agree completely with George Adams's assertion that "what begins as a riot ends as a traumatic experience which transmutes the inarticulate and patient protagonist into an enraged and progressive one" (97), I would grant that multiple losses may potentially revitalize the previously supine Jones. Though he and Pink suffered the demoralizing pain of losing their second child in childbirth and the questionable imprisonment of their firstborn, the story's conclusion intimates Jones's potential regeneration, where he may be forced to give up the alternatively infantile and self-effacing ways that rendered him psychically and spiritually impoverished.

Conclusion

FROM THE 1960S TO THE 2000S AND BEYOND

Ann Petry's Prescient Vision

In her standard no-nonsense, borderline curt way, Ann Petry penned this response to a 1970 invitation to speak on racial matters at an institute called "The Young Adult in Conflict": "I have talked to too many audiences and given too many speeches and taken part in too many seminars, etc. I can't talk any more about what 'being black in white America' means. In a few years I will have done with writing about it, too."[1] Petry's weariness with addressing the misdiagnosed "Negro Problem" is unqualified here and, true to her word, she published no adult fiction between the years 1971 and 1986. However, her declaration of impending artistic self-muzzling on race—understandable given the oppositional and parochial way in which it is traditionally cast in stark "black-versus-white" terms—didn't dull her piercing insights into our everlasting "race problem," the reductive appellation applied to material, manifold issues that didn't magically vanish circa November 2008. In the 1960s and in the mid-1980s, Petry produced some of her most penetrating writing regarding issues as culturally relevant in the twenty-first century as they were topically germane when they were published—specifically the short stories "The New Mirror" (1965),"The Migraine Workers" (1967), "Mother Africa" (1971), and "The Moses Project" (1986). Given the scant ("Migraine") to nonexistent ("Moses") criticism on these works, I will concentrate primarily on them here. These stories are both period-specific and contemporarily relevant, confronting the fault lines underlying a burgeoning white, black, and *brown* America and the surveillance of the black body. Petry's foresight in dramatizing such abiding concerns attests to her acute grasp of the cracks in our national foundation that keep Americans of all hues, ethnicities, classes, and sexual orientations distressingly separate in what James Baldwin would prophetically classify as "these yet to be United States" (288). While exemplifying my central claims regarding her re-envisioning of white and black masculinity and her agile appropriation of gothic conventions, these stories reflect an expansion of her creative vision and insure her literary relevance long beyond her death in 1992.

Much like Ralph Ellison in the 1960s, Petry was relatively peripheral if not totally silent during the stentorian Black Arts Movement, where a cadre of Afro- and dashiki-bedecked younger artists preached to their adherents to "get whitey" and beseeched "niggers" to "kill" in the rabid, zero-sum rhetoric that often (but not always) privileged militancy over rumination. On the one hand, there was Gwendolyn Brooks, who in essence underwent a self-styled artistic makeover (not to mention her jettisoning her perm for a fro) after attending what for her was an aesthetic-altering event—the Second Black Writers' Conference at Fisk University in 1967; this resulted in a more radicalized Brooks poetic persona. Contrarily, Ellison abjured what he saw as outré Black Arts propagandistic writing which forsook the august, richly American artistic tradition established by Twain, Eliot, and Faulkner, not to mention the African American folk, vernacular, and musical traditions (folklore, spirituals, sermons, the blues, jazz) that bear witness to what Ellison disciple/novelist/blues theorist Albert Murray deems our inherent "omni-Americanism." While Petry would never vociferously denounce her younger black counterparts while elevating their white literary predecessors to some problematically rarified realm of "pure," politically unfettered "art," she would nevertheless mediate these two positions. As the aforementioned correspondence suggests, she remained keenly aware of our inestimable racial discordances, while at the same time resisting Afrocentrically orthodox notions of capital-b Black art. Her later work, like her entire fictive corpus, reflects an art ineluctably informed by her lower-case but irrepressibly *b*lack sensibilities—irrespective of the number of "race problem" colloquia or black writers' conferences she did or did not attend.

Published in 1965, a red-letter year that witnessed the Watts uprising and the assassination of African Americans' "shining black Prince" (actor Ossie Davis's honorific for Malcolm X), "The New Mirror" might be considered a sort of gadfly text. On the one hand, the "Black Is Beautiful" mantra was pulsating throughout African America, as "slogans like

'Black Power' and 'I'm Black and I'm Proud' were battle cries of an entire generation. . . . When the sixties ended the concept of Black identity became less clear" (Russell et al. 71–72). Indeed, Petry demonstrates how black identity in the mid-1960s was still laden with agonizing contradictions that too often proved psychically debilitating for the children of Hagar. Set again in the predominantly white suburb of Wheeling, New York, the story portrays the drugstore-owning Layen family and bears witness to the claim that "among less radical Blacks, old patterns of color prejudice remained" (Russell et al. 36). As in the story "Miss Muriel," where Petry introduced the family, the Layens' drugstore abuts their home, thereby inflaming a presentiment of dread in the unnamed fifteen-year-old narrator: while she "liked working in it on Saturdays and after school," she laments "but it often seemed to me a monstrous, mindless, sightless force that shaped our lives into any old pattern it chose, and it chose the patterns at random" (60). Infused with the gothicized horror coterminous with under- or unstated racial dyspepsia, the "old patterns" which Kathy Russell, Midge Wilson, and Ronald Hall outline intersect with but also depart from the "random" ones the narrator alludes to, the girl's observations speaking not so much to the blatant, recognizable forms of prejudice as to the vaguer, more amorphous ones that seem to emanate from within rather than from without.

By employing the mirror as the story's dominant leitmotif, Petry cannily invokes her black New England intellectual forebear W. E. B. DuBois and his eternally relevant axiom regarding "*double consciousness*"; the Layens' mirror functions as a distorting microscope through which they, like decades of blacks before, misapprehend and devalue themselves as insufficiently white. Though the narrator disparages what she construes as the deformed self reflected in the new mirror—"The bathroom walls were white, and under the brilliant, all-revealing light cast by the new fixture I looked like all dark creatures impaled on a flat white surface: too big, too dark" (59)—her father's self-detestation is even more acute. Without notice, Samuel Layen embarks upon a pilgrimage to Buffalo to purchase false teeth, an act that renders the family panic-stricken; his wife, fearing the potential scandal that might accompany news of his disappearance which might bring speculations of suicide, delays notifying the police.

Upon his return, the narrator recoils at his ghastly appearance: "'Look,' and he smiled, revealing a set of glittering, horrible, wolfish-looking false teeth. There was a dribble of dried blood at the corner of his mouth" (84). The mortified but perspicacious narrator subsequently queries her father about his ill-fated purchase and reveals the revulsion that occasioned his disastrous makeover:

> He sighed and said that that morning, while he was shaving, he had run through a solo he was to sing in church on Sunday. He stood in front of that new plate-glass mirror in the downstairs bathroom under all that brilliant white light, and he opened his mouth wide, and he saw himself in the mirror—the open mouth all red and moist inside, and the naked gums with a tooth here and there, and it was the mouth of an idiot out of Shakespeare, it was the mouth of the nurse in *Romeo and Juliet*, the mouth of the gravediggers in *Hamlet*, but most shocking of all, it was the mouth of Samuel Layen. This was what the congregation looked at and into on Sunday mornings. He said he couldn't bear the thought that that was what all those white people saw when he sang a solo. If he hadn't seen his mouth wide open like that in the new mirror under that new light . . . (85–86).[2]

Critic Jenijoy La Belle's observation about the horror that accompanies Frankenstein's monster's glimpse of himself in the pool resonates here: "The monster is radically self-alienated. It initially responds to its own image in the water in the same way the cottagers will—with horror" (104). In Petry's counter-discursive signifying, blacks now adopt the larger culture's bestializing gaze; they themselves strip the membrane barely separating their dark bodies and the monstrousness with which those bodies have historically and unfailingly been equated.

Another work of intraracial critique, "Mother Africa," like early 1970s works such as *The Third Life of Grange Copeland* and *The Bluest Eye*, unsparingly scrutinizes black cultural beliefs and practices—specifically, the extolling of a quasi-African ontology and epistemology by blacks born on American soil and the knotty gender politics underlying this "recuperation," as well as blacks' eternal search for a homeland. This tale chronicles the life of junkman Emanuel "Man" Turner, who answers to any number of sobriquets—"His neighbors called him Rags, Ole Rags, Junk, Ole Junk, Bottles, Ole Bottles. His friends called him Man or Mannie" (127). Through Emanuel's apotheosizing but subsequent repudiation of the "metal woman" statue he purchases and rechristens "Mother Africa," we witness the folly of compensatory fictions—Ibsenian "life-lies" that races and individuals construct in the face of intractable powerlessness and voicelessness. Barbara Puschmann-Nalenz succinctly describes one of the quasi-Afrocentric monument's core functions: "She represents the origins of black Americans, a symbolic 'home,' the roots of the African American" (35). Thus, the story seeks to demythologize two dominant cultural narratives emblematic of the black Zeitgeist during the late 1960s–early 1970s—one "Afrocentrically" proclaiming that "Black Is Beautiful," the other predicated on post-1920s Harlem being reclaimed and transformed into a racial holy land, a hallowed obsidian "nation within a nation" free of the imperialist white presence that would drive blacks from their two colonized, "lost" Edens: Africa and the American south. Through her poignant portrait of an alternatively absurd, idealistic, and egomaniacal Emanuel Turner, Petry unveils how racial platitudes and cant, despite all-too-real psychic and physical trauma, can preclude black self- and communal actualization.

Reflecting her expansive and forward-looking engagement of race beyond the overworked white-versus-black binary, "The Migraine Workers" again displays Petry's proleptic artistic vision in a work whose characters grapple with topics that continue to roil our national consciousness. Not only is the story an arabesque of many of the key issues addressed throughout this study—racialized terror, entombment, Edenic aspirations, male prerogative, social- and self-erasure—but it anticipates some of the most contentious concerns that bedevil twenty-first century America: ethnic tensions between blacks and Latinos and concomitant issues surrounding cheap labor and the economic exploitation of people of color. Evoking masterpieces of American short fiction such as "A Clean, Well-Lighted Place" and "A Good Man Is Hard to Find," this story dramatizes a day-in-the-life of Pedro Gonzales, the presumably Hispanic proprietor of an all-night truck stop, and his happenstance encounter with a group of black migrant workers. Mike, Pedro's employee of unidentified race, relays a request from the black driver of a "ramshackle truck": the "migraine workers" would like to use the restroom (114, 116). Petry isn't clear about the source of the malapropism—whether Mike or the driver garbles "migrant" into "migraine." In response to Pedro's puzzled query as to what this descriptor means, Mike pronounces: "It means these colored people who go from place to place to pick beans and stuff. The driver brings them from down South every year, and he's taking them upstate" (117).

The verbal gaffe aptly captures the plight of those perceived as an incurable headache in a xenophobic culture—a culture whose collective digestive and economic systems are sustained by the grueling labor of those it would just as soon cast aside as human detritus once the beans, lettuce, and other staples are harvested. Initially, Pedro is reluctant to admit these human nuisances onto his sacred turf: in a moment of divine assessment akin to the God of Genesis, Pedro "thought the station looked good, all of it—from the white one-story building that housed his office and the rest rooms and the salesroom where he sold car accessories, to the vast shed in the back where he stored truck tires and where Mike fed all the stray cats in the neighborhood" (113). But like Samuel Layen's pharmacy in "Miss Muriel" or the pastoral, white-picket-fence splendor in which Emanuel Turner cordons off the "Mother Africa" statue, these manufactured paradises are only transitory, for they can't keep at bay the ubiquitous Others and the ensuing conflicts.

A miniaturized and northernized precursor of contemporary neo-slave fiction—works such as Sherley Anne Williams's *Dessa Rose* (1986) and Charles Johnson's *Middle Passage* (1990)—"The Migraine Workers" is enshrouded in the vestiges of the primordial episode of black horror, the Middle Passage, and the subsequently nightmarish existences of enslaved Africans/African Americans on less-than-paradisal southern plantations. First, the seatless truck is "filled with black people—men, women, children and nursing babies. They were ragged, dirty, their dark skins covered with sores, and there were burrs and straw in their matted hair" (117). Once these South-based, economic captives begin disembarking to use the restrooms, the narrative describes Pedro's encounter with these Others, displaced African American peons who will in subsequent decades be supplanted by brown-skinned Hispanic Others with whom Pedro shares a common heritage:

> The last one out was an old black man, bearded, dirtier than the others, his work pants so filled with holes and torn places that he looked like a bundle of rags. After the flaps had swung back in place behind him, Pedro looked inside the truck. There was nowhere to sit except the floor. The stench made him cough, and over it was the yeasty smell of some kind of rotgut liquor. Then he moved away because there was someone lying way back in a corner—a very old woman who peered at him and then drew back in fear. (118)

Petry's stark etching of black misery and peonage, suffused with images of the nautical death traps and the stench, entombment, disease, and death that befell live cargo, vivifies the originating moment of American horror for a readership—the story was first published in the popular (white) woman's magazine *Redbook*—probably oblivious to or ignorant of it. The nauseating conditions Petry illumines here make the analogy between her latter-day slave-mover and its actual antecedent unmistakable: "Conditions were miserable. Slaves were forced to lie naked on wooden planks, and many developed bruises and open sores. The unbearable heat below deck, mixed with the human waste and vomit, produced an overwhelming stench" (Robinson 1302). The sanctuary-less "migraine workers" are descendants of "Miss Muriel's" Chink "All us black folks is lost" Johnson, peripatetic blacks for whom America has yet to be America, thereby leaving them psychically and physically unanchored. The effluvia and dread Petry animates here instantiates Leonard Cassuto's observation that "human objectification can result from all kinds of perceived differences, but in American culture it happens most readily to people with dark skin" (3).

However, Petry seasons the story's denouement with a perceptibly Christian flavor, recalling O'Connor's southern gothic parable "A Good Man," where the sententious grandmother is redeemed by the providential grace she bestows upon the serial killer who instantly snuffs out her life. Overcoming his initial cynical trepidation upon seeing the truck but not its inhabitants—he speculates that the truck might "have cobras in it or boa constrictors or lions" (115), serpentine and feral predators invading his sacrosanct, blissful space—Pedro evokes comparisons to his Anglicized biblical namesake, the Galilean fisherman who would upon Christ's miracle of feeding the multitude be converted to "fisher of men." After providing these black wayfarers manna that includes "loaves of bread" and "six quarts of milk" (119), Pedro will soon thereafter give sanctuary to the aforementioned "smelly old man" (124), who escapes shortly after the truck leaves its momentary refuge. Despite Pedro's reluctance to harbor the man (named Ben, we eventually learn) who confesses to his curt inquiry "Where'd you come from?" with the racially existential rejoinder "I don't know" (123), Mike both convinces Pedro to offer refuge and utters the parable's inscrutable message: "Didn't you [Pedro] hear him say if he hadn't jumped off the truck when he did, he couldn't 'a found the *fat* white man's place?" (125). This blues-like "turn," where the author troubles the ending, indicates the radicalness of this modern parable. As she did most keenly in "The Bones of Louella Brown," Petry elucidates the arbitrariness of the racial markers that disunite Americans. From Ben's limited epistemological perspective, Pedro's relative prosperity—em*bodied* in his girth—and freedom render him decidedly un-black and, therefore, *white;* a contemporary analog might be Miami's *white* Cubans, who've parlayed their rabid anti-Castroism/anticommunism into an economic and political colossus that is often the bane of other minorities, mainly African Americans and Haitians. But in her signification upon our blurred racial lenses, the conclusion imagines a truly diverse or, dare I say, multicultural and inclusive brotherhood, hearkening back to the multi-ethnic heirs to the Gramby estate in *Country Place* and the interracial sisterhood that Louella Brown and the Countess of Castro posthumously achieve. To affix the moniker of "Christian writer" to Petry may be a bit hyperbolic, but in betokening Alice Walker's tropological quilt, Petry dares to dream a world where racial and ethnic ruptures can be sutured in the formation of a polyethnic tapestry.

I will conclude this study by briefly remarking on her entirely neglected last-published story, "The Moses Project," which appeared in the relatively obscure *Harbor Review.* This story evolved from the author's being "intrigued by newspaper stories about 'house arrest'" (Ervin, "Just a Few Questions" 102). This deceptively straightforward tale—at least vis-à-vis technically sophisticated and richly labyrinthine ones like "Miss Muriel" or "The Witness"—depicts the travails of Sam Cooper, a black mechanic who has recently divorced his wife (whom he derisively refers to as "Diana the Kindergarten teacher" throughout the story) and has racked up $3,000.00 in unpaid traffic tickets. An exceptionally talented and much-sought-after mechanic ("anything with a motor or an engine that needs fixing I can fix. A one-of-a-kind black man," 53), Sam nevertheless is sentenced by a judge alternatively described as "a small black man," "wizened," and "wearing little rimless eyeglasses" (52). What this jurist lacks in stature he makes up for with his judicially authorized power to sentence Sam to six months of home detention, which would effectively kill Sam's livelihood. As a concession, the judge offers an alternative sentence. This "new form of probation," dubbed the "Moses Project," involves Sam being attached to an electric device: The judge decrees, "You can go to work but you cannot go anywhere else. You will be monitored constantly" (55). Subsequently, "a couple of young white guys . . . fitted [Sam] with a small transmitter, placed on his leg just above his ankle. They told him that it was impossible to remove it, that he would be wearing it day and night, even when he took a shower, for the next six months, and that the transmitter sent out inaudible bleeps every thirty seconds" (55). But given his acumen for repairing things, Sam recalls the protagonist's "thinker-tinker" reference in *Invisible Man*, as well as the jive-talking but indefatigably resourceful trickster Petie Wheatstraw of the same novel. Intoning "White man invent. Black man circumvent" as his motto, Sam guarantees he will "outwit the transmitter and the monitor and the whole damn Moses Project" (60). After three hours, he finally detaches the electronic shackle and calls his employer, who sends "Joe" to bring Sam to work; Sam defiantly and victoriously "went outside and stood in the driveway of his suburban one-story two-car garage ranch type house waiting for Joe, thinking screw you, Moses" (61).

Her futuristic vision reminiscent of that of George Orwell, Petry, like the story's protagonist, foresaw so many of the concerns with which we wrestle in our technically profligate twenty-first century. Looking back to the harrowing vision of technology run amok portrayed by fellow New Englander George Schuyler in *Black No More* (1932), where blacks voluntarily subject themselves to convulsive shocks administered by an electric-chair-like contraption that will racially alchemize and *Nordicize*, and foreshadowing our contemporary cultural moment in which government agencies can eavesdrop and spy on Americans in the name of some procrustean "war on terror," Petry was especially prescient in dramatizing the implications of these "advances" for African Americans. That this regulatory enterprise is christened the "Moses Project" gives it an especially ominous tincture, as if the policing of black bodies is ordained and to be governed by the strictest, most draconian social laws. Even more ill-boding is that this state-sponsored detention and surveillance take place in the black man's putatively "safe space," his own home. The conflation of home and prison is evinced in Houston Baker's reflections on the *panopticon*, about which Foucault theorized in *Discipline and Punish*. Baker expatiates upon Foucault's contention that prisons are geometrically designed to permit untrammeled observation, which in turn engenders self-regulation: "Individuals incarcerated in the panopticon are inserted in a fixed place where their slightest movements are supervised and all events recorded. . . . Shackled in the panopticon, individuals are constantly located, examined, distributed among living beings, the sick and the dead" (Baker 97). Images of the warehousing of black bodies via the Prison Industrial Complex come to mind—what some have perhaps exaggeratedly deemed an updated version of the plantation. Still, that white males *oversee* the Moses Project and employ a prime implement of enslavement gives the story both a historical and contemporary pertinence.

Thus, we come full circle. Recall this book's first chapter, where I discussed Petry's profound, heartfelt veneration of her male and female ancestors—figures such as Willis Samuel James, her grandfather who was a runaway slave, and her great-aunt Hal, who sold roots and herbs. While a Sam Cooper most explicitly evokes memories of her unruly and irrepressible grandfather, the writer herself emerges as a neo–conjure woman who audaciously and innovatively subverted the male-dominated literary establishment, an establishment that attempted to shackle her to the dwarfing milieu of black protest. Whether it was cunningly crafting ghost stories that comically but earnestly condemned "race science," or a deceptively "pulp"-inflected novel that turned the racial tables by "pathologizing whiteness," Petry refused to hew to any literary or racial line. While a tribute written immediately after her death would avow that she "had little tolerance for fools or academics, two categories she regarded as essentially synonymous" (Streitfeld C6), it is my utmost hope that this study, along with her daughter Elisabeth's publication of biographical tomes both historicizing the James/Lane families and reflecting upon her personal relationship with Ann Lane Petry, will inaugurate a critical reassessing and reengaging of a writer whose imagination remained unbounded.

Notes

Introduction

1. I'm alluding here, of course, to Howe's controversial 1963 essay "Black Boys and Native Sons" (*Dissent* magazine), in which he chided "young Turks" Baldwin and Ellison for failing to match the same degree of righteous racial anger that pulsates through the fiction of the man he considered their literary father, Wright. In effect, Howe called out the younger writers for apparently eschewing the genre of protest, which he seemed to think should have been theirs by racial-artistic birthright; in effect, he scolds them for not being angrier-than-thou. Howe found their insufficiently bellicose artistic endeavors an affront to Wright and the price he paid so that they might pursue their art-for-art's-sake agenda.

2. For a discussion of the voice-performance-race nexus in Petry's works, see the following: Lindon Barrett's *Blackness and Value: Seeing Double* (Cambridge: Cambridge University Press, 1999), which focuses on *The Street* and *The Narrows;* Gayl Jones's "Jazz/Blues Structure in Ann Petry's 'Solo on the Drums'" in her study *Liberating Voices: Oral Tradition in African American Literature*, 90–98 (Cambridge, MA: Harvard University Press, 1991); and Johanna X. K. Garvey's "That Old Black Magic? Gender and Music in Ann Petry's Fiction" in *Black Orpheus: Music in African American Fiction from the Harlem Renaissance to Toni Morrison*, ed. Saadi A. Simawe, 119–51 (New York: Garland, 2000).

Chapter One

1. One recent exception to this critical pattern is Melina Vizcaino-Aleman's essay "Counter-Modernity, Black Masculinity, and Female Silence in Ann Petry's Fiction" in *Revising the Blueprint: Ann Petry and the Literary Left*, ed. Alex Lubin, 120–36.

2. For theoretical discussions of the hypervirility and braggadocio exalted in masculinist boast/toasts in African American vernacular traditions, see Gates's treatment of H. Rap Brown in the chapter "The Signifying Monkey and the Language of Signifyin(g): Rhetorical Differences and the Orders of Meaning," in *The Signifying Monkey*, 72–75, and James W. Coleman's introduction to *Black Male Fiction and the Legacy of Caliban*, where he outlines what he labels "Calibanic phallicism" (6), a discursive trope black male writers consciously and unconsciously employ in response to black men's presumed sexual licentiousness and brutishness in the American cultural imaginary. Both scholars deconstruct how black male figures from folkloric and literary traditions recoup the myth

of the sexually bestial black male and redeploy it in verbal narratives of unencumbered sexual dominance/authority to signify on or to subvert their perceived emasculation and agencylessness.

3. Discussions of several of these folk/historical figures can be found in the following: Cecil Brown, *Stagolee Shot Billy* (Cambridge, MA: Harvard University Press, 2003); *The Book of Negro Folklore,* ed. Langston Hughes and Arna Bontemps (New York: Dodd, Mead, 1958); Zora Neale Hurston, *Mules and Men* (1935; Bloomington: Indiana University Press, 1978); and Lawrence Levine, *Black Culture and Black Consciousness: Afro-American Folk Thought from Slavery to Freedom* (Oxford: Oxford University Press, 1977). For discussion of literary iterations of the baad nigger archetype, see John Roberts, *From Trickster to Badman: The Black Folk Hero in Slavery and Freedom* (Philadelphia: University of Pennsylvania Press, 1989).

4. I borrow the phrase "moderated masculinity" from critic/gender theorist Marlon Ross's *Manning the Race: Reforming Black Men in the Jim Crow Era.*

5. See my essay "'From a Thousand Points of View': The Multiple Masculinities of 'Miss Muriel'" in *Ann Petry's Short Fiction: Critical Essays,* ed. Hazel Arnett Ervin and Hilary Holladay, 76–96.

6. I take the phrase "walking palimpsest" from literary/gender theorist Maurice Wallace, who uses it in his study *Constructing the Black Masculine.* However, I alter the term slightly: whereas Wallace uses it as a pejorative to describe how "the West has created out of the black male body a walking palimpsest of the fears and fascinations possessing our cultural imagination" (2), I invoke the phrase to underscore how Petry's father shatters anachronistic notions of "true manhood" by troubling binaristic gender constructs.

7. Robert Hemenway's "Gothic Sociology: Charles Chesnutt and the Gothic Mode" is one of the few studies that identify and investigate the gothic undercurrents of Chesnutt's fiction.

Chapter Two

1. With Petry yet to be the subject of a scholarly biography, recent publications have provided a more extensive look at her personal life and history. At the vanguard in retrieving her from the literary margins is her and George Petry's only child, Elisabeth, who co-edited (with Farah Jasmine Griffin) and compiled *Can Anything Beat White? A Black Family's Letters* (2005) and authored the memoir *At Home Inside: A Daughter's Tribute to Ann Petry* (2008; both published by University Press of Mississippi). For pertinent biographical information, see Hilary Holladay's *Ann Petry* and Petry's autobiographical essay "Ann Petry" (*Contemporary Authors*).

2. The 2007 film revolved around the premise that hordes of black gay men are stealthily and diabolically on the "Down Low," a colloquialism popularized by J. L. King in *On the Down Low: A Journey into the Lives of "Straight" Black Men Who Sleep with Men* (with Karen Hunter; New York: Broadway, 2004). In the film the black male protagonist, a

psychologist, is part of a clandestine group of married men who sleep with each other, unrepentantly cheating on "innocent," unsuspecting wives. The film's thesis, such as it is, makes it clear that these "DL" brothers, arranging trysts through cryptic, fraternity-like codes (at one point in the most stereotypically gay-identified environment, the restroom), are disease-spreading scourges to the black community (one DL character goes as far as to characterize himself as a "monster"). For more thoughtful forays into the facilely reductive conceptualization of black men as alternatively victimized/victimizing, see "The Black Man Is in Terrible Trouble: Whose Problem Is That?" *New York Times Magazine*, December 4, 1994; and "Being a Black Man," a series that appeared in the *Washington Post* from June 2 to December 31, 2006.

3. I'm thinking here of Schuyler's masterful 1932 novel *Black No More*, where almost nearly every black person checks into a national chain of sanatoriums to undergo a torturous "black no more" complexion-lightening treatment that Anglicizes them. Her pulse on so many racially tender issues, Hansberry in *A Raisin in the Sun* (1959) touches upon many blacks' self-loathing "lookism" that classifies their hair as "good" or "bad"; the African character Joseph Asagai berates the young Beneatha for straightening—in his words, "mutilating"—her hair. Spike Lee's 1988 *School Daze* audaciously confronted blacks' self-abnegating but hard-to-dislodge beliefs about white skin as "right" and straightened/straighter hair as "good."

4. Sybil Weir likewise observes how different characters offer a countervision to Abbie's Brahmin-informed class and racial viewpoints: "One of Petry's techniques in *The Narrows*, then, is to provide an Afro-American response to Abbie's New England Way" (86).

5. In *American Patriots: The Story of Blacks in the Military from the Revolution to Desert Storm*, Gail Buckley describes the heroism of Miller, "a messman on the burning deck of the U.S.S. *West Virginia*" at Pearl Harbor on December 7, 1941: "Miller, the shy twenty-two-year-old son of a Texas sharecropper, carried the ship's mortally wounded captain to safety, then manned an antiaircraft gun to bring down what witnesses said were four Japanese planes (officials listed two). Miller had never been taught to fire the antiaircraft gun; it was against Navy regulations for blacks to do so" (275). Buckley then comments on the too-familiar response to Miller's valiant acts, which weren't recognized until three months later: "The first Navy dispatches from Pearl Harbor described him as an 'unidentified Negro messman.' Apparently embarrassed that the first hero of the war was black, the Navy found a white hero in Captain Colin Kelly, killed on December 9 in a crash-dive onto the Japanese battleship he had just bombed. . . . In May, after considerable pressure from civil rights organizations, [Miller] became (to the disapproval of Secretary Knox) the first black to win the Navy Cross" (275). Given Petry's long-standing commitment to filling the lacunae in an American history that too often expunges African Americans' contributions (she has authored books and articles on a range of icons—Harriett Tubman, Venture Smith, Tituba, and John Henry), I would conjecture that she was well aware of (Dorie) Miller's fate and was paying homage to him in naming the Major "Dory."

6. Despite Petry's description of the relationship as less than convivial, she nevertheless credits "Miss Avery" with kindling her interest in writing. Having been assigned to write an "imaginary scene" from *A Tale of Two Cities*, Petry "listened in horror" as the teacher read hers to the class: "I thought she was going to say: 'This is an example of what you should never, ever do!' But instead she said that I had written it; and she said, 'You know, I honestly believe that if you wanted to, you could become a writer'" (Wilson 73–74). In the early autobiographical short story "Doby's Gone," Petry portrays her own childhood encounters with racial hostility at school. Her fictive surrogate is Sue Johnson, whose family moves to an all-white Connecticut hamlet not unlike Petry's native Old Saybrook. As the only black child in her first-grade class, she undergoes a racial initiation that includes the de rigueur taunts—"'How do you comb that kind of hair?' 'Does that black color wash off?'" (303). When the verbal jabs turn physical, Sue "started hitting out with her fists. Kicking. Pulling hair. Tearing at clothing." Her physical resistance is rewarded when two of the white children befriend her, making her imaginary friend "Doby" dispensable. Though a relatively ordinary *Bildung* vis-à-vis the more nuanced "Miss Muriel," the story is also noteworthy for its portrayal of a warm relationship between Sue and her white teacher, Miss Whittier.

7. Commenting on the potential damage incurred from a failed mother-son relationship, theological counselor Fred Gustafson adduces: "I am convinced that much of the violence done by men toward women occurs because the women in their lives unknowingly failed to be nourishing, and instead aroused in the male's unconscious the negative" (167). Lest he be accused of scapegoating mothers for sons' shortcomings, Gustafson also expatiates upon the aborted father-son relationship, especially germane in light of the deleterious effect that Hod has on Link's psychosexual development: "When the father-son bond is not intact in a way that nourishes the son's growth, and when the father does not act as a vehicle for transmitting some of the masculine mysteries to the son, that child will grow up with a limited and crippling sense of his masculinity" (168).

8. I credit Petry scholar Hilary Holladay for pointing out the euphonic link between Hod and "hard," with its attendant corporeal and sexual connotations.

9. Michael Barry makes a persuasive case regarding Link's chauvinistic attitudes, which may be attributable to Hod's own pernicious enactment of patriarchal, phallocentric praxes. See "'Same Train Be Back Tomorrer': Ann Petry's *The Narrows* and the Repetition of History," especially 148–49. In *Ann Petry* Holladay makes a similar point regarding how Link copes with chronic racial and gendered apprehensions: "Never quite sure who he is supposed to be in regard to others, he strikes a cocky, aggressive pose to hide his self-doubts" (80).

10. Not to be overlooked here is Mamie's real-life counterpart, the blues singer from the 1920s of the same name. For a fuller discussion of the actual Mamie Smith's importance as "one of the early 'blues queens'" (139) and the fictional Mamie's transgressive role in challenging the community's class and sexual strictures, see Johanna Garvey's "'That

Old Black Magic'? Gender and Music in Ann Petry's Fiction." In "Women on the Go: Blues, Conjure, and Other Alternatives to Domesticity in Ann Petry's *The Street* and *The Narrows*" Kimberly Drake elaborates upon Mamie's role in troubling an amalgam of oppositions: "Through her blues praxis, Mamie breaks boundaries between home and street, between 'housewife' and 'streetwalker'; she also breaks down the moral and ideological boundaries in other people, luring them into her world of sensuality and pleasure" (81). For a scholarly treatment of dandyism from a racial, historical, and multi-genre perspective, see Monica L. Miller's original and groundbreaking *Slaves to Fashion: Black Dandyism and the Styling of Black Diasporic Identity* (Durham, NC: Duke University Press, 2009).

11. Drake makes a similar case, astutely addressing Powther's self-serving attraction to Mamie, as well as her function in relation to her husband's psychically impaired sexual/gender identity: "Powther's emasculation by Mamie in matters of home and family upsets him (and no doubt many readers as well), but his experiences of 'femininity' during sex with Mamie give him a life-sustaining pleasure that tends to affirm Mamie's disruption and revision of domestic ideology and gender identity" (87).

12. Powther's invocation of the English butler (163) takes on particular import in light of his nefarious actions. Cultural theorist Homi Bhabha's trenchant discussion of the genealogical/historical significance of the British butler as the sentient emblem of good breeding and servitude is particularly compelling in light of Powther's relationship with the Treadways. Bhabha melds issues of masculinity, class, and nationhood in his reading of the British butler's tropic function in the novel *The Remains of the Day:* "Is it possible to read Kazuo Ishiguro's *The Remains of the Day*, centered on the very British bathos of the butler Stevens, a 'gentleman's gentleman,' as a parable of the masculinist ritual of 'service' to the nation, with the domestic sphere as a substitute for the public sphere? In the British context, 'service' has a double cultural genealogy. It represents an implication in the class structure where domestic service normalizes class difference by extravagantly 'acting it out' as an affiliative practice, perfectly exemplified in the metonymic mimicry of the idiomatic naming of the butler as a 'gentleman's gentleman': 'A butler's duty is to provide good service,' Stevens meditates, 'by concentrating on what *is* within our realm . . . by devoting our attention to providing the best possible service to those great gentleman in whose hands the destiny of civilization truly lies'" (61–62; author's emphasis). I would extrapolate from Bhabha's reading that Powther's function is manifold: He too "normalizes" African Americans' hierarchically lower place on the race/class totem, where black mammies/butlers/retainers similarly "affiliate" with their white employers and imbibe their values, no matter how antiblack, and thereby self defeating those values. Moreover, as an unwitting cog in a plot that reenacts our nation's cancerous extermination of black—particularly male—bodies, Powther in effect metaphorically and actually functions as the "powder" that fuels the "Treadway Gun People['s]" (9) diabolical hunting and executing of Link.

13. As J. C., Powther and Mamie's youngest child, begs his mother for the "pretty-

pretty"—the cigarette case the child has taken from Link's room that leads Powther to falsely conclude that Link and Mamie are sleeping together—she "laughed because he looked just like Bill when Bill was being pure nigger" (292).

14. Margaret McDowell also sees a connection between mother and (adopted) son with respect to their incorrigible sense of racial inferiority: "In her emphasis on the relationship of past and present in her penetration into the depths of consciousness, Petry emphasizes the sense of inferiority which hangs over certain Blacks and makes them experience a general and irrational guilt for something that they cannot define. Because of the denigration that Blacks have suffered over the generations, both Abbie and Link are plagued at times by a feeling that Blacks perhaps deserve, in part, this denigration" (137).

Chapter Three

1. Petry's "New England's John Henry," published in the venerable *Negro Digest* in 1945, is an early indicator of what will become her abiding interest in African American history, reflected in works on such figures as Tituba, the Bajan woman enslaved in Salem and tried as a witch, and Harriet Tubman of "Underground Railroad" fame. This essay is a paean to the enslaved African Venture Smith, who was brought to Connecticut and, through his physical and intellectual fortitude, secured not only his own freedom but that of his entire family and some fellow slaves.

2. A subsequent episode to Johnson's imagined battering of Mrs. Scott involves yet another white woman, not only dramatizing the depth of Johnson's repressed racial rage but also foreshadowing the brutal beating of his wife Mae: his inability to contextualize the racial offenses that take a steep physical and psychological toll. When he finally gets to the front of a long line of customers waiting to be served coffee after work, "the white girl looked past him, put her hands up to her head and gently lifted her hair away from the back of her neck, tossing her head back a little. 'No more coffee for a while,' she said." This event stokes the same seething rage that accompanied the demeaning encounter with Mrs. Scott, as Johnson desires to "hit her [the coffee server] so hard that the scarlet lipstick on her mouth would smear and spread over her nose, her chin, out toward her cheeks, so hard that she would never toss her head again and refuse a man a cup of coffee because he was black" (207). Petry skillfully captures what I call Johnson's *race neurosis*, his propensity to reduce every encounter to a racial zero-sum death match in which he is the inevitable loser. The conclusion of this episode emblematizes this point: having him irately depart the restaurant without looking back, Petry writes: "If he had [looked back] he would have seen the flickering blue flame under the shiny coffee urn being extinguished"; the woman then proceeds to make more coffee.

3. Eva Tettenborn also emphasizes the markedly gendered nature of the violence Johnson displaces onto Mae: "Since the barrier of race is removed at home, this time

Johnson's body and mind truly reenact the original event [Mrs. Scott's racial insult] without holding back. Johnson's racial anger and fury become fully gendered" (160).

4. Critics over the last twenty or so years have argued that sexually veiled texts such as Johnson's *The Autobiography of an Ex-Colored Man* are as much about sexual(ity) passing as they are about troubling the color line, the more fraught and titillating subject in the period in which they were published. Representative examinations include Siobhan B. Somerville's *Queering the Color Line: Race and the Invention of Homosexuality in American Culture* (Durham, NC: Duke University Press, 2000), especially chap. 4, "Double Lives on the Color Line: 'Perverse' Desire in *The Autobiography of an Ex-Coloured Man*" (111–30); and Philip Brian Harper's *Are We Not Men?: Masculine Anxiety and the Problem of African-American Identity* (New York: Oxford University Press, 1996), especially "The Feminine Function of the Ex-Colored Man" (108–13).

5. The specific works to which I allude here are as follows: Baldwin's *Go Tell It on the Mountain* (1953), *Another Country* (1962), and *If Beale Street Could Talk* (1974); Kennedy's *Funnyhouse of a Negro* (1964); Bambara's *The Salt Eaters* (1980); Fuller's *A Soldier's Play* (1981); and Kenan's *A Visitation of Spirits* (1989). Bambara's protagonist, Minnie Ransom, actually survives an attempted suicide.

6. In the *MELUS* interview Petry remarks briefly on the inspiration for Forbes: "Actually there *was* a man who did commit suicide, and my family did conjecture about it—about what happened, what caused it" (Wilson 76).

7. Though "Has Anybody Seen Miss Dora Dean?" has received little scholarly attention, a few critics have pondered the historical significance of "The Creole Show" and Petry's allusion to it. Gladys Washington notes that the story "takes its title from a song in an all-black minstrel show of the late 1800s called 'The Creole Show,' which is credited with having revived the dance called the cakewalk" (25). Barbara Lewis draws more extensive connections between two late-nineteenth century acts: the minstrel team of Williams and Walker and the husband-and-wife cakewalk dancing tandem of Charles Johnson and Dora Dean from the actual "Creole Show." Lewis goes as far as comparing the physical proximity between the older, more physically ample Sarah Forbes and one of the minstrel performers: "George Walker, the dandy half of the cakewalking blackface-comedy team of Williams and Walker, was famous for 'throwing his chest and buttocks out in opposite directions, until he resembled a pouter pigeon more than a human being' (Emery 212). It was as though Sarah's posture, in later years, had settled into the alignment of her finest hour" (126). While Forbes may have been attracted to the younger Sarah, who in actuality was based on the beautiful real-life Dora Dean, the older, more masculinized version of Sarah also lends credence to my reading of Forbes's possibly repressed homosexuality.

8. Those most rabid in their condemnations of homosexuality often summon biblically charged terminology—"wicked," "abomination," "unnatural" being among the preferred epithets flung at sexual minorities. Using a purposefully provocative (and offensive) song by the less popular members of the prominent gospel-singing Winans

clan, literary critic Sheila Smith McKoy characterizes the mainstream African American church's chronic hostility toward its gay and lesbian brethren and sistren: "The controversial release of the gospel duo Angie and Debbie Winans' 'Not Natural' is only one of many titles we might add to this list of songs with anti-gay lyrics. . . . The sentiments the Winans express in 'Not Natural' represent the black church's public view of homosexuality although, within the private histories of most black churches, black lesbians and gay men have been continually and typically present" (17).

9. Barbara Lewis in fact offers a more racial-historical interpretation of the story. Connecting Forbes's lifelong servitude to post-Reconstruction African Americans' dashed hopes for autonomy and integration, she asserts that "Mrs. Wingate symbolizes the subservient [i.e., southern] past from which John Forbes attempted to escape, without total success" (135). I would take slight issue with this reading: though the Wingates are clearly northern replicas of aristocratic, plantation/slaveholding southerners, I would argue that Forbes did little to "escape"; on the contrary, it was his very *freedom*—in effect, his manumission—brought about by Mrs. Wingate's death that re-ignited the masculine panic that compels his suicide.

10. Brief portions of this section appeared in an essay published in Ervin and Holladay's collection *Ann Petry's Short Fiction: Critical Essays*, "'From a Thousand Different Points of View': The Multiple Masculinities of Ann Petry's 'Miss Muriel'" (79–96).

11. Several critics in the last decade or so have scrutinized the tortured gender politics underwriting parochial notions of *authentic* black manhood in the volcanic 1960s; especially perceptive is Marlon Ross's 1994 essay "Some Glances at the Black Fag: Race, Same-Sex Desire, and Cultural Belonging."

12. In the *MELUS* interview with Mark Wilson, Petry discusses in some detail how specific episodes from her childhood and adolescence provided the basis for theme and characterization in the story—for instance, she talks about how the drugstore, though spatially abutting the family living quarters, "was the public space in our lives. My parents never let it intrude on their private lives" (77). She further recalls that her father, like Samuel, "sang in the church choir" and that there was in fact "a Mr. Bemish"; in answer to the interviewer's asking whether "he was in fact run out of town?" Petry coyly replies, "Well, let's say he left (laughs)."

13. Hilary Holladay befittingly proffers connotative meanings of the male suitors' names: She notes the "squeamish" feeling Bemish's glass eye evokes in the narrator, and this encounter "set[s] the stage for an unsettling portrait of a distinctly undignified old white man"; she observes that the name Chink sounds "hard and tough" compared to the "soft, yielding sound of 'Bemish'" and that as an ethnic slur, Chink is "considered an outsider among fellow blacks"; and she construes Dottle's name as "ambiguous" and "plump sounding," thereby "open to interpretation, as are his swaying walk and theatrical mannerisms" (95). About the latter I would add its proximity to "waddle," which dovetails with the young narrator's observation of "his very fat bottom" that sashays "from side to side as he walks"—hence Dottle exemplifying a pansified, diluted masculinity.

14. In the *Encyclopedia of Homosexuality*, Wayne Dynes provides sexual-historical context for the centuries-old homosexuality–lavender/purple connection: "According to the poet Martial, several colors were associated with effeminate homosexuality in imperial Rome. He limns an exquisite 'who thinks that men in scarlet are not men at all, and styles violet mantles the vestures of women'" (249). Further, Dynes notes: "In American culture the word lavender—a blend of red and blue (as in 'lavender lover,' *The Lavender Lexicon*, etc.)—almost speaks for itself. Gershon Legman (in his 1941 glossary published as an appendix to George Henry's *Sexual Variants*) claimed to relay popular lore when he wrote of seven stages of homosexuality, 'from *ga-ga* to the "deeper tones" of lavender.' This shade has a secondary association with scented powder and aromatic flowers, producing an unconscious synaesthetic effect" (250).

15. In making this point, Ross in *Manning the Race* credits what he calls Wayne Koestenbaum's "compelling" theorizing of the "queer voice" in Koestenbaum's *The Queen's Throat: Opera, Homosexuality, and the Mystery of Desire* (New York: Poseidon, 1993).

16. In an interview Petry elaborates on her inspiration for both characters: "In 'Miss Muriel,' there was only one person who had a real existence as far as—no, two people: one was my uncle (I think I refer to him as 'Uncle Johno') and the other one is the man who arrives every summer as a guest of Uncle Johno. Now the man who arrived every summer really existed. He had been a teacher of English. He had been an actor" (Mrtek 78). Again, I reiterate that she doesn't comment on or even speculate about the men's sexual orientation. Even more intriguing is Petry's selection of the name "Johno Ecckles." Ironically and appropriately enough, John Eccles was a married gay man and activist in the late 1950s/early1960s on the west coast. His papers and other materials (pamphlets, poems) are housed in the special collections section of the University of Washington library in Seattle. "The Lesbian, Gay, Bisexual, and Transgender Religious Archives Network" Web site provides a brief bio-sketch: "John Eccles was a gay man whose missionary parents lived in Buckley, Washington. He tried unsuccessfully to establish a chapter of the Mattachine Society [one of the first gay rights organizations] in Washington State in 1959–1960. Eccles subsequently moved to Los Angeles. He was active in the Los Angeles Mattachine Society in the 1960s but resigned as Vice President in 1963 [the year "Miss Muriel" was published] following a dispute" (www.lgbtran.org). I have no tangible evidence that Petry knew of John Eccles and his significance in LGBT history. Nevertheless, despite the slight difference in how she spells his surname, the fact that her character, like the activist Eccles, was a married gay man opens the door for speculation that Petry may have at some point run across the name and remembered it as she imagined a character negotiating his stigmatized sexuality and the austere social mores that rendered it such.

17. The following films/television programs have trafficked in some of the most notoriously stereotypical representations of hyper-effeminate black gay men: *Carwash* (1976); *Mannequin* (1987) and *Mannequin: On the Move* (1991); and *In Living Color* (1990–94). For critical interrogations of these and other gay (mis)representation, see E. Patrick John-

son's chapter "Manifest Faggotry: Queering Masculinity in African American Culture" (48–75) in his study *Appropriating Blackness.*

18. Discussing the meta-narratological significance of the "Miss Muriel" folk story, Paul Wiebe insightfully remarks that it "becomes the site of a struggle over discourse, the struggle of deciding how a term should be coded or recoded and deciding who has the authority to use the term" (62). Wiebe further comments on what he calls Chink's "counternarrative," his revision of the racially and masculinely disempowering version of the "Miss Muriel" story the narrator has absorbed from Dottle: "He [Chink] protects himself from the primary racist narrative by taking the offensive and writing his own narrative about how things should be" (70).

19. In her seminal reading of cloaked lesbian desire in the introduction to Larsen's *Passing,* the eminent black feminist literature/theory critic Deborah McDowell makes a comparable argument regarding Irene's projection of her own repressed desire for Clare onto the object of her desire: "Because Clare is a reminder of that repressed and disowned part of Irene's self, Clare must be banished, for, more unacceptable than the feelings themselves is the fact that they find an object of expression in Clare. In other words, Clare is both the embodiment and the object of the sexual feelings that Irene banishes" (xxix). Of course the comparison isn't exact; there's little evidence in "Miss Muriel" to suggest that Dottle desires Mr. Bemish. Moreover, McDowell makes a convincing case that Irene in fact does push Clare out the window—contrary to Irene's declarations that Clare jumped—by considering the homoerotic symbolism of an act that immediately precedes the push: "To suggest the extent to which Clare's death represents the death of Irene's sexual feelings for Clare, Larsen uses a clever objective correlative: Irene's pattern of lighting cigarettes and snuffing them out. Minutes before Clare falls from the window to her death, 'Irene finished her cigarette and threw it out, watching the tiny spark drop slowly to the white ground below.' Clearly attempting a symbolic parallel, Clare is described as 'a vital glowing thing, like a flame of red and gold' who falls from (or is thrown out of) the window as well" (xxix). By way of analogy, Dottle's puffing on the more symbolically phallic and "masculinely correct" *cigar* as he extols Chink's sexual prowess achieves the same homoerotic effect.

Chapter Four

1. By no means do I intend to suggest that the gothic dimensions of many African American works have gone unnoticed and unexamined. Early seminal articles by Wright scholar Michel Fabre—"Black Cat and White Cat: Richard Wright's Debt to Edgar Allan Poe," *Poe Studies* 4 (1971): 17–19—and Robert Hemenway—"Gothic Sociology: Charles Chesnutt and the Gothic Mode," *Studies in the Literary Imagination* 7 (1974): 101–19—opened a critical space for illuminating critical studies by Goddu and Justin Edwards, both of whom theorize black literature's gothic resonances. Fabre and Hemenway's pioneering

essays directed our critical gaze to how works such as *The Conjure Woman*, *Black Boy*, *Native Son*, and *Invisible Man* abound with gothic underpinnings: the psychoracial function of conjure as an inherently black gothicized response to egregious racial crimes and black disempowerment; the psychosexual and racial dimensions of misogynistic violence perpetuated by Bigger Thomas and the socio-pathological behavior of young Dick Wright (see young Wright's "lynching" of a cat, which Fabre directly correlates to Poe's "The Black Cat"); and recent critics such as Mary Sisney would expound upon Ellison's gothic-tinged descriptions of Invisible Man's encounters with whites who, in a canny reversal, came to embody the very essence of dread and death that had heretofore been assumed to be inherently black (e.g., Invisible Man's description of Mr. Norton as a "formless white death"). Expanding the terrain of black gothic studies, some critics have combined African American and Anglo-American gothic traditions, examined crosscurrents between black men's and women's gothic writings, and explored recent authors' forays into the literature of terror: see Sisney, "The Power and the Horror: Wright and Ellison Respond to Poe," *CLA Journal* 29, no. 1 (1985): 82–90; Keith Sandiford, "Gothic and Intertextual Constructions in *Linden Hills*" in *Gloria Naylor: Critical Perspectives Past and Present*, ed. Henry Louis Gates, Jr., and K. A. Appiah, 195–214 (New York: Amistad, 1993); Wesley Britton, "The Puritan Past and Black Gothic: The Haunting of Toni Morrison's *Beloved* in Light of Hawthorne's *The House of Seven Gables*," *Nathaniel Hawthorne Review* 21, no. 2 (Fall 1995): 7–23; Ellen J. Goldner, "Othere(ed) Ghosts: Gothicism and the Bonds of Reason in Melville, Chesnutt, and Morrison," *MELUS* 24, no. 1 (Spring 1999): 59-83; and Cedric Gael Bryant, "'The Soul Has Bandaged Moments': Reading the Gothic in Wright's 'Big Boy Leaves Home,' Morrison's *Beloved*, and Gomez's *Gilda*," *African American Review* 39, no. 4 (2005): 541–53.

2. Evie Shockley considers how Petry's interest in authors such as Wilkie Collins preceded the writing of *The Street* and thereby provides a window into what Shockley calls "Petry's recourse to the gothic" (440).

3. I credit one of *The Street*'s early commentators, Ben Burns, for discerning the gothic cadences of the novel. Writing in the historically black newspaper the *Chicago Defender*, he compared the novel in "mood and tempo" to Edgar Allan Poe's "The Pit and the Pendulum" (Ervin, *Ann Petry* 22). I would also pinpoint Petry's frequently expressed interest in the otherworldly to uncover the origins of her texts' gothic qualities. She has frequently and fondly recalled the presence of conjure in her family history: "My father told us many wonderful stories about his family: his great-great-aunt was a conjure woman who sold roots and herbs in Hartford" (Petry, "Ann Petry" 259); at another time, she forthrightly avowed, "I have had relatives with conjuring powers" ("An Interview with Ann Petry" 100). In another interview, she revealed that she abandoned one book project "because I became interested in—actually fascinated by—a slave, Tituba, who was one of three women charged with witchcraft at the beginning of the trials for witchcraft in Salem, Massachusetts" (O'Brien 158); hence, her belief in conjure as a specifically female form of empowerment and agency resulted in a book for adolescents, *Tituba of Salem Vil-*

lage, which engages the tragedy of the diasporan "conjurer/witch" who was persecuted in Tituba and Petry's native New England.

4. Tracing the historical and cultural origins of evil, Annie S. Perkins offers an innovative reading of the novel: see "The Effects of Evil in Ann Petry's *The Street:* Invoking Biblical and Literary Tradition" in *The Critical Response to Ann Petry*, ed. Hazel Arnett Ervin, 333–41 (Westport, CT: Praeger, 2005).

5. Using the critical lens of fairy tale discourse, J. Lee Greene also notes how Lutie's own predatory nature coincides with that of the overtly bestial Jones: "And Lutie, like Little Red Riding Hood in some versions of the tale, is an unconscious contributor to her predicament. The beast in her is attracted (even if unconsciously) to the bestial nature of some of the wolves [Junto, Mrs. Hedges, Boots Smith, and Jones] she encounters" (196).

6. For discussions of how economics, race, gender, and spatiality intertwine, see William Scott, "Material Resistance and Agency of the Body in Ann Petry's *The Street*"; the subsection "Holes and Walls" (93–101) focuses exclusively on space and physical edifices. In "The Opacity of Everyday Life: Segregation and the Iconicity of Uplift in *The Street*," Meg Wesling explores what she calls the novel's "preoccupation: African American women attempting to circulate through public space always find their mobility compromised" (120).

7. Andrews similarly concludes that Lutie problematically adopts a belief system inimical to black subjectivity in a racially hostile America: "What counts is what other resources one has with which to act on these perceptions—folk wisdom, flight, conjuring, communal support. Tragically, Lutie relies instead on rationalism, individualism, and the American myth of success until at the end violence explodes from her uncontrollably" (201).

8. Several critics have commented on the intertextual salience of Benjamin Franklin's life in both thematization and characterization in *The Street.* Representative studies include Marjorie Pryse's insightful essay "'Pattern against the Sky': Deism and Motherhood in Ann Petry's *The Street*" in *Conjuring: Black Women, Fiction, and Literary Tradition*, ed. Marjorie Pryse and Hortense J. Spillers, 116–31 (Bloomington: Indiana University Press, 1985); Gayle Wurst, "Ben Franklin in Harlem: The Drama of Deferral in Ann Petry's *The Street*" in *Deferring a Dream: Literary Sub-Versions of the American Columbiad*," ed. Gert Buelens and Ernst Rudin, 1–23 (Basel: Birkhauser, 1994); and Wesling, "The Opacity of Everyday Life."

9. Writing about Junto's sexual predation and attendant moral torpor as the byproduct of a physiological deformity, Greene adduces, "The images of food and consumption Petry uses to portray Junto's desire for Lutie indicate that his congenital physical deformities reflect his innate moral aberrations" (196).

10. The infamous Tuskegee syphilis experiment—the "study" of untreated syphilis in African American men that occurred over several decades beginning in the early 1930s—has been widely examined since the 1990s; James H. Jones's *Bad Blood: The Tuskegee Syphilis Experiment* (New York: Free Press, 1993) is the foundational study of this ignominious episode in American medical-racial history. In this vein, Harriet A. Washington's *Medi-*

cal Apartheid (New York: Random House, 2006) also explores African Americans' abuse as medical guinea pigs over several decades, demonstrating that the ignoble Tuskegee episode is but one node on a cancerous body of American medical "research."

11. Informed by the theoretical treatments of the gaze by scholars such as Mary Anne Doane, Martin Jay, Laura Mulvey, and Griselda Pollock, Heather Hicks in "'This Strange Communion': Surveillance and Spectatorship in Ann Petry's *The Street*" offers a convincing reading of the link between "ocular acts" (23) and the intersectionality of the sexual gaze, the racial gaze, and forms of domination. Her analysis concentrates primarily on Jones and Mrs. Hedges; about the former she argues that it is "the Super's dogged pursuit of Lutie that becomes truly emblematic of a voyeuristic gaze" (24).

12. For extended discussion of what he calls the "extraordinary, nightmarish character of most of the sensory detail" (198), see Andrews's "The Sensory Assault of the City."

13. Jones's maniacal actions might also be read as another instance in which he, like Mrs. Hedges, exhibits behaviors that connect him to ostensibly victimized and innocent Lutie. Though he focuses exclusively on commodity fetishism, Bill V. Mullen in "Object Lessons: Fetishization and Class Consciousness in Ann Petry's *The Street*" in *Revising the Blueprint: Ann Petry and the Literary Left*, ed. Alex Lubin, 35–48, explores Lutie's materialist fascinations, thereby amplifying the notion that she and Jones may have more in common than she'd ever acknowledge.

14. Greene also speaks to Jones's sexual pathology: "Among those who desire Lutie sexually, Jones's desire is the most intense, the most sexually aberrant, the most psychologically and physically threatening, the most diabolical, and thus the most frightening to Lutie" (194).

Chapter Five

1. Amy Lee pays particular attention to the pivotal role Peabody's mother plays in Louella's posthumous elevation to family member status, since it was she who insisted that Louella be buried in Yew Tree Cemetery: "Mrs. Peabody's request suggests a new level of feminine consciousness during her time among some individuals, for her decision to treat her laundress as her equal challenges the issues of value and property in the public and political realms" (123).

2. Gates uses this phrase in describing an instance of "unmotivated signifying," which is how he describes the intertextual relationship between Alice Walker's *The Color Purple* and Zora Neale Hurston's *Their Eyes Were Watching God.* In Walker's reclaiming and celebrating of her literary foremother's novel, Gates argues that she appropriates and revises the themes and tropes of Hurston's classic novel, doing so with "an absence of negative critique" (xxvi).

3. For a different perspective on the function of laughter and comedy in the story, see Gene Fendt's "Apartheid among the Dead; Or, on Christian Laughter in Ann Petry's

'The Bones of Louella Brown.'" Fendt argues that "such erasures [of "forms of apartheid" separating the story's audience] have a lightness of touch that exhibit Petry as a masterful writer rather than a heavy-handed apologist or embittered racialist" (112). He also notes how the story effects a "purification through laughter" and a "catharsis" in the reader.

4. For a compelling and comprehensive history of towns that summarily purged blacks and/or denied them the right to reside within their boundaries, see sociologist James W. Loewen's *Sundown Towns: A Hidden Dimension of American Racism* (New York: W.W. Norton, 2005). According to Loewen, these towns existed fairly openly from the 1930s to the 1960s; further, surprisingly—or not—they were located mostly *outside* the South in places such as Hawthorne, California, which posted the following chilling forewarning: "Nigger, Don't Let The Sun Set on YOU in Hawthorne." Petry's own life was touched by the offense of what in contemporary parlance has been called "being while black": Hilary Holladay notes that one of the tales in the family's lore concerned a "great-uncle arrested for being in a Georgia town after sundown," and Petry's father, "who was threatened by a white man when he [her father] opened the drugstore [in Old Saybrook]" (9). Finally, Petry alludes to this disturbing historical legacy in another of her Wheeling stories, where Chink Johnson in "Miss Muriel" corroborates the very real existence of such uncongenial burgs. When the twelve-year-old narrator rather tartly asks the itinerant bluesman whether he's familiar with Atlanta, he doesn't miss a beat: "Yeah. 'Nigger, read this. Nigger, don't let sundown catch you here. Nigger, if you can't read this, run anyway. If you can't run—then vanish. Just vanish out.' I know the place. I came from there" (36).

5. Krüger-Kahloula references three sources in this quotation pertaining to the racialized politics of interment in early New England: "George Tolman, *John Jack, the Slave, and Daniel Bliss, the Tory* (Concord, Mass., c. 1902): 4"; "Lorenzo Johnston Greene, *The Negro in Colonial New England* (New York: 1942): 284"; and "*Inscriptions from the Burial Grounds in Worcester, Massachusetts, from 1727 to 1859* (Worcester, 1878), map of 1798" (Krüger-Kahloula 146).

6. This, of course, is the title of the controversial—radioactive, to many—1994 "study" by psychologist Richard Herrnstein and political scientist Charles Murray, who sum up what might be regarded as the book's thesis thusly: "It seems highly likely to us that both genes and the environment have something to do with racial differences" (311). This dubious "scholarship" demonstrates that there's an umbilical cord linking the more indecorously racist "science" of Gliddon and Nott et al. and twentieth-century researchers whose primary objective is to "prove" blacks' genetic difference, congenital shortcomings, and overall social depravity.

7. Eugenia DeLamotte speaks to the "fear" she delineates as the underlying apprehension on which nineteenth-century "Anglo-Gothic" literature was based, racelessness: "Behind the fears of dark, racialized others on which the Gothic construction of whiteness hinges is the unspeakable Other of that construction: the fear that there is no such thing as whiteness, or even race" (17).

8. Justin Edwards addresses the abiding concern of white "race men" such as novelist/social critic Thomas Dixon (especially in Dixon's 1902 white supremacist treatise *The Leopard's Spots*) and "race scientists" like Joseph Alexander Tillinghast, who addressed what he found to be unimpeachable racial differences and the perils of miscegenation in his 1902 essay "The Negro in Africa and America"; writes Edwards: "Here, Chesnutt [in his essay "The Future American: What the Race is Likely to Become in the Process of Time"] plays upon the amalgamation hysteria at the heart of Dixon's and Tillinghast's writings. For them, intermixture inspired fear because it not only threatened to corrupt Southern racial purity, but it had the potential to destabilize the Southern caste system and shed doubt on the legacy of a great Southern 'civilization'" (92).

9. See chap. 1, "Outraged Mother and Articulate Heroine: Linda Brent and the Slave Narrative Genre" (10–38), of Joanne Braxton's study *Black Women Writing Autobiography*. Here Braxton conceptualizes what she calls the "outraged mother archetype," where Brent/Jacobs and her grandmother, "Aunt Marthy," employ language—specifically "sass and invective"—as "a weapon, dueling with Dr. Flint, gaining psychological space and strength. The many references to 'sass' and 'impertinence' underscore the importance of its use in regaining self-esteem; they also suggest the feminine reflection of the trickster figure" (30).

10. Carol Henderson notes Petry's deliberate or coincidental invocation of Kafka in Woodruff's degrading self-perception: "Specifically, in this example, Woodruff's alien status animalizes him—makes him a freak reminiscent of Kafka's beetle-man in his haunting tale *The Metamorphosis*. Like Gregor, Woodruff searches for wholeness in an environment that has mongrelized him, encrusted him in flesh that is spiritually and culturally contaminated due to the way others view him" (145).

11. In a section entitled "Cannibal Gothic," H. L. Malchow expounds upon the "deep revulsion" of cannibalism in "European popular culture," despite the prevalence of man-eating figures in that culture's folklore; he cites Sweeney Todd, the "demon barber of Fleet Street" in nineteenth-century London (45). He notes a tangible *reversal* with respect to this character's origin: "If the late-nineteenth-century Sweeney is more sharply delineated as ethnic Other than earlier, this was by then an ethnicity that was not merely the result of custom and upbringing, but of inherent, 'racial' difference" (48). In effect the barbaric act of cannibalism became yet another signifier of inherently racial—read dark-skinned—savagery. Hence, Malchow concludes, "White cannibalism came to be read as racial primitivism, a blackness under the skin, until, at the end of the century, [Conrad's] Kurtz's savagery is merely a form of 'going native'" (48). I contend, then, that Petry recuperates the former notion of whites as potentially innately savage, as she employs lexical descriptors "darkness" and "black/ness" not to Africanize Rambler, but to *Anglicize* him, given the history of white cannibals in European folklore that Malchow delineates. Note her distinct Europeanizing of Rambler and his minions: their "great quilted dark jackets" had "been designed for European ski slopes" (217); "they could pass

for the seven dark bastard sons of some old and evil twelfth-century king" (218). And though Woodruff casts them as "black," he does so with a difference: "This was not the blackness of human flesh . . . it was the blackness and coldness of the hole from which D.H. Lawrence's snake emerged" (218).

12. Eva Tettenborn notes how America's acidic history of place, gender, and race percolates in Woodruff's consciousness once he begins processing Nellie's rape and his multiply irreconcilable roles—as victim of physical assault, as forced participant, and, ultimately, as terrified black man unwilling to risk being branded a rapist; thus, he chooses the expedient "safety" of silence over identifying the perpetrators of Nellie's violation: "Once Woodruff returns home from his ordeal, he faces the social implications of his witnessing. While he is at first determined to call the police, he neglects to do it. I want to suggest that Woodruff suddenly recalls, as it were, the communal trauma of African American men falsely accused of raping white women. Significantly, he has this kind of realization, a traumatic flashback to collective African American memory, in one of his rooms that 'had a southern exposure' (229). This southern perspective seems to allude to the fate of many black men from the South accused of rape and brought to 'justice' with a lynching" (Tettenborn 165). The glaring irony, of course, is that Woodruff ultimately chooses to return to Virginia, an *ur*-Confederate space and the scene of the very injustices he imagines await him in the quasi-southern North if he dares to "witness" for Nellie. Even more inconsonant, of course, is Woodruff's positioning himself into the historical narrative of what Tettenborn labels "the communal trauma of African American men falsely accused of raping white women"; I would counter that his accessing of this familiar script is willfully self-serving, given the chasm between his fastidious, assimilative mien and the rampaging black brute with whom he, at least in Tettenborn's reading, now claims an imaginative, historical kinship. I concur with Hilary Holladay's speculation that "it is possible that he would be believed—and that the minister, among others, would vouch for his honor" (110).

Chapter Six

1. Petry took umbrage with critics who mistakenly assumed her second novel could be ghettoized as yet another fictional treatise on/treatment of the "race problem." In his introduction to *Revising the Blueprint: Ann Petry and the Literary Left*, Alex Lubin quotes her corrective letter to Trinity College professor Kenneth Reeves, "who sought to include Petry's 'white life' novel *Country Place* in a list of novels about race" (Lubin, "Introduction" 9); Petry wrote, "The following novels by black authors do not deal with racism in the United States: Baldwin, James GIOVANNI'S ROOM, Motley, Willard, KNOCK ON ANY DOOR, Petry, Ann, COUNTRY PLACE, Yerby, Frank, THE VIXENS, FOXES OF HARROW, etc. Yerby is a black author who has written at least 20 novels—they have nothing to do with the ghetto or with the black experience. I am enclosing re-

views of 2 new books. Don't you think that Cleaver's POST-PRISON WRITINGS AND SPEECHES sounds as though it would be more stimulating and thought-provoking than Yerby's JUDAS, MY BROTHER?" (9–10). Conspicuously absent from this list is Zora Neale Hurston's final novel, *Seraph on the Suwanee* (1948), which depicted the plight of a "white trash" heroine, Arvay Meserve. For a relatively recent and comprehensive examination of Petry within the context of other "raceless" novels of the period, see Emily Bernard's 2005 essay "'Raceless' Writing and Difference: Ann Petry's *Country Place* and the African-American Literary Canon," especially the section entitled "The Trials of Black Authorship," where Bernard examines what she calls the "tensions between the African-American writer and her audience"; here Bernard considers the travails of early black writers such as Phillis Wheatley and how twentieth-century authors/critics such as James Weldon Johnson, Langston Hughes, and W. E. B. DuBois have addressed this metadiscursive issue.

2. In "A Neglected Study in 'Whiteness'—Ann Petry's *Country Place*," Martin Japtok also takes issue with this faulty misclassification—the underlying assumption that whiteness fails to constitute a "race" in the African American author's literary imagination, given that the always-racially marked African American self should constitute the totality of her creative vision: "I suggest that rather than merely being a 'raceless' novel, Petry's *Country Place* actually focuses on 'race,' albeit 'whiteness'" (354).

3. Laura Dubek argues that *Country Place* "mocks the sentimentality of postwar white family narratives such as William Wyler's award-winning film *The Best Years of Our Lives* (1946), which dramatizes the difficult homecoming of three veterans. *Country Place* tells a similar story about white folks, but without the happily-ever-after ending." Dubek goes on to provide an informative historical, contextualizing discussion; see the section of her essay titled "The Best Years of 'Our' Lives: Marriage and Family in Postwar America."

4. John Charles makes a similar argument about the liberatory potential of centering whiteness/decentering blackness, though he presents an intriguing notion of "racial privacy" as part of his argument: "In *Country Place*, I argue that Petry's emphasis on white characters enacts a form of racial privacy for both the character Neola, a black maid, and the author herself; this shift in focus allows Petry an identificational mobility and creative freedom that was radically circumscribed for black novelists in mid-twentieth-century America" (98).

5. Allan Lloyd-Smith expounds upon the gothic convention in which the feline becomes the embodiment of the feminine, best exemplified in Poe's "The Black Cat," where the protagonist's pent-up gynophobia, ostensibly exteriorized in the titular creature, results in his axing his wife to death: "As we have seen, the cat's blackness may suggest a racial inflection, its lynching a southern trauma. More openly, the cat seems to represent the wife, onto whom the blow is so easily deflected. . . . Attentive readers will have noticed that his wife, who was superstitious, had 'made frequent allusion to the ancient popular notion, which regarded all black cats as witches in disguise. Not that she was ever serious upon this point[. . .]' (200). Not, in any event, as serious as the

narrator proves to be. The cat is an avatar of the witch; the wife is killed instead of the cat. Misogyny, then, is part of that strangeness within the familiar: the *woman* is walled up, only to break out and return" (77).

6. Japtok concentrates on the correlation between whiteness and materialism in the novel, though his focus differs from my emphasis on the gothic. In illuminating how ownership and acquisitiveness shape many of the white characters' actions and relationships, he expatiates upon how the diamond ring given to her by the late Mr. Gramby triggers his widow's remembrance of him during the storm: "While connecting an object with the memory of a person appears unremarkable enough in and of itself, the context makes clear that Mrs. Gramby expects solace from putting on her jewelry—no other strategy for seeking relief or sympathy occurs to her, indicating that objects connected to wealth and power substitute here for spiritual solutions" (362).

7. Also worth noting in the juxtaposition of Mrs. Gramby and Lil as possible doubles is Lil's own invocation of the feline-feminine during her adulterous cavorting with Ed Barrell; from the omniscient narrator comes this: "She had hungered for the sound of pet names and endearments, and had lavished them on him, hoping he would reciprocate. But he had brushed them aside, never remembering them from one week to the next. She had asked him to call her 'Kittikins.' And whenever she reminded him of this special name he was to call her, he shrugged and started unfastening her dress" (117). Moreover, not to be lost is how Lil's self-indulgent, paperback- romance fantasies cohere with Glory's equally juvenile musings; Glory daydreams that her own affair with Ed "would be like a movie. . . . They would lie close to each other, near the hearth, so they could watch the flames licking up the chimney as Ingrid Bergman and Cary Grant did in that last picture—or was it Jennifer Jones?" (59).

8. Petry's penchant for the theatrical may have its origins in her early, brief stint as an actor with the American Negro Theatre in 1940; she performed in *On Striver's Row* at the Schomburg Center for Research in Black Culture (Ervin, *Ann Petry* xiii). She herself makes the theater-novel connection: "In *Country Place* I tried to *under*write, if there is such a word for writing, a word which corresponds to underplaying in the theatre. Despite the obvious violence of the storm, and the violent action of some of the characters, I tried to get into the style something of the surface quiet of a small country town—a slowness of tempo which I hoped the reader would absorb almost unconsciously" (Petry, "The Great Secret" 217).

9. Japtok offers both a materialist and a moral interpretation of Mrs. Gramby's posthumous beneficence: "Connected to her earlier statement of the futility of arbitrarily deciding who is to own 'the earth,' a phrase ringing with imperialist pretensions, and with Biblical overtones, Mrs. Gramby's will may be seen as an act of restitution of stolen goods, of returning possessions to those who have been wronged or exploited" (363). Along the same lines, Emily Bernard also interprets the book's ending as potentially envisioning forward-thinking alternatives to fusty classist and racist prerogatives that maintained their currency in postwar America: "*Country Place* represents Petry's ambition

to imagine a new society in which traditional, small town American culture would join forces with changing racial and ethnic demographics in order to combat ideologies of the shameless pursuit of materialism and white supremacy." Alternatively, Rachel Peterson offers a less-sanguine but equally plausible reading of the denouement, measuring the presumed generosity and potentially progressive race-class prospects which Mrs. Gramby's bequests adumbrate against the realities of a still-xenophobic, classist New England: "The house's stature as a class marker, as noted by Lennox's less privileged inhabitants, raises questions about the degree to which the household staff's ownership of the house can 'change' Lennox (184). Given that the story ostensibly centers on a returning G.I. who finds Lennox limited and intolerant, the book's ending may reflect an optimism regarding the potential for changes in the racial order in the post-war moment. However, Lil's abuse of Neola [Lil uses the word nigger at least once in her presence albeit not directly to her face] complicates this, as does the persistence of anti-Semitism in Lennox. Instead, Neola's rise in status to homeowner is the product of a random turn of events that reflect capitalism's volatility. Similarly, the will fails to affirm the right to private intermarriage and property between Portalucca [sic] and Neola, through the instillation of the Irish Cook as co-owner, who can be seen as either an overseer in this interracial union or whose inclusion in the will can more generously be viewed as Mrs. Gramby's attempt to turn over the means and site of production to all of the household laborers" (90–91).

Chapter Seven

1. I refer here to some of the nation's most vicious antiblack—and in one instance, antiblack *and* antigay—crimes: the so-called "Wilmington, North Carolina, Race Riot of 1898," where a white mob, including policemen and former Confederate soldiers, murdered up to one hundred black citizens; the Tulsa "Black Wall Street" massacre in which the city's thriving black business community was violently razed and several blacks slaughtered; Fannie Lou Hamer, the indefatigable Civil Rights activist from Mississippi who was arrested and beaten within an inch of her life for attempting to register blacks to vote; the "Four Little Girls" in Birmingham who were killed in the bombing of the Sixteenth Street Baptist Church in 1964; James Byrd, Jr., the victim of a barbaric massacre by dragging in Jasper, Texas, in 1998; Arthur Warren, a black gay man murdered by two white teens in Grant Town, West Virginia, in 2000; and Sean Bell, a young, unarmed African American male who was gunned down by New York City's finest while leaving his bachelor party in 2006.

2. I take the term from Sharon Gleeson-White, who uses it to describe Amelia in Carson McCullers' novella *The Ballad of the Sad Cafe:* "The text constructs her as 'the phallic woman' of psycho-analytic theory, the female equivalent . . . of the pregnant man. Like the pregnant man, the phallic woman suggests a pre-Oedipal plentitude, representing

'the child's fantasy of an omnipotence and absolutely powerful, sexually neutral figure' (Grosz, "Phallic Mother" 314)" (Gleeson-White 101).

3. Farah Jasmine Griffin constructs a convincing theory of "safe space": "First, hegemonic ideology can exist even in spaces of resistance. Second, these sites are more often the locus of sustenance and preservation than of resistance. While sustenance and preservation are necessary components of resistance, I do not believe they are in and of themselves resistant acts. Moreover, safe spaces can be very conservative spaces as well" (9). William Jones is clearly sustained by the homo-gendered environment, an antipode of the not-so-safe homespace and workplace; as well what Griffin deems the "conservative" components of such a space surface in Jones's anti-Japanese slurs, akin to the same epithets used in a "conservative" 1940s America which victimized and/or killed black soldiers with seeming impunity.

4. The unseen character Sam Jones may be a composite of two of Petry's relatives/ancestors. In the autobiographical essay "Ann Petry," she recalls her "extraordinary uncles," one of whom fought in the Spanish-American War; another, Uncle Bill, "had spent time on a chain gang in Georgia, sentenced to five years for being caught in a small town in Georgia after sundown" (257).

5. For an account of the actual historical event upon which Petry bases this episode, see John Charles's essay "The Home and the Street."

6. I borrow this concept from Trudier Harris's study *From Mammies to Militants*. Though she didn't include Pink in her discussion (she does offer extensive analysis of *The Street*'s Lutie), her classification of northern literary domestics is fitting: "At their various stages of development, they [northern maids] illustrate degrees of militancy. For all of them, territory is symbolic reality; the North means freedom and sassiness, the antithesis of confinement and self-denial. It suggests no need for the same kind of mask that the moderates wear. For the northern maid, indirection gives way to direct confrontation" (32).

7. It is certainly valid to suggest, as Robin Lucy does, that the story is a "radical text which inscribes the revolutionary energy of black women, their capacity to analyze and resist the machinations of the war against the domestic front and reclaim the home" (16). To be sure, Pink's actions to some degree reflect such a noble intervention. But I would take issue with Lucy's insistence that Annie May almost solely reflects this resistive impulse; glaringly absent from Lucy's discussion is how Pink fits into this narrative of black female recuperation and reclamation, which I find problematic given Pink's treatment of Jones and the subsequent actions which precipitate her death. Egging on a group of young black male rioters with her entreaty, "Come on, you niggers . . . drink up the white man's liquor," which she facilitates by destroying the store's protective gate so that the men can loot and drink to their hearts' content, Pink acts in a way that's a bit more ambiguous. Her reference to these young men with a racial slur seems more hostile than colloquially benign; this and her enjoining them to drink raises a nagging concern that informs my reading: Is she abetting revolutionary action or conversely undermining

such possibilities by ensuring that the young men remain defanged by the anesthesia of alcohol?

Conclusion

1. I found this and many other Petry letters during my research at Boston University's Howard Gotlieb Archival Research Center, which houses a great deal of the author's materials—original manuscripts, personal correspondences, etc. The excerpt I cite is taken from a February 26, 1970, letter Petry penned to Dorothy M. Broderick, director of an institute on "The Young Adult in Conflict." Broderick's original letter and Petry's reply reveal some sort of miscommunication: the first line of Broderick's letter—"This is to confirm our telephone conversation concerning our Institute on 'The Young Adult in Conflict'"—suggests that Petry had agreed to participate, while the first line of Petry's response—"I am the wrong person for your Institute on 'The Young Adult in Conflict' because *I am the wrong age*" (Petry's emphasis)—conveys otherwise.

2. Though there's no indication that Petry's father, Peter Clark Lane, sought false teeth, Petry does note that he, like Samuel, "sang in the church choir. He and three other men used to sing stuff from Gilbert and Sullivan all over the country" (Wilson 77). With respect to African Americans' continual struggle with skin color hierarchies—often imposed and perpetuated by blacks themselves—I think Morrison, more than any writer in the early 1970s, pinpointed the contradictory racial impulses. Underneath the affirming cries of "Black Is Beautiful" lay a more heartfelt and painful belief among too many blacks that didn't quite uplift the race. Morrison speaks of the pain and pathos of the Breedloves in *The Bluest Eye* (1970), a family described as draped in "a cloak of ugliness" that bestowed upon them the commandment-like truth that "You are ugly people." Inculcating this edict, the ironically named Breedloves "had looked about themselves and saw nothing to contradict the statement; saw, in fact, support for it leaning at them from every billboard, every movie, every glance" (39). I thus see Morrison continuing this anguished but necessary intraracial introspection—one that I would say Petry not so much inaugurated as entered at an especially pivotal moment—regarding why so many blacks, as the Civil Rights Movement was cresting, still weren't quite convinced of their beauty.

Works Cited

Adams, George R. "Riot as Ritual: Ann Petry's 'In Darkness and Confusion.'" 1972. Reprinted in *Ann Petry's Short Fiction: Critical Essays*, ed. Hazel Arnett Ervin and Hilary Holladay, 97–103. Westport, CT: Praeger, 2004.

Andrews, Larry R. "The Sensory Assault of the City in Ann Petry's *The Street*." In *The City in African-American Literature*, ed. Yoshinobu Hakutani, 196–211. Madison, NJ: Fairleigh Dickinson University Press, 1995.

Anolik, Ruth Bienstock, and Douglas L. Howard, eds. *The Gothic Other: Racial and Social Constructions in the Literary Imagination.* Jefferson, NC: McFarland, 2004.

Baker, Houston A., Jr. *Turning South Again: Re-thinking Modernism/Re-thinking Booker T.* Durham, NC: Duke University Press, 2001.

Bakhtin, Mikhail. *Rabelais and His World.* Trans. Helene Iswolsky. Bloomington: Indiana University Press, 1984.

Baldwin, James. "*A Man's Life: An Autobiography* by Roy Wilkins." 1982. Reprinted in *The Cross of Redemption: Uncollected Writings*, ed. Randall Kenan, 287–89. New York: Pantheon, 2010.

Barry, Michael. "'Same Train Be Back Tomorrer': Ann Petry's *The Narrows* and the Repetition of History." *MELUS* 24, no.1 (Spring 1999): 141–59.

"batty man." http://www.urbandictionary.com/define.php?+batty+man. June 15, 2010.

Beavers, Herman. "'The Cool Pose': Intersectionality, Masculinity, and Quiescence in the Comedy and Films of Richard Prior and Eddie Murphy." In *Race and the Subject of Masculinities*, ed. Harry Stecopoulos and Michael Uebel, 253–85. Durham, NC: Duke University Press, 1997.

Becker, Susanne. *Gothic Forms of Feminine Fictions.* Manchester, NY: Manchester University Press, 1999.

Bernard, Emily. "'Raceless' Writing and Difference: Ann Petry's *Country Place* and the African-American Literary Canon." *Studies in American Fiction*, 33, no. 1 (Spring 2005): 87–117. (http://go.galegroup.com. . . . GALE%7CN2812040308, MLA International Bibliography, July 11, 2010.)

Bhabha, Homi K. "Are You a Man or a Mouse?" In *Constructing Masculinity*, ed. Maurice Berger, Brian Wallis, and Simon Watson, 57–65. New York: Routledge, 1995.

Bodziock, Joseph. "Richard Wright and the Afro-American Gothic." In *Richard Wright: Myths and Realities*, ed. C. James Trotman, 27–42. New York: Garland, 1988.

Bone, Robert A. *The Negro Novel in America.* 1958. Revised edition. New Haven: Yale University Press, 1965.

Braxton, Joanne M. *Black Women Writing Autobiography: A Tradition within a Tradition.* Philadelphia: Temple University Press, 1989.

Buckley, Gail. *American Patriots: The Story of Blacks in the Military from the Revolution to Desert Storm.* New York: Random House, 2001.

Buell, Lawrence. *New England Literary Culture: From Revolution through Renaissance.* London: Cambridge University Press, 1986.

Butcher, Philip. "Our Raceless Writers." *Opportunity* 26, no. 3 (1948): 113–15.

Carpenter, Lynette, and Wendy K. Kolmar. "Introduction." *Haunting the House of Fiction: Feminist Perspectives on Ghost Stories by American Women*, ed. Carpenter and Kolmar, 1–25. Knoxville: University of Tennessee Press, 1991.

Cassuto, Leonard. *The Inhuman Race: The Racial Grotesque in American Literature and Culture.* New York: Columbia University Press, 1996.

Charles, John. "The Home and the Street: The Dialectics of Racial Privacy in Ann Petry's Early Career." In *Revising the Blueprint: Ann Petry and the Literary Left*, ed. Alex Lubin, 97–119. Jackson: University Press of Mississippi, 2007.

Chesnutt, Charles W. "Mars Jeems's Nightmare." 1899. In *The Conjure Woman and Other Conjure Tales*, ed. Richard H. Brodhead, 55–69. Durham, NC: Duke University Press, 1993.

Clarke, Cheryl. "Ann Petry and the Isolation of Being Other." *Belles Lettres* 5 (Fall 1989): 36.

Coleman, James W. *Black Male Fiction and the Legacy of Caliban.* Lexington: University Press of Kentucky, 2001.

Creed, Barbara. *The Monstrous-Feminine: Film, Feminism, Psychoanalysis.* London: Routledge, 1993.

Davis, Arthur P. *From the Dark Tower: Afro-American Writers, 1900–1960.* Washington, DC: Howard University Press, 1974.

DeLamotte, Eugenia. "White Terror, Black Dreams: Gothic Constructions of Race in the Nineteenth Century." In *The Gothic Other: Racial and Social Constructions in the Literary Imagination*, ed. Ruth Bienstock Anolik and Douglas L. Howard, 17-31. Jefferson, NC: McFarland, 2004.

Douglass, Frederick. *Narrative of the Life of Frederick Douglass, an American Slave, Written by Himself.* 1845. Reprint. New York: Penguin, 1982.

Drake, Kimberly. "Women on the Go: Blues, Conjure, and Other Alternatives to Domesticity in Ann Petry's *The Street* and *The Narrows*." *Arizona Quarterly* 54, no. 1 (Spring 1998): 65–94.

Dubek, Laura. "White Family Values in Ann Petry's *Country Place*." *MELUS* 29, no. 2 (Summer 2004): 55–76. (*www.jstor.org/stable/4141819*, July 11, 2010.)

duCille, Ann. *The Coupling Convention: Sex, Text, and Tradition in Black Women's Fiction.* Oxford: Oxford University Press, 1993.

Dynes, Wayne R. "Color Symbolism." In *The Encyclopedia of Homosexuality*, ed. Dynes, 249–50. New York: Garland, 1990.

Early, Gerald. *The Culture of Bruising: Essays on Prizefighting, Literature, and Modern American Culture.* Hopewell, NJ: Ecco Press, 1994.

Edwards, Justin D. *Gothic Passages: Racial Ambiguity and the American Gothic.* Iowa City: University of Iowa Press, 2003.

Ellis, Kate Ferguson. "Can You Forgive Her? The Gothic Heroine and Her Critics." In *A Companion to the Gothic*, ed. David A. Punter, 257–68. Oxford: Blackwell, 2000.

Ellison, Ralph. *Invisible Man.* 1952. Reprint. New York: Vintage, 1995.

———. *Shadow and Act.* 1964. Reprint. New York: Vintage, 1995.

Ervin, Hazel Arnett. *Ann Petry: A Bio-Bibliography.* New York: G. K. Hall, 1993.

———. "Just a Few Questions More, Mrs. Petry." In her *Ann Petry: A Bio-Bibliography*, 101–3. New York: G. K. Hall, 1993.

Ervin, Hazel Arnett, and Hilary Holladay, eds. *Ann Petry's Short Fiction: Critical Essays.* Westport, CT: Praeger, 2004.

Fanon, Frantz. *Black Skin, White Masks.* New York: Grove, 1967.

Feldman, Jessica R. *Gender on the Divide: The Dandy in Modernist Literature.* Ithaca, NY: Cornell University Press, 1993.

Fendt, Gene. "Apartheid among the Dead; Or, on Christian Laughter in Ann Petry's 'The Bones of Louella Brown.'" In *Ann Petry's Short Fiction: Critical Essays*, ed. Hazel Arnett Ervin and Hilary Holladay, 111–17. Westport, CT: Praeger, 2004.

Fiedler, Leslie A. *Love and Death in the American Novel.* 1966. Revised edition. Briarcliff Manor, NY: Stein & Day, 1975.

Flannigan Saint-Aubin, Arthur. "Testeria: The Dis-ease of Black Men in White Supremacist, Patriarchal Culture." *Callaloo* 17, no. 4 (1994): 1054–74.

Fleenor, Juliann. "Introduction: The Female Gothic." In *The Female Gothic*, ed. Fleenor, 3–28. Montreal: Eden, 1983.

Freud, Sigmund. *The Uncanny.* 1899. Reprint. London: Penguin, 2003.

Garvey, Johanna X. K. "That Old Black Magic? Gender and Music in Ann Petry's Fiction." In *Black Orpheus: Music in African American Fiction from the Harlem Renaissance to Toni Morrison*, ed. Simawe Saadi, 119–51. New York: Garland, 2000.

Gates, Henry Louis, Jr. *The Signifying Monkey: A Theory of African-American Literary Criticism.* New York: Oxford University Press, 1989.

Gayle, Addison, Jr. *The Way of the New World: The Black Novel in America.* Garden City, NY: Anchor/Doubleday, 1975.

Gibbs, Jewelle Taylor. "Anger in Young Black Males: Victims or Victimizers?" In *The American Black Male: His Present Status and His Future*, ed. Richard G. Majors and Jacob U. Gordon, 127–43. Chicago: Nelson-Hall, 1994.

Gibson, Donald B. *The Politics of Literary Expression: A Study of Major Black Writers.* Westport, CT: Greenwood, 1981.

Gleeson-White, Sarah. *Strange Bodies: Gender and Identity in the Novels of Carson McCullers.* Tuscaloosa: University of Alabama Press, 2003.

Goddu, Teresa A. *Gothic America: Narrative, History, and Nation.* New York: Columbia University Press, 1997.

Gooding-Williams, Robert. "Look, a Negro!" In *Reading Rodney King/Reading Urban Uprising,* ed. Gooding-Williams, 157–77. New York: Routledge, 1993.

Green, James. *The World of the Worker: Labor in Twentieth-Century America.* New York: Hill & Wang, 1980.

Greene, J. Lee. *Blacks in Eden: The African American Novel's First Century.* Charlottesville: University of Virginia Press, 1996.

Griffin, Farah Jasmine. *"Who Set You Flowin?" The African-American Migration Narrative.* New York: Oxford University Press, 1995.

Gross, Louis S. *Redefining the American Gothic from "Wieland" to "Day of the Dead."* Ann Arbor. MI: UMI Research Press, 1989.

Gross, Theodore L. "Ann Petry: The Novelist as Social Critic." In *Black Fiction: New Studies in the Afro-American Novel since 1945,* ed. Robert A. Lee, 41–53. New York: Barnes & Noble, 1980.

Gustafson, Fred R. "Fathers, Sons and Brotherhood." In *Betwixt and Between: Patterns of Masculine and Feminine Initiation,* ed. Louise Carus Mahdi, Steven Foster, and Meredith Little, 159–74. LaSalle, IL: Open Court, 1987.

Harper, Phillip Brian. *Are We Not Men? Masculine Anxiety and the Problem of African-American Identity.* New York: Oxford University Press, 1996.

Harris, Trudier. *From Mammies to Militants: Domestics in Black American Literature.* Philadelphia: Temple University Press, 1982.

———. *Saints, Sinners, Saviors: Strong Black Women in African American Literature.* New York: Palgrave, 2001.

Harris-Lopez, Trudier. "Architecture as Destiny? Women and Survival Strategies in Ann Petry's *The Street.*" In *South of Tradition: Essays on African American Literature,* 68–90. Athens: University of Georgia Press, 2002.

Hartman, Saidiya V. *Scenes of Subjection: Terror, Slavery, and Self-Making in Nineteenth-Century America.* New York: Oxford University Press, 1997.

Hemenway, Robert. "Gothic Sociology: Charles Chesnutt and the Gothic Mode." *Studies in the Literary Imagination* 7 (1974): 101–19.

Henderson, Carol E. "The 'Walking Wounded': Rethinking Black Women's Identity in Ann Petry's *The Street.*" *Modern Fiction Studies* 46, no. 4 (2000): 849–67.

Henry, Katherine. "Slavery and Civic Recovery: Gothic Interventions in Whitman and Weld." In *The Gothic Other: Racial and Social Constructions in the Literary Imagina-*

tion, ed. Ruth Bienstock Anolik and Douglas L. Howard, 32–53. Jefferson, NC: McFarland, 2004.

Herrnstein, Richard J., and Charles Murray. *The Bell Curve: Intelligence and Class Structure in American Life.* New York: Free Press, 1994.

Hicks, Heather. "'This Strange Communion': Surveillance and Spectatorship in Ann Petry's *The Street.*" *African American Review* 37, no.1 (Spring 2003): 21–37.

Hoeveler, Diane Long, and Tamar Heller, eds. *Approaches to Teaching Gothic Fiction.* New York: Modern Language Association of America, 2003.

Hogle, Jerrold E. "Teaching the African American Gothic: Its Multiple Sources to *Linden Hills* and *Beloved.*" In *Approaches to Teaching Gothic Fiction*, ed. Diane Long Hoeveler and Tamar Heller, 215–22. New York: Modern Language Association of America, 2003.

Hogue, W. Lawrence. *Discourse and the Other.* Durham, NC: Duke University Press, 1986.

Holladay, Hilary. *Ann Petry.* Boston: Twayne, 1996.

Holland, Sharon Patricia. *Raising the Dead: Readings of Death and (Black) Subjectivity.* Durham, NC: Duke University Press, 2000.

Holloway, Karla F. C. *Moorings and Metaphors: Figures of Culture and Gender in Black Women's Literature.* New Brunswick, NJ: Rutgers University Press, 1992.

———. *Passed On: African American Mourning Stories.* Durham, NC: Duke University Press, 2002.

hooks, bell. *Ain't I a Woman: Black Women and Feminism.* Boston: South End Press, 1992.

———. *Black Looks: Race and Representation.* Boston: South End Press, 1992.

———. *Killing Rage: Ending Racism.* New York: Henry Holt, 1995.

———. "Representing Whiteness in the Black Imagination." In *Displacing Whiteness: Essays in Social and Cultural Criticism*, ed. Ruth Frankenberg, 165–79. Durham, NC: Duke University Press, 1997.

———. *We Real Cool: Black Men and Masculinity.* New York: Routledge, 2004.

Hopkins, Pauline. *Contending Forces.* 1900. Reprint. New York: Oxford University Press, 1988.

Horner, Avril, and Sue Zlosnik. *Gothic and the Comic Turn.* New York: Palgrave Macmillan, 2005.

Hughes, Carl Milton. *The Negro Novelist, 1940–1950.* New York: Citadel, 1970.

Hurston, Zora Neale. *Their Eyes Were Watching God.* 1937. Reprint. New York: Harper & Row, 1990.

"An Interview with Ann Petry from *Artspectrum* (Windham Regional Arts Council)." In *Ann Petry: A Bio-Bibliography*, by Hazel Arnett Ervin, 98–100. New York: G. K. Hall, 1993.

Jacobs, Harriet A. *Incidents in the Life of a Slave Girl, Written by Herself.* 1861. Reprint, ed. Jean Fagan Yellin. Cambridge, MA: Harvard University Press, 1987.

Japtok, Martin. "A Neglected Study in 'Whiteness': Ann Petry's *Country Place.*" In *The Critical Response to Ann Petry*, ed. Hazel Arnett Ervin, 354–65. Westport, CT: Praeger, 2005.

Jefferson, Thomas. *Notes on the State of Virginia.* 1787. Reprint, ed. William Peden. New York: W. W. Norton, 1972.

Johnson, Charles. "A Phenomenology of the Black Body." In *Traps: African American Men on Gender and Sexuality*, ed. Rudolph P. Byrd and Beverly Guy-Sheftall, 223–35. Bloomington: Indiana University Press, 2001.

Johnson, E. Patrick. *Appropriating Blackness: Performance and the Politics of Authenticity.* Durham, NC: Duke University Press, 2003.

Jordan, Margaret I. *African American Servitude and Historical Imaginings.* New York: Palgrave, 2004.

Kelley, Robin D. G. *Race Rebels: Culture, Politics, and the Black Working Class.* New York: Free Press, 1994.

Kristeva, Julia. *Powers of Horror: An Essay on Abjection.* Trans. Leon S. Roudiez. New York: Columbia University Press, 1982.

Krüger-Kahloula, Angelika. "On the Wrong Side of the Fence: Racial Segregation in American Cemeteries." In *History and Memory in African-American Culture*, ed. Geneviève Fabre and Robert O'Meally, 130-49. New York: Oxford University Press, 1994.

La Belle, Jenijoy. *Herself Beheld: The Literature of the Looking Glass.* Ithaca, NY: Cornell University Press, 1990.

Lamothe, Daphne. "*Cane:* Jean Toomer's Gothic Black Modernism." In *The Gothic Other: Racial and Social Constructions in the Literary Imagination*, ed. Ruth Bienstock Anolik and Douglas L. Howard, 54–71. Jefferson, NC: McFarland, 2004.

Larsen, Nella. *Quicksand.* 1928. Reprint. In *"Quicksand" and "Passing,"* ed. Deborah E. McDowell, 1–135. New Brunswick, NJ: Rutgers University Press, 1989.

Lee, Amy. "The Narrator as Feminist Ally in Ann Petry's 'The Bones of Louella Brown.'" In *Ann Petry's Short Fiction: Critical Essays*, ed. Hazel Arnett Ervin and Hilary Holladay, 119–24. Westport, CT: Praeger, 2004.

"The Lesbian, Gay, Bisexual, and Transgender Religious Archives Network." www.lgbtran.org; June 10, 2011.

Lewis, Barbara. "Taking the Cake: Ann Petry's 'Has Anybody Seen Miss Dora Dean?'" In *Ann Petry's Short Fiction: Critical Essays*, ed. Hazel Arnett Ervin and Hilary Holladay, 125–39. Westport, CT: Praeger, 2004.

Liggins, Saundra. "The Urban Gothic Vision in Colson Whitehead's *The Intuitionist.*" *African American Review* 40, no. 2 (Summer 2006): 359–70.

Lloyd-Smith, Allan. *American Gothic Fiction: An Introduction.* New York: Continuum, 2004.

Lubin, Alex. "Introduction." *Revising the Blueprint: Ann Petry and the Literary Left*, ed. Lubin, 3–14. Jackson: University Press of Mississippi, 2007.

Lucy, Robin. "Fables of the Reconstruction: Black Women on the Domestic Front in Ann Petry's World War II Fiction." *CLA Journal* 49, no. 1 (2005): 1–27.

Mahdi, Louise Carus, Steven Foster, and Meredith Little, eds. *Betwixt and Between: Patterns of Masculine and Feminine Initiation.* LaSalle, IL: Open Court, 1987.

Majors, Richard, and Janet Mancini Billson. *Cool Pose: The Dilemmas of Black Manhood in America.* New York: Touchstone, 1992.

Majors, Richard, Richard Tyler, Blaine Peden, and Ron Hall. "Cool Pose: A Symbolic Mechanism for Masculine Role Enactment and Coping by Black Males." In *The American Black Male: His Status and His Future*, ed. Majors and Jacob U. Gordon, 245–59. Chicago: Nelson-Hall, 1994.

Malchow, H. L. *Gothic Images of Race in Nineteenth-Century Britain.* Palo Alto, CA: Stanford University Press, 1996.

McDowell, Deborah E. "Introduction." *"Quicksand" and "Passing,"* by Nella Larsen. Reprint, ed. McDowell, ix–xxxvii. New Brunswick, NJ: Rutgers University Press, 1989.

McDowell, Margaret B. "*The Narrows:* A Fuller View of Ann Petry." *Black American Literature Forum* 14, no. 4 (1980): 135–41.

McKay, Nellie Y. "Introduction." *The Narrows*, by Ann Petry. 1953. Reprint, ed. McKay, vii–xx. Boston: Beacon Press, 1988.

McKoy, Sheila Smith. "Rescuing the Black Homosexual Lambs: Randall Kenan and the Reconstruction of Southern Gay Masculinity." In *Contemporary Black Men's Fiction and Drama*, ed. Keith Clark, 15–36. Urbana: University of Illinois Press, 2001.

Miles, Margaret. "The Female Body as Grotesque." In *The Grotesque in Art and Literature*, ed. James Luther Adams and Wilson Yates, 83–112. Grand Rapids, MI: W. B. Eerdmans, 1997.

Moers, Ellen. *Literary Women.* Garden City, NY: Doubleday, 1976.

Morrison, Toni. *Beloved.* New York: Knopf, 1987.

———. *The Bluest Eye.* 1970. Reprint. New York: Plume, 1994.

———. "Rootedness: The Ancestor as Foundation." In *Black Women Writers, 1950–1980*, ed. Mari Evans, 339–45. New York: Anchor, 1988.

Mrtek, Robert. "A Visit with Ann Petry, May 16, 1984." In *Ann Petry: A Bio-Bibliography*, by Hazel Arnett Ervin, 77–88. New York: G. K. Hall, 1993.

Naylor, Gloria. *Linden Hills.* New York: Ticknor & Fields, 1985.

Neal, Larry. "The Black Arts Movement." 1968. Reprinted in *The Norton Anthology of African-American Literature.* Second edition, ed. Henry Louis Gates, Jr., and Nellie Y. McKay, 2039–50. New York: W. W. Norton, 2004.

Neal, Mark Anthony. *New Black Man.* New York: Routledge, 2006.

Nero, Charles. "Gay Men." In *Oxford Companion to African American Literature*, ed. William L. Andrews, Trudier Harris, and Frances Smith Foster, 312. New York: Oxford University Press, 1997.

O'Brien, John. "Ann Petry." *Interviews with Black Writers*, ed. O'Brien, 153–63. New York: Liveright, 1973.

Peterson, Rachel. "Invisible Hands at Work: Domestic Service and Meritocracy in Ann Petry's Novels." In *Revising the Blueprint: Ann Petry and the Literary Left*, ed. Alex Lubin, 72–96. Jackson: University Press of Mississippi, 2007.

Petry, Ann. "Ann Petry." *Contemporary Authors: Autobiography Series*, ed. Adele Sarkissian, 253–69. Vol. 6. Detroit: Gale Research, 1988.

———. *Country Place*. 1947. Reprint. New York: Signet, 1950.

———. "The Great Secret." *The Writer* 61, no.7 (July 1948): 215–17.

———. Letter to Dorothy M. Broderick. February 2, 1970. MS. Ann Petry Collection. Howard Gotlieb Archival Research Center. Boston University.

———. *"Miss Muriel" and Other Stories*. 1971. Reprint. Boston: Beacon, 1989.

———. "The Moses Project." *Harbor Review* 5–6 (1986): 52–61.

———. *The Narrows*. 1953. Reprint. Boston: Beacon, 1988.

———. *The Street*. 1946. Reprint. Boston: Houghton Mifflin, 1992.

———. "What's Wrong with Negro Men?" *Negro Digest* 5 (March 1947): 4–7.

Pleck, Joseph H. *The Myth of Masculinity*. Cambridge, MA: MIT Press, 1984.

Poe, Edgar Allan. "The Fall of the House of Usher." In *Eighteen Best Stories by Edgar Allan Poe*, ed. Vincent Price and Chandler Brossard, 21–40. New York: Dell, 1965.

Punter, David. *The Literature of Terror: A History of Gothic Fictions from 1765 to the Present Day*. Vol. 1. London: Longman, 1996.

Puschmann-Nalenz, Barbara. "Ann Petry: 'Mother Africa' (1971)." In *The African American Short Story, 1970 to 1990: A Collection of Critical Essays*, ed. Woolfgang Karrer and Puschmann-Nalenz, 29–39. Trier: Wissenschaftlicher Verlag Trier, 1993.

Raynor, Deirdre. "'Ain't No Room for Us Anywhere': Reading Ann Petry's 'In Darkness and Confusion' as a Migration Narrative." In *Ann Petry's Short Fiction: Critical Essays*, ed. Hazel Arnett Ervin and Hilary Holladay, 105–10. Westport, CT: Praeger, 2004.

Riggs, Marlon. "Black Manhood Revisited: Reflections of a SNAP! Queen." 1991. Reprinted in *Traps: African American Men on Gender and Sexuality*, ed. Rudolph P. Byrd and Beverly Guy-Sheftall, 292–96. Bloomington: Indiana University Press, 2001.

Roberts, Diane. *The Myth of Aunt Jemima: Representations of Race and Region*. London: Routledge, 1994.

Roberts, Nora Ruth. "Artistic Discourse in Three Short Stories by Ann Petry." 1999. Reprinted in *Ann Petry's Short Fiction: Critical Essays*, ed. Hazel Arnett Ervin and Hilary Holladay, 31–47. Westport, CT: Praeger, 2004.

Robinson, Alford James, Jr. "The Middle Passage." In *Africana: The Encyclopedia of the African and African American Experience*, ed. Kwame Anthony Appiah and Henry Louis Gates, Jr., 1302. New York: Basic Civitas Books, 1999.

Rosenblatt, Roger. *Black Fiction*. Cambridge, MA: Harvard University Press, 1974.

Ross, Marlon. *Manning the Race: Reforming Black Men in the Jim Crow Era*. New York: New York University Press, 2004.

———. "Some Glances at the Black Fag: Race, Same-Sex Desire, and Cultural Belonging." 1994. Reprinted in *African American Literary Theory: A Reader*, ed. Winston Napier, 498–522. New York: New York University Press, 2000.

Rotundo, E. Anthony. *American Manhood: Transformations in Masculinity from the Revolution to the Modern Era*. New York: Basic Books, 1993.

Ruse, Michael. *Homosexuality: A Philosophical Inquiry*. Oxford: Blackwell, 1988.

Rushton, J. Philippe. *Race, Evolution, and Behavior: A Life History Perspective*. Second special abridged edition. Port Huron, MI: Charles Darwin Research Institute, 2000.

Russell, Kathy, Midge Wilson, and Ronald Hall. *The Color Complex: The Politics of Skin Color among African Americans*. New York: Anchor, 1992.

Sanday, Peggy Reeves. *Divine Hunger: Cannibalism as a Cultural System*. New York: Cambridge University Press, 1986.

Sandiford, Keith. "Gothic and Intertextual Constructions in *Linden Hills*." In *Gloria Naylor: Critical Perspectives Past and Present*, ed. Henry Louis Gates, Jr., and K. A. Appiah, 195–214. New York: Amistad, 1993.

Schechter, Harold. "Symbols of Initiation in *Adventures of Huckleberry Finn*." In *Betwixt and Between: Patterns of Masculine and Feminine Initiation*, ed. Louise Carus Mahdi, Steven Foster, and Meredith Little, 67–68. LaSalle, IL: Open Court, 1987.

Schuyler, George. "The Negro-Art Hokum." 1926. Reprinted in *Speech and Power: The African-American Essay and Its Cultural Content, from Polemics to Pulpit*. Vol. 2, ed. Gerald Early, 85–87. New York: Ecco, 1993.

Scott, William. "Material Resistance and the Agency of the Body in Ann Petry's *The Street*." *American Literature* 78, no.1 (March 2006): 89–116.

Sedgwick, Eve Kosofsky. *Between Men: English Literature and Male Homosocial Desire*. New York: Columbia University Press, 1985.

———. *The Coherence of Gothic Conventions*. New York: Methuen, 1986.

Seshadri-Crooks, Kalpana. *Desiring Whiteness: A Lacanian Analysis of Race*. London: Routledge, 2000.

Sexton, Patricia C. *The Feminized Male: Classrooms, White Collars, and the Decline of Manliness*. New York: Vintage, 1970.

Shockley, Evie. "Buried Alive: Gothic Homelessness, Black Women's Sexuality, and (Living) Death in Ann Petry's *The Street*." *African American Review* 40, no. 3 (Fall 2006): 439–60.

Sonser, Anna. *A Passion for Consumption: The Gothic Novel in America.* Bowling Green, OH: Bowling Green State University Press, 2001.

Stein, Karen F. "Monsters and Madwomen: Changing Female Gothic." In *The Female Gothic*, ed. Juliann Fleenor, 123–37. Montreal: Eden, 1983.

Stoltenberg, John. "Healing from Manhood: A Radical Meditation on the Movement from Gender Identity to Moral Identity." In *Masculinities: Interdisciplinary Readings*, ed. Mark Hussey, 379–88. Upper Saddle River, NJ: Prentice-Hall, 2003.

Streitfeld, David. "Ann Petry's Storied Life." *Washington Post*, May 3, 1992, C1, 6.

Sundquist, Eric J. *Faulkner: The House Divided.* Baltimore: Johns Hopkins University Press, 1983.

Tate, Claudia. *Psychoanalysis and Black Novels: Desire and the Protocols of Race.* New York: Oxford University Press, 1998.

Tettenborn, Eva. "Traumatic Reenactment and the Impossibility of African American Testimony in Ann Petry's 'Like a Winding Sheet' and 'The Witness.'" In *Ann Petry's Short Fiction: Critical Essays*, ed. Hazel Arnett Ervin and Hilary Holladay, 153–69. Westport, CT: Praeger, 2004.

Thomas, Calvin. *Male Matters: Masculinity, Anxiety, and the Male Body on the Line.* Urbana: University of Illinois Press, 1996.

Thomas, Kendall. "'Ain't Nothin' like the Real Thing': Black Masculinity, Gay Sexuality, and the Jargon of Authenticity." In *Representing Black Men*, ed. Marcellus Blount and George E. Cunningham, 55–69. New York: Routledge, 1996.

Tithecott, Richard. *Of Monsters and Men: Jeffrey Dahmer and the Construction of the Serial Killer.* Madison: University of Wisconsin Press, 1997.

Trafton, Scott. *Egypt Land: Race and Nineteenth-Century American Egyptomania.* Durham, NC: Duke University Press, 2004.

Tuan, Yi-Fu. *Space and Place: The Perspective of Experience.* Minneapolis: University of Minnesota Press, 1977.

Turner, Patricia A. *Ceramic Uncles and Celluloid Mammies: Black Images and Their Influence on Culture.* 1994. Reprint. Charlottesville: University of Virginia Press, 2002.

"A Visit with Ann Petry, May 16, 1984." In *Ann Petry: A Bio-Bibliography*, by Hazel Arnett Ervin, 77–88. New York: G. K. Hall, 1993.

Vizcaino-Aleman, Melina. "Counter-Modernity, Black Masculinity, and Female Silence in Ann Petry's Fiction." In *Revising the Blueprint: Ann Petry and the Literary Left*, ed. Alex Lubin, 120–36. Jackson: University Press of Mississippi, 2007.

Wallace, Maurice O. *Constructing the Black Masculine: Identity and Ideality in African American Men's Literature and Culture, 1775–1995.* Durham, NC: Duke University Press, 2002.

Warren, Joyce W. "The Challenge of Women's Periods." In *Challenging Boundaries: Gender and Periodization*, ed. Warren and Margaret Dickie, ix–xxiv. Athens: University of Georgia Press, 2000.

Washington, Gladys J. "Folk Traditions in the Short Fiction of Ann Petry." In *Ann Petry's Short Fiction: Critical Essays*, ed. Hazel Arnett Ervin and Hilary Holladay, 19–29. Westport, CT: Praeger, 2004.

Washington, Mary Helen. "'I Love the Way Janie Crawford Left Her Husbands': Zora Neale Hurston's Emergent Female Hero." In *Invented Lives: Narratives of Black Women, 1860–1960*, ed. Washington, 237–54. New York: Anchor-Doubleday, 1987.

———. "'Infidelity Becomes Her': The Ambivalent Woman in the Fiction of Ann Petry and Dorothy West." In *Invented Lives: Narratives of Black Women, 1860–1960*, ed. Washington, 297–306. New York: Anchor-Doubleday, 1987.

Weir, Sybil. "*The Narrows:* A Black New England Novel." *Studies in American Fiction* 15, no. 1 (1987): 80–93.

Wesling, Meg. "The Opacity of Everyday Life: Segregation and the Iconicity of Uplift in *The Street.*" *American Literature* 78, no.1 (March 2006): 117–40.

West, Cornel. *Race Matters.* Boston: Beacon, 2001.

———. "Readings and Conversations: Cornel West." Lannan Foundation, June 6, 2003. (*http://www.lannan.org/docs/cornel-west-030625-trans-read.pdf.* Transcript.)

Wiebe, Paul. "'Miss Muriel': Rewriting Innocence into Experience." In *Ann Petry's Short Fiction: Critical Essays*, ed. Hazel Arnett Ervin and Hilary Holladay, 59–78. Westport, CT: Praeger, 2004.

Wilson, Mark K. "A *MELUS* Interview: Ann Petry—The New England Connection." *MELUS* 15, no. 2 (Summer): 71–84.

Wilt, Judith. "'And Still Insists He Sees the Ghosts': Defining the Gothic." In *Approaches to Teaching Gothic Fiction: The British and American Traditions*, ed. Diane Long Hoeveler and Tamar Heller, 39–45. New York: Modern Language Association of America, 2003.

Wright, Richard. *Black Boy.* 1945 and 1977. Reprint. New York: HarperPerennial, 1993.

———. *Native Son.* 1940. Reprint. New York: HarperPerennial, 1992.

Index